TOTAL SPORTSCASTING

TOTAL SPORTSCASTING
PERFORMANCE, PRODUCTION, AND CAREER DEVELOPMENT

Marc Zumoff and Max Negin

Focal Press
Taylor & Francis Group

NEW YORK AND LONDON

First published 2015
by Focal Press
70 Blanchard Road, Suite 402, Burlington, MA 01803

and by Focal Press
2 Park Square, Milton Park, Abingdon, Oxon OX14 4RN

Focal Press is an imprint of the Taylor & Francis Group, an informa business

© 2015 Taylor & Francis

The right of Marc Zumoff & Max Negin to be identified as author of this work has been asserted by them in accordance with sections 77 and 78 of the Copyright, Designs and Patents Act 1988.

Notices
Knowledge and best practice in this field are constantly changing. As new research and experience broaden our understanding, changes in research methods, professional practices, or medical treatment may become necessary.

Practitioners and researchers must always rely on their own experience and knowledge in evaluating and using any information, methods, compounds, or experiments described herein. In using such information or methods they should be mindful of their own safety and the safety of others, including parties for whom they have a professional responsibility.

Product or corporate names may be trademarks or registered trademarks, and are used only for identification and explanation without intent to infringe.

Library of Congress Cataloging-in-Publication Data

Zumoff, Marc.
   Total sportscasting : performance, production, and career development / Marc Zumoff & Max Negin.
     pages cm
   Includes index.
  1. Television broadcasting of sports—Handbooks, manuals, etc.   2. Television broadcasting of sports—Vocational guidance.   3. Radio broadcasting of sports—Handbooks, manuals, etc.   4. Radio broadcasting of sports—Vocational guidance.   I. Negin, Max.   II. Title.
   GV742.3.Z86   2014
   070.4′49796—dc23
   2014008688

ISBN: 978-0-415-81392-1 (pbk)
ISBN: 978-1-315-84840-2 (ebk)

Typeset in Times New Roman
By Apex CoVantage, LLC

Printed and bound in the United States of America
by Edwards Brothers Malloy, Inc.

CONTENTS

PREFACE AND ACKNOWLEDGEMENTS

It was cold and damp inside the press box of the Yale Bowl. This was November 15, 1980, and co-author Marc Zumoff was the fill-in color announcer alongside play-by-play man Howard David. The two were broadcasting Princeton University football on radio and at half time, David would leave the booth to take a break. Alone, Zumoff decided to let his eyes wander, peering outside of the ancient stadium. There, he saw a television production truck with a logo he'd never seen before. When David returned to the press box, Zumoff asked him about it.

"Howard, what's ESPN?"

Today, young sports fans learn the letters E.S.P.N. shortly after learning their ABCs. The self-proclaimed worldwide leader in sports is largely indicative of the wild, symbiotic growth of sports and media in the past 35 years. With it have come other all-sports networks at both the national and regional levels, as well as channels owned by leagues and teams at both the professional and collegiate levels. Add to that over-the-air television and radio stations that continue to serve hungry sports fans with coverage of live events and sports news. Most if not all of these entities have enhanced and expanded their coverage utilizing the World Wide Web, mobile services, and social media. And have we mentioned the unlimited opportunities for individuals to set up their own video broadcasts, podcasts, blogs and social media postings, thus proclaiming themselves "sportscasters"?

While all of this growth offers unprecedented opportunities in the business, the increase in aspiring sportscasters has been exponential. Associated with that are two things: the need for college graduates to be equipped with the expertise to thrive in a career in sports broadcasting along with the skills needed to break into such a competitive field.

We believe this book is one of the primary tools to help you accomplish that. It offers the most comprehensive overview of the industry as it exists today. Performance aspects are broken down by individual discipline such as anchoring, reporting, play-by-play, and so forth. The same is true with the production side of the business such as producing, directing, camera, audio, etc. Performance and production were both included in this book because they have become increasingly integrated. Performers are frequently called upon to exhibit abilities in the production area, not only in television and radio but also when contributing to digital content as well. The same can be said for being able to write for a particular entity's website. Media are, after all, converging, so broadcasters need to know how to write while writers are being asked to broadcast.

Another important aspect of the book, as we just alluded to, is career development. We often say that there are no career fairs for aspiring sportscasters because the pool of candidates exceeds the demand. After all, who wouldn't want to be paid to cover something that people pay good money to see? Because the competition is so fierce, we felt compelled as authors to provide several chapters that will help with career development.

Other chapters include a historical overview of sportscasting, another on what it's like to be a woman in a predominantly man's world, a chapter that examines the financial aspects of the business, and a final chapter where some of sportscasting's more prominent names analyze current trends and future possibilities.

Sportscasting (as opposed to broadcasting in general) has become its own area of specialization, from performance to production and everything in between. As a business and as a field of study, it has never been bigger. When asked by the publisher, Focal Press, to provide evidence of the need for a book such as this, the authors uncovered a study by Marie Hardin, the associate director of research at the John Curley Center for Sports Journalism at Penn State University. The study said in part:

> "As sports-related news has become a major cultural force in recent years— expanding its presence on television and the Internet and dominating the nation's newsprint—it's also become a staple part of many US journalism programs."

> "A survey of 384 university programs in journalism and mass communication found that more than 40 percent offer at least one sports media-related course on a regular basis.[1] The most frequently offered are courses in sports journalism and sports broadcasting, representing 151 courses in 127 programs. In all, 155 programs offer more than 200 sports-focused courses . . ."

> "Fourteen institutions report offering minors, certificates or other formal emphases in sports media. Thirty-six programs reported that they provide two or more

sports media courses, and seven—Penn State, Oklahoma State, Southern Cal, Marist College, Suffolk University, Boston University, and Utica College—reported offering four or more courses."

The concept of *Total Sportscasting*, allows the reader to wade at least ankle-deep into just about every aspect of the business, knowing that he or she may be called upon to dip into that knowledge base in many different situations. This is why we became co-authors, not only our combined half-century in sportscasting, but also our different perspectives (performance and production). Thus, readers are encouraged to take in the entire book, whether your heart is set on becoming the next great sports host, director, or sports programming executive.

Here is a thumbnail of each chapter:

Chapter 1: A history and overview: A history of sportscasting, from sports reporting before the electronic age to the early days of radio, the advent of television, the impact of satellite and cable, and the innovators who helped to make the business what it is today.

Chapter 2: The production plan: The overall scope of producing the broadcast of a sporting event or a studio show, including planning, storylines, coordinating talent and crew, and preparing for what could go wrong.

Chapter 3: Research and relationships: How talent and producers determine the best sources of information, how best to gather that information along with what and who to trust.

Chapter 4: Writing: The difference between writing for the ear versus the eye, scripting good sportscasts for both radio and television as well as reporter packages and of course the paramount importance of being right.

Chapter 5: Performance theory: How to become a good performer in each sportscasting discipline, including such topics as individual development of a personal broadcasting style, specific exercises for promoting certain performance and speech mechanics and working on having a good on-camera look.

Chapter 6: Reporter, anchor, sideline, host, sports talk: The requirements necessary for excelling at each of these disciplines including interview skills, reading from the teleprompter and properly preparing for each of these roles.

Chapter 7: Play-by-play and analyst: The requirements necessary for excelling at each of these disciplines including preparation, the difference between radio and television, as well as developing good chemistry between you and your broadcast partner.

Chapter 8: Women in sportscasting: The opportunities available for women in a predominantly male world, dealing with sexism and other issues in the workplace, dressing and looking the part as well as trying to answer the question, "do you have to be a blonde to be a sideline reporter?"

Chapter 9: Social media and the Web: The need for sportscasters to become comfortable and proficient at both, utilizing them to your advantage—both as a reporting tool and as a source of information—and avoiding the pitfalls associated with each.

Chapter 10: Producing: The producer as the point person for a sports production, ensuring that everyone and everything is in place to fulfill the production plan, planning for what they can, and preparing for the uncertainties—all while wearing a variety of hats.

Chapter 11: Cameras and visual communication: The eyes of the sports production, a primer on what it takes to be a good cameraperson at an event or as part of an electronic news-gathering organization.

Chapter 12: Audio: The ears of the sports production, this chapter will include microphone placement, audio design, mixing, and other aspects of producing good sound.

Chapter 13: Editing, replays, and post-production: The roles of tape and non-linear editors in a sports production, including editing packages, being a source for replays as well as what needs to be done after the event or show is finished.

Chapter 14: Graphics and design elements: The use of graphics and how best to produce them.

Chapter 15: Directing and the flow of the crew: How the director helps to implement the production plan, possessing skills that include the ability to focus on multiple tasks simultaneously, and a discussion of the various permutations of directing including technical and assistant directing.

Chapter 16: The demo: What broadcast performers should and should not include in a demo as well as how to generate good demo material and why production personnel frequently do not need a demo.

Chapter 17: Career development: Step-by-step suggestions for performers and production personnel alike on how to break into this competitive business, including developing a wide network of contacts, putting less emphasis on employment ads, and why the secret to starting your sportscasting career lies deep within . . . yourself.

Chapter 18: Finance: The flow of the money necessary to pay for productions, the relationship between teams, advertisers, and fans and why it's important for you to know all of this.

Chapter 19: Current trends and future possibilities: Taking a look at what's happening in the business today and how it might portend where the business of sportscasting is headed in the future.

Companion Website

With any textbook, a natural lag exists between the typing of the manuscript and the process of publishing to get this textbook into your hands. To help make up for that gap, we have developed a robust website full of additional up-to-date materials to help keep the textbook alive. These items include slides summarizing the main points of each chapter, more in-depth interviews from folks featured in the book as well as play-by-play charts, forms, diagrams and additional material and resources. The website for this book will allow for extensions of the text where new trends have emerged. Please go to www.totalsports casting.com for more information.

ACKNOWLEDGEMENTS

Our heartfelt thanks and gratitude go out to our editor at Focal Press at Taylor & Francis Group, Kathryn Morrissey, whose guidance, responsiveness and general handholding was superb. Also thanks to Dennis McGonagle, Melissa Sandford, and former editor Michele Cronin for initially believing in and helping to develop the original book proposal. Marie Hardin, associate director for research at John Curley Center for Sports Journalism, Penn State University, provided the data showing there is indeed a need for a textbook such as this one. Marty Kenney and Micah Kleit, two long-time veterans of the publishing industry, selflessly spent many hours counseling two neophytes.

While the co-authors do bring their own knowledge to the table, there is the need to substantiate, refute, or simply provide additional or different perspectives on that information. That came through interviews with experts in sportscasting or those in businesses that are strongly or loosely allied with the field. Their contributions are gratefully acknowledged and they are identified with the titles they held at the time of their interviews: J.R. Aguila, event producer and director at Comcast SportsNet in Philadelphia; Greg Aiello, senior vice-president of communications at the National Football League; Geoff Arnold, play-by-play announcer for Frisco RoughRiders; Kurt Badenhausen at *Fortune Magazine*; Dr. Murali Balaji, assistant professor for media Studies and production at Temple University; Brian Baldinger, NFL analyst; Jason Benetti, play-by-play announcer for the Syracuse Chiefs; Tom Boman, broadcast manager, Learfield Sports; Scott Brady, news director at KYTV-TV, Springfield, MO; Mike Breen, NBA play-by-play announcer, ESPN and ABC; Carie Brescia, make-up artist; Doris Burke, sideline reporter and color analyst for NBA and college basketball on ABC and ESPN; Rick Burton, David B. Falk professor of sport management at Syracuse University; Dr. Robert Chope, founder of the Career and Personal Development Institute; Scott Cook, news director at WENY-TV, Elmira, NY; Bob Costas, sportscaster at NBC; Chris Dachille, executive sports producer at WBAL-TV, Baltimore; Nicholas Dalley, president of Intentional Communication, Inc.; J.P. Dellacamera, play-by-play announcer, Philadelphia Union; Dr. Marsha Della Giustina, professor of journalism, Emerson College; Wes Durham, play-by-play announcer, Georgia Institute of Technology and Atlanta Falcons football; Mike Emrick NHL play-by-play announcer, NBC and NBC Sports Network; Marc Ernay, sports director, WINS, New York; Colin Evans, vice-president, content and business development, Spreecast, Inc.; Greg Farnese, freelance cameraman; Brian

Feldman, sports anchor/reporter for KMOV-TV St. Louis; Kevin Finch, news director at WRTV-TV, Indianapolis; Randy Flick, audio engineer; Tim Frank, senior vice-president, basketball communications, NBA; Scott Franzke, radio play-by-play Philadelphia Phillies; John Gambadoro, sports talk show host, KTAR Phoenix; Phil Giubileo, play-by-play announcer, Bridgeport Sound Tigers; Paul Gluck, associate professor, Department of Broadcasting, Telecommunications, and Mass Media, School of Media and Communication, Temple University; Adam Goldberg, director of marketing, Memphis Redbirds; Dr. Carol Goldberg, psychologist; Ron Harig, news director at KOTV-TV, Tulsa, OK; Dave Harmon, HBO Sports; Fred Hickman, sports director, WVUE-TV, New Orleans; Mike Joy, lap-by-lap voice, NASCAR Sprint Cup, Fox Sports; Charles Kelly, attorney; Ed Kilgore, sports director, WGRZ-TV, Buffalo; Russ Kilgore, news director, WINK-TV, Fort Meyers, FL; Allison Kimmich, executive director, National Women's Studies Association; John Kincade, sports talk show host, WCNN, Atlanta; Dr. Robert Kriegel, sports psychologist and motivational speaker; Mike Lacett, sports anchor and reporter, WTOL-TV, Toledo, OH; Chris Lanni, news director, WJAR-TV, Providence; Daniel Lawrence, managing partner and founder of Elmrox Investment Group; John Lewis, author of *Radio Master: The Life and Times of Sports Broadcasting Great Ted Husing*; Bridget Lovelle, news director, KSPR-TV, Springfield, MO; Wayne Lynch, news director at Northwest Cable News; Mark Mancini, sports podcaster; Meredith Marakovits, New York Yankees clubhouse reporter, Yes Network; Alexis McCombs, freelance journalist, producer, and host; Brandon Mercer, news director, KTXL-TV, Sacramento; Caleb Mezzy, social media strategist; Rudy Mezzy, news and sports anchor and reporter, KOLN-TV/KGIN-TV, Grand Island, NE; Jon Mozes, play-by-play announcer for Abilene Prairie Dogs; Owen Murphy, sports radio talent coach; Jim Nantz, sportscaster, CBS; Kelley O'Brien, director of social media at Krispy Kreme Doughnuts; Larra Overton, sideline reporter, Big Ten Network; Steve Paino, owner of Total Production Services; Todd Palladino, freelance camera operator; Professor Sandy Padwe, special lecturer at Columbia University Journalism School; Marc Payton, director, HBO; Peggy Phillip, news director, KSHB-TV, Kansas City, MO; Bill Rasmussen, founder of ESPN; Amber Roessner, assistant professor at the University of Tennessee School of Journalism and Electronic Media; Craig Sager, sideline reporter for Turner Sports; David Schuster, sports reporter for WSCR radio, Chicago; Vin Scully, play-by-play announcer for the Los Angeles Dodgers; Frank Shorr, director of the Sports Institute at Boston University; Steven Shutt, associate athletic director, athletic communications, Wake Forest University; Jerod Smalley, sports director, WCMH-TV; Dennis Smith, retired news director, WLBT-TV, Jackson, MS; Rick Smith, audio engineer, Instructor New England Institute of Art; Suzanne Smith, director, CBS Sports; Russ Thaler, host, NBC Sports Network; Susan Tully, news director, KXAS-TV, Dallas; Norby Williamson, executive senior vice-president of studio and event production; Max Utsler, associate professor, School of Journalism and Mass Communications, University of Kansas; Dr. Ann Utterback, author of *The Broadcast Voice Handbook: How to Polish Your On-air Delivery*;

Lesley Visser, sports reporter, CBS; Suzyn Waldman, color analyst, New York Yankees, WCBS Radio; Dave Winder, assistant director of athletics/media relations, Murray State University; Gregg Winik, CEO and founder of CineSport; Dr. Stacey Woelfel, news director, KOMU-TV, Columbia, MO, and associate professor, University of Missouri School of Journalism; Craig Wilkie, graphics designer; Eva Zaccaria, sports director, WICZ-TV, Binghamton, NY.

Research is one of those things you have to love, and fortunately, Jared Browsh loves it. We thank him for his dedication and fastidiousness. We're also thrilled he was willing to format our footnotes. Others who helped with researching material for this book include Daniel Kurish and Deidre Snively.

Once the book was complete, both Focal Press and the authors beseeched a number of worthy experts to provide peer reviews. We would especially like to thank Dr. Phillip Thompsen, professor in the Department of Communication Studies at West Chester University, as well as Professor Tammy Trujillo, Mt. San Antonio College, for their extensive and valuable feedback. Others who were kind enough to provide the same include: Dr. Murali Balaji, assistant professor of media studies and production, Temple University; Paul Gluck, associate professor, Department of Broadcasting, Telecommunications, and Mass Media, School of Media and Communication, Temple University; Tom McCarthy, play-by-play announcer, Philadelphia Phillies; and Jon Slobotkin, vice-president and executive producer, live events, NBC Sports Regional Networks.

A terrific cast of folks provided everything from arranging an interview to simply making a referral in an email. We would like to particularly give a big thank you to Whitney Burak, Robyn Callahan, and Tom Feur of Fox Sports West for helping to arrange the interview with the greatest of them all, Vin Scully, and Dave Goren, executive director of National Sportscasters and Sportswriters Association and Hall of Fame, who pointed the way to Bob Costas and Jim Nantz, both of whom were not only gracious and giving of their time but, as luck would have it, returned phone calls on the same day. Assistant Professor Matt Fine of Temple University was awesome in helping to secure student examples of work for our companion website. Others we need to thank include, in alphabetical order, Adam Bagni, Brian Baker, Kyle Blackstone, Mark Burghart, Caroline Carter, Doug Carter, Roymieco Carter, Paul Castro, Matt Celli, Pam Davis, Jim DeLorenzo, Colin Donohue, Sam Dostaler, Oliver Frazier, Jr., Josh Getzoff, Gisela Gier, Joanne C. Gerstner, Jim Gray, Eric Handler, Anthony Hatcher, Leslie Hicks, Paul Hicks, Jeff James, Joe Jareck, Mark Levy, J. McMerty, Ann Meyers-Drysdale, Melissa Miller, Tom Monfiletto, Brian Monihan, Eddie Motl, Tom Nelson, Shawn Oleksiak, Youssef Osman, Paul Parsons, Maureen Quilter, John Reynolds, Jim Rosenhaus, Dan Sabreen, Mike Sheehan, Curt Smith, John Stoviak, Ray Tipton, Pat Taddei, and Elizabeth Weinreb Fishman.

We would also like to thank our wives, families, and significant others for their unwavering support, including Marc's wife Debbie and sons Jake and Pace, and Max's children Ben and Abbey, his father Michael, sister Emily, brother Sam, and sister-in-law Beth.

ENDNOTE

1. An updated 2011 study done by the Curley Center revealed more than 200 US colleges and universities offering at least one sports media-related course.

Chapter 1

SPORTSCASTING: A BRIEF HISTORY AND OVERVIEW

A SPECTACULAR CENTURY'S WORTH OF GROWTH

These were men who had to invent what to say. Sportscasting pioneers painting word images and creating phrases. Sketchy descriptions of baseball games and boxing matches transmitted over scratchy radio signals heard by relatively few.

These were the early 1920s.

Not even a century later, sportscasting is a multibillion-dollar business. Entire entities are built around sports content, often delivering round-the-clock coverage of events and sports news on multiple platforms. These include outlets on both the national and regional levels as well as individual channels owned and operated by leagues, conferences, teams, and universities. Thousands of conventional, over-the-air television and radio stations have also included extensive coverage of live event and sports news coverage starting after World War I. And the World Wide Web has opened the way for thousands of portals, adding words such as "streaming," "webcasting," and "podcasting" to the lexicon.

"Sports unifies us," says Rick Burton, the David B. Falk professor of sport management at Syracuse University. "It's a universal language. It tends not to be pensive in the way talking about politics or religion or sex can be. And I think in large part it equalizes all parties. It's a place where, in a lot of cases, we set aside racism and sexism and present [instead] the concept of the balanced universe. I'm speaking in the abstract but I think we see the best of ourselves in sports. We almost nightly see some

Rick Burton, courtesy of Syracuse University

form of heroism. We see some form of personal or individual courage. We see some form of equality—as long as you make the cutoff throw or you make the basket, I don't care what your race is, your sexual preference, or your country of origin. For that shining moment, sports delivers the best in all of us."

IN THE BEGINNING

News involving sports and sporting events, along with the stories and results behind them, have been communicated throughout much of recorded history. Cave paintings by early man depicted sports like hunting, sprinting, and wrestling.[1] In the eighth century BC, Homer's *Iliad* Book 23 describes the so-called funeral games for Patroclus, including detailed accounts of the participants, the outcomes, and even disputes about the results.[2] Greek poets like Pindar, who lived from c. 518 to 438 BC, would write victory odes for participants at the ancient Olympic games.[3] And while he wasn't reporting on a sporting event per se, the ancient Greek hero Pheidippides was said to have run from the Battle of Marathon to Athens to announce the defeat of the Persian Army in 490 BC, only to collapse and die after delivering the news. The distance Pheidippides ran set the stage for today's marathon.

REALIZING THAT SPORTS SELLS

In the United States, newspapers began writing about sports as early as the 1790s with reports of explorations by outdoor sportsman. A March 1796 issue of *The New York Magazine* included an article that chronicled a bear hunting expedition in Russia. More frequent newspaper reporting on sports surfaced in the early 1800s. In 1823, for example, the *New York Evening Post* featured the first round-by-round account of a prize fight.[4] So-called "penny papers," such as the *New York Herald*, used articles on sports along with simpler writing and lower prices to draw readers away from the competition. According to reader-interest surveys of the time, certain features of the sports section were rated "higher than anything else except the most striking news story, the comics, and picture pages."[5]

Before the Civil War, the growth of baseball led to more journalists dedicated to covering sports. Henry Chadwick, a former cricket player, began covering baseball for the Long Island Star in 1847. Chadwick is credited with creating the first box score.[6]

After the Civil War, newspapers dedicated even more resources to sports coverage. After Joseph Pulitzer purchased the *New York World* in 1883, he dedicated a special newsroom to sports and was the first person to hire a sports editor.[7]

SPORTS: ORGANIZED

Throughout the 1890s and into the early twentieth century, sports coverage continued to expand as more sports were developed and organized:

- College football expanded greatly from 1880 to 1900 with the number of football programs growing from eight to 43 after the establishment of uniform rules of the game[8]
- Professional baseball continued to grow in popularity after the establishment of the National League in 1876 and the American League in 1901. The two leagues formed the National Agreement in 1903 leading to the development of the World Series. At the same time, minor league baseball came under the control of the National Association of Professional Base Ball Leagues[9]
- Baseball cards, which were distributed by tobacco and candy companies, helped familiarize children with baseball and its players throughout the late nineteenth and twentieth centuries[10]
- Basketball was invented in 1891 and would spread quickly throughout the country, leading to several Ivy League and Midwest schools starting basketball programs[11]

ALMOST THERE

This evolution of organized sports created fans and their attendant need to keep up with their teams. The telegraph was used to communicate not only the results of games and matches, but also to describe the action during the game. Famously, during the 1912 World Series between the Boston Red Sox and New York Giants, telegraphers stood outside railroad stations and in Times Square, announcing what was going on during the games as they progressed.[12]

In 1911, more than 1,000 fans watched a mechanized re-creation of a college football game between the University of Kansas and the University of Missouri. First, the result of each play was received via telegraph. Then, as each play was announced, a ball would be moved back and forth depending on its actual position on the field.[13]

FINALLY . . . ON THE AIR

While radio technology was improving during this time, live broadcasting was still a struggle. However in 1920, there would be a turning point in radio history when KDKA in Pittsburgh provided live coverage of election results.[14]

Sportscasting as we know it today (specifically event coverage) would begin to flourish from this confluence of sports growth and technological advances. This growth intrigued the Radio Corporation of America (RCA), a broadcasting giant that not only owned several radio stations but also manufactured and sold radio receivers as well. RCA founder David Sarnoff felt that broadcasting baseball would be an important element in an overall strategy of developing radio programming as well as enticing the growing number of baseball fans to buy the units needed to listen to that programming.[15]

RCA owned an interest in Pittsburgh's KDKA. On April 11, 1921, KDKA broadcasted the first play-by-play of an event in a major city, as *Pittsburgh Post* writer Florent Gibson would deliver the blow-by-blow descriptions of a prize fight at Motor Square Garden. Nearly three months later, on July 2, would be the first sporting event broadcasted simultaneously on two stations as New York's WJY and WJZ brought listeners a title fight between Jack Dempsey and Georges Carpentier in Jersey City. KDKA would continue to spearhead sports coverage, first with its broadcast of the first baseball game on radio between the Pittsburgh Pirates and the Philadelphia Phillies on August 5th and the next day by broadcasting the Davis Cup on August 6th. Harold Arlin, a foreman at RCA, announced that game and is widely recognized as the first full-time sports announcer, even though the station would not cover every game.[16] Arlin would again make history on October 8 of the same year when he provided play-by-play for the so-called Backyard Brawl between the University of Pittsburgh and the University of West Virginia, the first college football game to be broadcast live on radio.[17]

THE SPORTSCASTER

Despite Arlin's status, most early radio broadcasters were newspaper reporters. Sandy Hunt, from Newark, New Jersey's *Sunday Call*, convinced WJZ to cover the World Series since two New York teams, the Yankees and Giants, were competing. But Hunt had to be creative since the telephone company would not install a line to the press box, so he got a phone line run to a box seat that he had purchased. His descriptions of the games had to be called in to a man named Thomas H. Cowan, who in turn repeated Hunt's descriptions word-for-word for broadcast. Later, WJZ covered the 1922 World

Series featuring the same teams, only this time the great sportswriter Grantland Rice did the announcing live. That same year, WJZ would also start covering college football from the Polo Grounds. Then on October 28, 1922, the first long-distance broadcast of a sporting event occurred when New York's WEAF broadcasted a college football game from Stagg Field in Chicago.[18]

By 1923, the term "sportscaster" or "sports announcer" became more formalized as radio stations began looking for voices to represent them and the sports they broadcasted. Graham McNamee took a job as a radio announcer after a failed singing career and, in 1923, announcing the World Series for WEAF in New York. McNamee was one of the first announcers to use the time in between plays to talk to the listeners and include descriptions of what was going on beyond the field of play, including crowd descriptions and action in the bullpen.[19] The next year Edward Britt "Ted" Husing would gain popularity as a sports announcer and along with Phil Carlin would make up half of one of the first popular announcing teams.[20]

GROWING PAINS

While some events were actually described by an announcer at the stadium utilizing play-by-play, particularly in larger cities like New York and Chicago, many were still being "recreated" in a studio. By the end of the 1920s, the teleprinter would begin to replace the telegraph as the station's method of receiving in-game information. The teleprinter allowed for more detailed descriptions of the action and would eliminate the need to understand Morse code, allowing announcers to directly receive and decipher the game information. So instead of radio stations requiring someone to decipher the dots and dashes, they would receive easily translatable letters and numbers that gave a fuller description of the action on the field.[21]

Game recreation became the method of choice for stations with skimpy budgets that couldn't afford to provide live coverage of games. In fact, some stations would schedule broadcasts at their convenience, going as far as to literally hide the results of events from their listeners until what they declared was "game-time." At that point, they would "announce" the game as if it was live, but instead actually read the play-by-play of an already completed event from the telegraph or teleprinter. Gordon McLendon was one of the more popular re-creators of his time.[22]

Dr. Murali Balaji is an assistant professor of media studies and production at Temple University. He says radio in the 1920s was very much a case of trial and error.

> "There had not yet been a standard set of laws governing radio," says Dr. Balaji. "The Communications Act was not passed until 1934 (establishing the Federal Communications

Commission). Plus, the limitations of technology and the fundamental limitations of training at the time really made sportscasting hit or miss for the duration of the 1920s."

■ **From Play-by-Play to President**

In 1932, after graduating from Eureka College in Illinois, a young man traveled to Iowa to pursue a career in broadcasting. After arriving at WOC radio in Davenport, Iowa, he told the program director he wanted to be a sportscaster. His audition was to announce a fictitious game. He passed, becoming the play-by-play announcer for University of Iowa football games for the rest of the season. He would make $10 a game.

He would eventually move to the bigger WHO radio in Des Moines, Iowa, after telling management he was able to cover track and field, a popular sport on radio at the time. He also recreated Cubs games for the station. Once while doing just that, the telegraph machine stopped working. He covered up by having a batter foul imaginary balls off for almost seven minutes. The telegraph was revived, allowing him to finish the game. In 1937, this sportscaster took a screen test while covering the Cubs' spring training. It led to a contract with Warner Brothers Studios and a 25-year career in film and television including—ironically—a role as George "Gipper" Gipp in the 1940 film *Knute Rockne, All American*. The nickname "Gipper" would stick for the rest of his life. He would also serve as the Screen Actors Guild president for seven years, helping to vault him into the world of politics. From there, two terms as governor of California starting in 1967 and two terms as president of the United States in 1980 and 1984 . . . for one Ronald Reagan.

GROWTH, MILESTONES, AND REGULATING ALL OF IT

More milestones would be reached in sportscasting through the 1920s and 30s:

- 1927: On New Year's Day, NBC launched its first coast-to-coast broadcast of any kind, with coverage of the Rose Bowl game[23]
- 1930: The invention of the car radio made rush hour an important programming time for radio, particularly during the post-World War II phenomenon known as "suburbanization." Since most sports were played during the day, the car radio increased the daytime audience for sportscasts[24]
- 1935: United Press International started selling news and sports information to radio stations, allowing stations to provide sports news coverage to complement their game broadcasts[25]

Despite the growth of sportscasts and its audiences, some sports teams were still suspicious. There was apprehension about radio's impact on their sports, with some fearing broadcasts would convince people to listen at home instead of attending games. In 1929, the American League of Baseball attempted to ban radio broadcasts of their games altogether. When the Great Depression held down crowds, some blamed radio instead. In 1932, the Eastern Intercollegiate Association also banned radio broadcasts of their college football games.[26] This same fear led the New York City baseball teams (Giants, Yankees, Dodgers) to delay broadcasting regular season games until 1939, when the Dodgers finally took to the air on WHN and WOR.[27]

At the same time, the legal framework surrounding sports broadcasts began to take shape. Baseball was the first sport to establish its teams' right to dictate who broadcasted their games. The Federal Communications Commission (FCC) would rule in several cases, saying that stations could not broadcast or recreate games of certain teams without their consent. Still, stations would infringe on the rights of other stations. For example, in 1934 in Jamestown, New York, a station broadcasted play-by-play of the 1934 World Series after listening to a live broadcast of the game from another station. In 1938, KQV in Pittsburgh was caught recreating games after listening to broadcasts from other Pittsburgh stations, including KDKA. In both cases, the FCC threatened to revoke each station's broadcasting license. In 1936, baseball commissioner Kenesaw Mountain Landis ordered major league teams to limit alternative stations, aside from the team's flagship station, from broadcasting games.[28]

As broadcasters and teams worked through the legalities, sports broadcasting would flourish. By 1935, the Mutual Radio Network began its national broadcasts of the World Series with the team of Red Barber and Bob Elson after baseball commissioner Landis sold the rights to all three major radio networks.[29] Both Barber and Elson would eventually be honored with the National Baseball Hall of Fame's Ford C. Frick Award, given to broadcasters who make major contributions to baseball.[30] On New Year's Day 1937, radio would feature its first international sports broadcast when Villanova played Auburn in the Bacardi Bowl in Havana, Cuba.[31] The Mutual Radio Network would continue to grow, attracting more affiliates and raising the profile (and value) of sports broadcasts. The Mutual Radio Network would also be the first to air a national broadcast of the NFL Championship when the Chicago Bears met the Washington Redskins from Washington, DC, on December 8, 1940.[32] By 1950, most Major League Baseball teams were commanding more than $200,000 a year for rights to their games, partly due to the competition created by the Mutual Radio Network.[33]

■ **Marty Glickman—from Olympian to Broadcaster**

Marty Glickman's story is one of multiple layers. He was one of the early play-by-play sportscasters who invented several well-known phrases that are still used today. But before that, he was a great athlete in his own right, denied an opportunity to win gold in the 1936 "Nazi Olympics" because of apparent anti-Semitism.

Glickman was born August 14, 1917, to Harry and Molly Glickman, two Romanian immigrants. The title of his autobiography, *The Fastest Kid on the Block*, tells of Glickman's ability as a track athlete. According to a synopsis of the documentary *Glickman*, which aired on HBO, when Glickman competed at the Olympic trials for the 1936 squad:

> Glickman was announced as having finished third in the 100-meter race, although the officials, who were likely biased, dropped him to fifth place. Still, he made the team as part of the 400-meter relay, joining Jesse Owens and others bound for Berlin.
>
> With Adolf Hitler in the stands, Owens won three gold medals, shattering the illusion of Nazi supremacy. Avery Brundage, chairman of the US Olympic Committee, along with assistant track coach Dean Cromwell, then declared that Owens and Ralph Metcalfe would replace Glickman and Sam Stoller—the only Jews—on the relay team, ostensibly because "secret" German runners were expected to challenge for the gold. The US team won by 15 yards, while the Germans finished a distant fourth.

www.hbo.com/documentaries/glickman/synopsis.html

Glickman would return to Syracuse University and continue to compete in track events while also playing basketball and football, earning All-American honors in football. After a game in 1937 in which he scored two touchdowns, a local businessman asked him to do a weekly 15-minute radio sports broadcast, which lead to his interest in broadcasting. After graduating in 1939, he joined WHN in New York, becoming their sports director in 1943. He was the first radio announcer for the New York Knickerbockers when they were formed in 1946. It was then that Glickman invented descriptions for locations on the court, coining phrases like "swish" for a basket that hit nothing but net. He was also the NBA's first national announcer. He would continue to work in sports broadcasting, particularly around the New York area, across six decades. He was the broadcaster for the New York Giants for 23 years, the Knicks for 21 years, and the Jets for 11 years. He was also hired by NBC to mentor their young broadcasters, including Marv Albert, who had met Glickman while working as a ball boy for the Knicks in the 1950s.

Glickman would continue working into his 70s after being hired for a second time as the Jets radio announcer. He would retire in 1992 and would pass away due to surgical complications in 2001 at the age of 83.[34]

TELEVISION: THE BEGINNING

During the 1930s, as radio firmly established broadcasting's role in delivering sports to fans, television technology was being developed to send images as well as sound throughout a region, and eventually, throughout the country.

Here's a list of some famous television firsts:

- The 1936 Summer Olympic Games in Berlin was the first sporting event broadcast live on television. Four areas of the games, including the track and field stadium, were covered. More than 72 hours of live coverage were featured in so-called "Public Television Offices" throughout Berlin and Potsdam. Each of these offices included a television set broadcasting certain events along with a sitting area so people could watch[35]
- The first time a sporting event was broadcast on television in the United States was May 17, 1939, a baseball game between Columbia University and Princeton University. This happened only a few weeks after television was exhibited and sets were sold at the New York World's Fair in April[36]
- The first professional baseball game on television was broadcast throughout New York on August 26, 1939. The game featured the Brooklyn Dodgers and Cincinnati Reds and was broadcast to the 400 or so sets existing in New York City at the time. The announcer, Red Barber, did his own commercials between innings, advertising products such as Wheaties cereal[37]
- The first college football game broadcasted on television was on September 30, 1939, between Fordham University and Waynesburg University[38]
- The first professional football game to be broadcast on television was on October 22, 1939, featuring the Brooklyn Dodgers and Philadelphia Eagles[39]
- The NHL aired its first television broadcast of a game on February 25, 1940, through NBC. The game between the Montreal Canadiens and the New York Rangers from Madison Square Garden was seen in New York City[40]
- Three days later, on February 28, the first basketball on television was broadcast on NBC featuring the University of Pittsburgh and Fordham University[41]

Further development of television was delayed as the world turned its focus to World War II. Throughout this time, radio remained the main source for news and information. Many Americans first heard about the attack on Pearl Harbor during a broadcast of a football game between the New York Giants and Brooklyn Dodgers.[42]

After the war, the price of television sets was still prohibitive, with most televisions purchased by restaurants, hotels, and other businesses. The novelty of television helped these establishments to attract crowds because viewers could now watch a game without going to the stadium. The increasing popularity of baseball led to more games being broadcast on television and an increase in the sale of television sets. In 1947, the first World Series to air on television would be broadcast on three stations throughout New York, featuring the Yankees and Brooklyn Dodgers.[43]

TELEVISION: UNEVEN GROWTH

Throughout the late 1940s and early 50s, broadcasters continued to work out the myriad of kinks involved in televising sports. At many stations, the maintenance personnel became more important than the on-air personalities due to frequent equipment issues. Also, members of the broadcast crews, such as cameramen, often came over from radio and were still learning how to use the new technologies in coordination with the on-field action. These cameramen, as well as the announcers, were often faked out by play-action and trick plays in football. Cameras would often focus only on the ball-carrier while ignoring the rest of the action. The capabilities of the equipment were also limited. In a 1948 football game between University of Oklahoma and University of Texas, the marching bands had to stay between the 35-yard markers because the cameras could only cover that portion of the field.[44]

In these formative years, television stations were still organizing regular schedules and broadcasting companies were forming national networks. Sporting events were an easy way to provide entertaining programming, thus enticing households to buy sets. Stations did not have to organize or finance the source of the programming (the games), but rather they just had to show up with the equipment and produce the telecast.[45]

The early financial model for covering sports on television was similar to that of early radio. That is, income came primarily from the sales of the television sets themselves. Many sports programs, like other radio and early television programming, did have a single sponsor. The first regularly scheduled sports program was *The Gillette Cavalcade of Sports*. It debuted on radio in 1942 after Gillette grouped its sports sponsorships under one name. The same show would make its television debut in 1944. It wasn't until the 1960s that sports would move toward the multi-company sponsorship and advertising model we see today.[46]

THE COAXIAL CONNECTION

Televising sports outside the city of the event continued to be an issue. However by 1948, coaxial cables were installed between New York, Philadelphia, and Washington, DC, allowing stations from those cities to share broadcasts with one another. Other cities had to rely on copies of events taped through a kinescope, a device used before the advent of videotape, which recorded a live broadcast from a small television monitor. These kinescope recordings had to be physically delivered, making same-day broadcasts of sporting events difficult.[47]

During this time, wrestling and boxing became popular on television for a variety of reasons. The events themselves were small and relatively easy to shoot, with some matches staged in a studio and shot by a single camera. But the location of these events in primarily larger cities ultimately meant better production facilities. And the popularity of boxing and wrestling on television showed station operators there was value to showing violent sports on television.[48]

But even as late as 1950, radio was still king, since only 9 percent of homes actually owned a television set. However, coaxial cable continued to be a boon for television as more cities were connected to New York and its sports programming. In September 1951, coaxial cable made its way to the West Coast just as baseball's post-season was getting underway. The first transcontinental television broadcast of a sporting event was on October 3, 1951, and featured the New York Giants and Brooklyn Dodgers in the third and deciding game of their National League playoff series. The game would end on the home run that became known as Bobby Thomson's "shot heard 'round the world." The historic homer was not only seen by those who had access to a television, but was heard on radio by servicemen listening while serving in Korea. The popular, long-time Detroit Tiger broadcaster Ernie Harwell did the national play-by-play for the game. Ironically, Russ Hodges' famous call "The Giants win the Pennant! The Giants win the Pennant!" after Thomson's home run was almost lost. Radio broadcasts were not recorded at this time, but a Brooklyn fan asked his mother to record the game while he was at work and she was able to capture the famous call for posterity.[49]

TV BECOMES KING

Technological improvements in televising sporting events came quickly through the 1940s and 50s. Innovations included increasing the number of cameras (from two to five, including one in centerfield for baseball broadcasts); multiple microphones for use by the announcers and to pick up crowd noise; the addition of an analyst to explain strategy and game play; and simple, two-line graphics to provide information on the players and games.[50]

By the mid-50s, television had surpassed radio in broadcasting sports. In 1954, the television industry would also surpass radio in overall advertising revenue, including more than $1 billion a year in advertising sales by 1955. In 1956, 80 percent of homes in the United States had at least one television. But radio maintained a sizeable portion of the sports broadcasting audience because of the introduction of the transistor in 1954. The transistor made radio even more portable, allowing people to listen anywhere they could receive a signal.[51]

Televised sports were a staple of early primetime television programming. But in the 1950s, it began to migrate more to the weekends as television matured and more inclusive programming was developed for an audience that was approximately 50 percent female.[52]

TV'S GREAT INNOVATIONS

The late 1950s and early 60s saw many additions and improvements to the way sports were broadcast, changes that are still in effect in some form or fashion today:

- In 1956, the videotape recorder (VTR) was introduced by Ampex, making it easier to duplicate copies of a game while also offering a clearer picture than the recordings from the kinescope[53]
- In 1959, the increased portability of television equipment gave us the first blimp shot. CBS would install a camera on the Goodyear Blimp, which gave aerial views of the 1960 Orange Bowl football game[54]
- In 1960, CBS paid $50,000 to televise the Winter Olympics, from Squaw Valley, California. This was the first live broadcast of the Olympics in the United States. During one race, it appeared that a skier missed a gate during the slalom. Race officials asked CBS if they could review the tape. This would inspire CBS to create instant replay for sports broadcasts[55]
- Later that same year in Rome, CBS would be the first to use a portable color camera in the Summer Olympics. Cameras were now small enough to fit on airplanes or portable enough to carry around (with a large backpack). This allowed cameramen to set up anywhere in order to get close-up shots of the action
- By 1961, NBC began offering color programming to entice people to buy new color television sets. NBC's parent company at the time was RCA, which manufactured and sold televisions. Ampex would also introduce the color VTR[56]

▪ Roone Arledge

Spanning the globe to bring you the constant variety of sports . . .
the thrill of victory . . . and the agony of defeat . . .
the human drama of athletic competition . . .
this is ABC's *Wide World of Sports*!

This was the introduction to ABC's *Wide World of Sports*, which debuted on April 29, 1961, and continued most Saturdays, every week, for some 37 years. The voice most associated with these words was that of the show's host, the late Jim McKay. But the main reason the show was one of the greatest, most innovative, and longest running sports shows in television history was its producer, Roone Arledge.

According to Arledge's biography *Roone: A Memoir*, Arledge took a different tack from NBC and CBS and their broadcasting of live sports. Instead, he "injected emotion and drama into the events on *Wide World of Sports*" through the use of videotape as well as the ability of jet travel to make available sporting events around the world. Due to the limited coverage of many of the sports they taped (such as Irish hurling and Mexican cliff-diving), *Wide World of Sports* was able to rebroadcast these events knowing that the majority of the audience did not know the result. At the same time, Arledge brought viewers closer to the action and closer to its participants by experimenting with different camera angles and microphone placement, often covering events in ways never seen nor heard before. *Wide World of Sports* would also feature the personal stories of the participants, allowing for a deeper, emotional connection between audience and athlete.

ABC (and Arledge) would forge the same audience/athlete connection in 1964 with their coverage of the Summer Olympics in Tokyo. ABC would continue to increase Olympic coverage, going from the 15 hours CBS provided in 1960 to more than 72 hours in 1972.

In 1970 Arledge would again change the televised sports landscape by introducing *Monday Night Football* on ABC. The show used the first three-man booth, featuring Keith Jackson (replaced in 1971 by Frank Gifford), Howard Cosell, and Don Meredith.

Arledge would eventually be hired as president of ABC News in 1977. He had only covered one "hard news" event, the tragedy at the 1972 Munich Summer Olympics (more on this later in the chapter), but ABC recognized his vision and creativity could help improve their low rated news department. He would go on to create the popular news programs *20/20*, *Nightline*, *Primetime*, *This Week*, and *World News Tonight*. Many of the innovations Arledge brought to ABC News, including eye-catching graphics and more on-location coverage, were successful in his previous productions for ABC Sports. Under Arledge, ABC News grew into one of the top news media outlets in the United States.

Arledge would continue to oversee both ABC Sports and ABC News until 1986. He would step down from ABC Sports in 1986, soon after the purchase of ESPN by ABC in 1984. He would continue to oversee the successful ABC News department until 1998, when he retired from television.

It is hard to realize the impact Arledge had on television throughout his career, but his creativity and innovation forever altered the way people around the world consume news and sports. Arledge would succumb to prostate cancer on December 5, 2002, in New York City.

- In 1961, the first remote pre-game show, *Pro Football Kickoff*, was introduced by CBS. A 15-minute program hosted by Johnny Lujack, the show would eventually expand to include interviews and news reports and would be a template for future pre-game shows[57]
- July 12, 1962 featured the first satellite transmission of images from the United States to Europe. One of the first transmissions was clips from a Philadelphia Phillies–Chicago Cubs game that aired on WGN[58]
- On December 7, 1963, CBS debuted instant replay during the Army–Navy football game in Philadelphia. Replay was possible before, but it would take several minutes to initiate. The instant replay machine, which was invented by CBS sports director

Tony Verna, weighed more than 1,300 pounds. When the replay was produced seconds after the original play, announcer Lindsey Nelson reassured viewers by saying "Ladies and gentlemen, Army did not score again!"[59]

■ On January 16, 1967, both CBS and NBC would broadcast the first NFL-AFL world championship football game. This occurred seven months after the leagues agreed to merge. The game, of course, would become known three years later as the Super Bowl[60]

The growth of sports and sports television was not without its issues. One of the more infamous events occurred on November 17, 1968, a hotly contested NFL matchup between the New York Jets and Oakland Raiders. As the two teams battled to the finish, fans in the eastern part of the country—local Jets fans included—were suddenly without the game. Instead, NBC began showing the heavily promoted movie *Heidi*. The Raiders would go on to win in dramatic fashion, scoring two touchdowns in the game's final 75 seconds. A colossal embarrassment for NBC, the "*Heidi* Game" would affirm the need for networks to broadcast games until their conclusion, delaying programs such as *Heidi* until after the clock showed all zeros.[61]

RIGHTS FEES BECOME A FACTOR

By the 1970s, programming rights for the major professional sports would be on the rise. While a mere fraction of some of the rights fees that are paid today, some of the dollars being forked over were unprecedented. Much of this growth was realized by the NFL, where rights to televise its product would reach a record $50 million by 1970. This figure far surpassed television rights fees being paid at that time to Major League Baseball ($18 million) and the National Basketball Association ($2 million).

■ **NFL rights fees: 1962 TO 2012**

1962: $7.4 million a year (CBS 4.7/NBC .6/ABC 2.1)
1965: $24.5 million a year (CBS 16/NBC 8.5)
1969: $33 million (CBS 24.5/NBC 8.5)
1970: First year for MNF and merger
1973: $47 million (ABC 8/CBS 22/NBC 17)
1977: $55 million (ABC 13/CBS 24/NBC 18)
1981: $162 million (ABC 60/CBS 54/ NBC 48)
1985: $420 million (115/120/107)
1989: $476 million (125/165/135)

1993: $900 million (225/265/188/ESPN 111/TBS 111)
1997: $1.097 billion (ABC 230/NBC 217/FOX 395/ESPN 131/TBS 124)
2002: $2.6 billion (ABC 550/CBS 500/FOX 500/ESPN 600/DirecTV 400)
2006: $3.735 billion (CBS 623/NBC 600/FOX 713/ESPN 1,100/DirecTV 700)
2012: $4.065 billion (CBS 613/NBC 610/FOX 743/ESPN 1,100/DirecTV 1,000)[62]

SOCIETY'S EFFECT

1970 was also a year of firsts in sports television for women and minorities. That year, *The NFL Today* show hired two of the first women sports reporters when they signed Marjorie Margolies and Carole Howey. By 1975, the same program would also employ one of the first minority analysts, former NFL player Irv Cross. Another woman, former Miss America Phyllis George, would later be hired by *The NFL Today* as a reporter.[63]

ABC would be the unwitting beneficiary of a tragedy that occurred during its coverage of the 1972 Summer Olympic Games in Munich. Palestinian terrorists attacked and captured members of the Israeli Olympic team, resulting in the death of 11 Israelis. ABC covered most of the Olympics in primetime, suddenly utilizing sports reporters to cover a dramatic, rapidly changing news event. ABC was able to keep viewers up-to-the-minute, utilizing some the latest in remote TV technology. This technology is said to have inspired the idea for today's sideline reporter (see Jim Lampley's comments in Chapter 6). All told, ABC netted 29 Emmys for its coverage of the disaster as well as the Olympic Games themselves.[64]

CABLE, SATELLITE, AND THE RSN

The 1970s would also mark a great leap forward in the cable television industry. To this point, cable was typically used to provide television programming to those who were out of reach of antenna signals. But now, cable was developing subscription services that consumers could purchase, giving them access to more programming than ever before. On November 8, 1972, Home Box Office (HBO) showed a New York Rangers–Vancouver Canucks game that would reach 365 people in the Wilkes Barre, PA, area.[65]

By the mid-70s, satellite would provide the means to transmit a station's signal to a cable company and then, ultimately, directly into a subscriber's home. In 1976, Ted Turner's WTCG in Atlanta (now TBS) became the first basic cable station to be launched via satellite, thus becoming the first so-called "Super Station." Before the end of the decade, several more channels would be developed, focused specifically on sports, movies, or children's programming.[66]

In 1969, the first of the regional sports networks (RSN) debuted. New York area sports fans got to see events originating from Madison Square Garden. The games were broadcast through a deal with Manhattan Cable Television. By 1978, this channel become known as the Madison Square Garden Network, or MSG as it's commonly known today.

RSN development continued in 1976 when SportsChannel America was started following the launching of New York City's Cablevision Sports 3. SportsChannel America would expand to several major markets throughout the 1980s. Today, many of those markets have come under the branding of two powerhouse RSN's, either Comcast SportsNet or Fox Sports.[67] PRISM (Philadelphia Regional In-Home Sports and Movies) also debuted in 1976, and like MSG, would focus on covering local and regional sports.[68]

■ ESPN

In 1978, a door closed on Bill Rasmussen. But another would soon open, leading to the creation of a sports television phenomenon.

Bill Rasmussen, courtesy of ESPN

That year, Rasmussen was fired from his job as a communications manager for the Hartford Whalers hockey club. Armed with time and an idea, Rasmussen, his son Scott, and his friend and insurance agent Ed Eagan decided to explore forming a cable network that would cover Connecticut sports. Originally, while Rasmussen was still with the Whalers, Eagan had pitched the concept of a weekly cable show on Connecticut sports to local cable operators. But after Rasmussen left the Whalers, his group decided to expand the original concept. So, they invited 12 local cable operators to listen to their proposal for a new network they were calling Entertainment and Sports Programming Network (ESP). Only five of the cable operators accepted, but it was enough for Rasmussen's group to incorporate the network on July 14, 1978, at the cost of $91. They had planned on providing the service throughout parts of New England through land lines, but satellite soon became a much more viable option. A representative from RCA convinced

Rasmussen that satellite use would be cheaper than landlines, while at the same time reaching the entire country. This changed the paradigm to a 24-hour national network. Rasmussen's company purchased a transponder for $30,000 and settled in Bristol, Connecticut. Six months before the network's planned September launch, private financing would allow the purchase of the rights to the early rounds of the 1980 NCAA Tournament. Rasmussen negotiated the deal just a few weeks before the 1979 tournament started, which included the seminal title game featuring Michigan State's Magic Johnson and Indiana State's Larry Bird. That contest garnered a 24.1 rating and raised the popularity of college basketball, prompting many to call and inquire about "that channel that has all the basketball." Also before their scheduled launch, they signed a substantial contract with Anheuser-Busch as a sponsor.

Eventually the network changed its name to ESPN to distinguish itself from the so-called "Big Three": ABC, NBC, and CBS. ESPN would debut at 7 pm EST on September 7, 1979, with the satellite being connected just five minutes before the first broadcast. The first telecast had Lee Leonard and George Grande anchoring the first SportsCenter, which featured videotaped highlights and scores. It lasted for half an hour before the broadcast of a slow-pitch softball game.

A little more than three decades after ESPN launched as a single cable network, the company now oversees several dozen properties that cover both professional and amateur sports as well as producing original programming and content. These properties include several domestic and international television networks, book and magazine publishing companies, a radio network and radio stations, websites and other digital properties, along with their film and television production companies. ESPN holds the rights to broadcast the NBA, NFL, MLB, MLS, NCAA basketball, football, and the NCAA championships for a number of sports, FIFA, NASCAR, and IndyCar. ESPN is responsible for the most sports coverage in the United States, including over half of all live coverage of sporting events. It is also the most popular network on cable, commanding the highest broadcasting fees of any cable network and earning its parent company, Disney, more than $8.2 billion in revenues in 2012.[69]

Like Turner's WTBS, WGN in Chicago would join the Super Station ranks, also becoming available through satellite in 1978. While WTBS broadcast Atlanta Braves baseball and Atlanta Hawks basketball games, WGN showed games of baseball's Chicago White Sox and Cubs along with Chicago Bulls basketball. The broadcasting of these sports nationally was a first for cable.[70]

THE 80S: THE COLD WAR, THE COURTS, AND THE EFFECTS OF CABLE

Through the 1980s, a number of events would sanctify the broadcasting of sports as a significant part of our culture.

In the midst of the Iranian Hostage Crisis and the Cold War, the United States' Olympic hockey team would all at once tap into its country's soul and latent patriotism. The so-called "Miracle on Ice" would take place on February 22, 1980 in Lake Placid, New York, as the USA pulled off one of the most remarkable upsets in all of sports history, a 4–3 victory over the Soviet Union in the gold medal game. The end-of-game call by ABC's Al Michaels, "Do you believe in miracles? Yes!" may very well be the most famous line in sports broadcasting history. Celebrants in cities and towns around the nation spontaneously took to the streets, waving and wearing the red, white, and blue.[71]

The Super Bowl continued to take strides toward becoming the virtual national holiday it's become. By 1982, the game would be the highest rated sporting event of all time. Super Bowl XVI, featuring the San Francisco 49ers and Cincinnati Bengals, received a rating of 49.1, a share of 73 and reached 40 million households in the US, making it—at the time—the highest rated sporting event ever.[72]

A 1984 Supreme Court ruling would pave the way for a flood of college football on television. In the case *NCAA* vs. *Board of Regents of University of Oklahoma*, the high court ruled the NCAA could not limit the amount of college football on television, nor could it limit the amount of times a specific team appeared on TV. The NCAA had originally limited televised college football games to one per Saturday and only allowed teams to appear on television once a year, fearing televising of games would hold down attendance.[73]

The growth in the popularity and programming of sports and sporting events along with the growth of cable began to have a negative economic effect on the televising of sports by broadcast networks. First, rights fees took a significant jump in the 1980s for a majority of leagues and conferences. Broadcast networks like ABC, NBC, and CBS were able to afford these fees before the arrival of cable. But with the development of cable and VHS tape products, the television audience now had more options through which to view their sports. All this led to a flattening of ratings. The major broadcast networks had tried raising advertising rates to cover the increasing rights fees, but the dilution of the audience caused advertisers to balk. To make up for the loss, the networks tried showing more sports to attract more ad money, but this strategy diluted the television sports market even more. This trend would continue through the 1990s forcing networks to re-evaluate their commitment to sports on the broadcast networks. In fact, after CBS signed a five-year contract with Major League Baseball for $1.06 billion in 1988, CBS Sports found itself deeply in the red. By 1993, the network would lose the rights to the NBA, MLB, and NFL's National Football Conference, although it regained the rights to the American Football Conference's games in 1998.[74]

The 80s also marked the introduction of one of the fastest growing segments of sports broadcasting today, the sports talk radio format. Actually as early as 1964, one of several early sports talk shows debuted on New York City radio when Art Rust, Jr. regularly took sports-related calls during his show on WWRL.[75] That same year, Bill Mazer launched the first regularly scheduled sports talk radio program.[76] On July 1, 1987, WFAN (formerly WNBC) was launched in New York City, becoming the first radio station dedicated completely to sports talk and play-by-play.[77] Philadelphia radio station WIP actually predates WFAN, shifting towards sports in 1986, but it would not become all sports and sports talk until 1988.[78] On January 1, 1992, ESPN would launch Sports Radio ESPN (later to become ESPN Radio), buttressing the all-sports radio format as a force in what at the time was an otherwise declining radio market.[79]

THE 90S: LEAGUE-OWNED NETWORKS, HIGH-DEFINITION, AND THE INTERNET

The 1990s would mark the arrival of some new players and interesting alliances in sports television. In 1993, ABC, NBC, and MLB joined forces to start The Baseball Network, thus becoming the first network to be owned by a professional sports league. The Baseball Network would ultimately fail a year later due to the baseball strike started in August 1994 that ended up in the cancellation of the World Series.[80] But the very concept of The Baseball Network would spur the National Basketball Association to launch the league owned and operated NBA-TV by the end of the decade. Eventually, all four major North American sports leagues would have their own networks by 2009. Also in 1993, the Fox broadcasting network would become a major player on the television sports scene as it outbid CBS for the rights to show the NFL's National Football Conference games starting in the 1994 season. Parent-company News Corp had also purchased several television station ownership groups, making it the largest network of stations in the United States by the early 90s.[81]

The concept of high-definition television was introduced to the public in 1994. The first high definition broadcast of a sporting event ever viewed in the United States occurred in a number of Los Angeles movie theaters when international broadcaster NHK connected audiences with its so-called "Hi-Vision" broadcasts of the 1994 World Cup.[82]

The increasing availability of cable and satellite services and the rapid commercialization of the Internet led to new and different portals for sports programming and services. In 1994, the NBA launched its League Pass followed by the NFL's Sunday Ticket, two services offering virtually every game on the schedule through a paid subscription. All of the major sports leagues in North America would launch similar services soon after.[83] On November 7, 1994, WXYC in North Carolina became the first radio station to stream online. This new way of broadcasting not only helped a flagging radio industry, but it also opened avenues for sports leagues to offer audio—and eventually video—online.[84] The NBA would be one of the first to do this when, in 1995, it became the first league to launch a fully integrated website with the introduction of NBA.com.[85]

The mid and late 90s also marked the rapid growth of the regional sports networks (RSNs). In 1996, News Corp partnered with Liberty Media to create Fox Sports Net, a large network of regional sports networks.[86] The following year, Comcast Corporation started Comcast Sportsnet Philadelphia in concert with its purchase of the NBA's Philadelphia 76ers and NHL's Philadelphia Flyers. The channel would serve as a model for other RSNs that Comcast would establish in other parts of the country.[87]

Sport management professor Rick Burton of Syracuse University says the rise of RSNs is traced to ESPN's limited ability to satisfy the hunger of the hometown fans for more news on their teams.

> "If I lived in Boston, I didn't want to spend a lot of time hearing about the Angels or the Mariners or the 49ers. I really wanted to hear mostly about the Red Sox, the Celtics, the Patriots and the Bruins. So the concept of a New England Sports network or a WGN with largely a Chicago focus is logical because you have enough of an audience in those locations to give them more specifically what they want."

High-definition television became more viable on baseball's Opening Day, 1998. That's when KXAS-TV showed the Fort Worth area the first commercial broadcast of a sporting event in HD as the Texas Rangers took on the Chicago White Sox.[88] Super Bowl XXXIV on January 30, 2000, became the first national broadcast of a sporting event in HD.[89]

The late 90s also saw two seismic shifts in broadcasting rights. In 1999, NASCAR consolidated its rights, selling its entire schedule to three networks—Fox, NBC, and TNT—for six years and $2.4 billion starting in 2001.[90] Fox alone acquired broadcasting rights to the World Series starting in 2000, expanding their portfolio of league broadcasting rights.[91]

For the 2002 season, Major League Baseball introduced MLB.tv, the first out-of-market streaming service for a professional sports league. The NBA and NHL would follow later in the decade. Streaming in general would also become an attractive, cost-effective alternative for smaller sports leagues and teams, allowing them to broadcast games without having to rely on over-the-air or cable broadcasters.[92]

Jason Benetti, the director of communications and play-by-play voice of Minor League Baseball's Syracuse Chiefs thinks that advent of streaming has raised the performance level of announcers.

"The smart announcers, when they have the opportunity, are clicking around to hear every other announcer to hear what they do well and what they don't do well and I think [as an announcer] you sort of become a composite of everybody while keeping your own ability and talent shining through. So [because of streaming] you know what's out there, you know who's good and you know who's not and you know what you like and don't like. But it's all helped to refine the craft and I think it's also given the people the feeling that, "hey, my job's not so bad—you're in single A ball or short-season single A—but anyone can listen to you."

In 1997, Cablevision became the sole owner of the broadcast rights for all seven, New York area NBA, MLB, and NHL teams. Cablevision was able to take these games and create an expensive, upper tier of digital cable channels. However, the New York Yankees were not happy with the arrangement. The club became frustrated with the way their games were distributed and how they were scheduled. So in 1999, the Yankees partnered with the NBA's New Jersey Nets to create their own network. The YES network debuted in March 2002, becoming the first regional sports network to be launched by a sports team in the United States.

In 2004, podcasting began to become popular in concert with the digital movement and the creation of the mp3 player. The podcast allowed a listener to take in any portion of a program they wanted to hear, any place they wanted to hear it. It also opened new opportunities for radio stations and hosts around the country to get their content out to listeners.[93]

In August 2007 the first regional network dedicated to a single, college conference emerged as the Big Ten and Fox Sports jointly launched the Big Ten Network.[94] By August 2011, the Longhorn Network became the first regional network dedicated to a single school, launched as a joint venture between ESPN, IMG College, and University of Texas-Austin.[95]

STILL GROWING

In January 2011, Comcast became an even bigger player in sports broadcasting with its acquisition of a majority stake in NBC. As a result of the sale, Comcast rebranded and reprogrammed the Versus network, creating the NBC Sports Network in its place. All of Comcast's regional sports networks were also placed under the NBC Sports umbrella.[96]

Murali Balaji, Ph.D, courtesy of Temple University

Fox and News Corp announced they are considering launching a national sports network in 2014, the last of the big four broadcast networks to do so. This would support Fox's growing portfolio of broadcasting rights which include the NFL, MLB, NCAA football and basketball, soccer (UEFA cup, Premier League, and FIFA World Cup starting 2015), Ultimate Fighting Championships, and NASCAR.[97]

Dr. Murali Balaji, assistant professor of media studies and production at Temple University sums up sportscasting's phenomenal growth this way:

> Sportscasting has become a multi-billion dollar a year business primarily because every aspect of global sports has become so monetized. What you've seen over the last 100 years is the internationalization of sports and the spectacle of sports. For example, with the Olympics, media would eventually serve a role in bringing live events to global audiences. First it was radio, allowing for sports to be broadcast internationally. Ultimately, sportscasting became a very powerful way for media companies and sports teams to build their brands.

POINTS FOR DISCUSSION 1

POINTS FOR DISCUSSION

1. What is it about sport that makes it valuable content for radio, television, and the Internet?
2. Describe what you think might have been some of the problems and challenges presented by the early sporting events broadcasted on radio and television.
3. After originally fearing that broadcasting their games on radio would affect attendance, baseball owners changed their minds. What factors do you think the owners considered when allowing radio stations to broadcast their games?
4. Choose an innovation and discuss its impact on sportscasting:
   a. Organizing sports through leagues and codification of rules.
   b. The establishment of the Federal Communications Commission.
   c. Coaxial cable.
   d. Color television.
   e. Instant replay.
   f. Portable camera equipment.
   g. Cable.
   h. Satellite.
   i. High-definition television.
5. What allowed radio to continue to flourish as a medium for sportscasts despite advancements in television and the Internet?

6. Choose a single event and discuss why you feel it was the most significant event broadcast in the history of sportscasting.

7. Explain the phenomenon that is ESPN.

ENDNOTES

1. Gary Barber, *Getting Started in Track and Field Athletics: Advice and Ideas for Children, Parents and Teachers* (Bloomington, IN: Trafford Publishing, 2007), 25.

2. Homer, *The Iliad*, trans. Samuel Butler, Book 23. http://classics.mit.edu/Homer/iliad.23.xxiii.html, accessed October 23, 2012.

3. Peter Armenti, "Pindar, Poetry, and the Olympics," *From the Catbird Seat: Poetry and Literature at the Library of Congress*, July 27, 2012. http://blogs.loc.gov/catbird/2012/07/pindar-poetry-and-the-olympics, accessed October 24, 2012.

4. Elliot Gorn, *The Manly Art: Bare-Knuckle Prize Fighting in America* (Ithaca, NY: Cornell University Press, 1986), 39.

5. Harry E. Heath, *How to Cover, Write, and Edit Sports,* (Ames, Iowa: Iowa State College Press, 1951).

6. Bruce J. Evenson, "Henry Chadwick" in *The Encyclopedia of American Journalism*, ed. Stephen Vaughn (New York: Taylor & Francis, 2008), 45.

7. Daniel Beck and Louis Bosshart, "Sports and Media," *Communication Research Trends* 22 (2003), 7.

8. "Final Football Standings 1900." www.shrpsports.com/cf/stand.php?season=1900&conf=Ind&week=final&B1=Submit, accessed November 2, 2012.

9. "The National Agreement for the Government of Professional Base Ball Clubs." http://roadsidephotos.sabr.org/baseball/1903NatAgree.htm, accessed November 3, 2012.

10. Kurt Snibbe and David Schoenfield, "A Brief History of Baseball Cards," *ESPN Page 2*, June 26, 2007. http://sports.espn.go.com/espn/page2/story?page=snibbe/cards/060726, accessed December 5, 2012.

11. "Yale Bulldogs Year-by-Year Results." http://www.yalebulldogs.com/sports/m-baskbl/2011–12/files/year-by-year_results.pdf, accessed October 23, 2012.

12. John R. Catsis, *Sports Broadcasting* (Chicago: Nelson-Hall, 1996), 2.

13. "100 Years Ago: Football Fans Enjoy a Mechanized Reproduction of KU-MU Game," *Lawrence Journal-World*, November 27, 2011. www2.ljworld.com/news/2011/nov/27/100-years-ago-football-fans-enjoy-mechanized-repro/?print, accessed October 25, 2012.

14. "Radio Station KDKA Historical Marker," *Explore PA History*. http://explorepahistory.com/hmarker.php?markerId=1-A-30F accessed October 22, 2012.

15. Brad Schultz, *Sports Broadcasting* (Boston: Focal Press, 2002), 3.

16. Catsis, *Sports Broadcasting*, 2–4.

17. "Pitt Football Firsts," Pittsburgh University. www.225.pitt.edu/story/pitt-football-firsts accessed December 2, 2012.

18. Catsis, *Sports Broadcasting*, 3–5.

19. Schultz, *Sports Broadcasting*, 240–242.

20. Ibid., 4–5.

21. Catsis, *Sports Broadcasting*, 8.
22. "Gordon McLendon," The Radio Hall of Fame. www.radiohof.org/pioneer/gordonmclendon.html, accessed December 3, 2012.
23. Catsis, *Sports Broadcasting*, 9.
24. "William P. Lear (1902–1978): Audio, Automotive, and Appartus," Lemelson-MIT, November, 1998, http://web.mit.edu/invent/iow/lear.html, accessed November 30, 2012.
25. Gwenyth L. Jackaway, *Media at War: Radio's Challenge to Newspapers: 1924–1939* (Westport, CT: Praeger, 1995), 35.
26. David George Surdam, *Wins, Losses, and Empty Seats: How Baseball Outlasted the Great Depression,* (Lincoln, NW: University of Nebraska, 2011), 202.
27. Catsis, *Sports Broadcasting*, 17.
28. Ibid., 15–16.
29. Ibid., 14–15.
30. "Ford C. Frick Award," The Baseball Hall of Fame. http://baseballhall.org/museum/awards/ford-c-frick, accessed December 2, 2012.
31. "Bowl History," Villanova University Athletic Department. www.villanova.com/sports/m-footbl/archive/nova-m-footbl-inbowls.html, accessed December 3, 2012.
32. "Football Firsts," The Pro Football Hall of Fame. www.profootballhof.com/history/release.aspx?release_id=1476, accessed December 4, 2011.
33. Catsis, *Sports Broadcasting*, 20.
34. "Mary Glickman (1917–2001)," Jewish Virtual Library. www.jewishvirtuallibrary.org/jsource/Holocaust/glickman.html, accessed March 14, 2014.
35. "Berlin 1936," Olympic.org. www.olympic.org/berlin-1936-summer-olympics, accessed December 4, 2012.
36. "Sports and Television," The Museum of Broadcast Communications. www.museum.tv/eotvsection.php?entrycode=sportsandte, accessed November 15, 2012.
37. "This Day in History: August 26," The History Channel, August 26, 2007. www.history.com/this-day-in-history/first-televised-major-league-baseball-game, accessed November 20, 2012.
38. "First TV Football Game," Waynesburg University Athletic Department. www.waynesburgsports.com/sports/2007/8/17/first_tv_game.aspx, accessed November 30, 2012.
39. "History: The Most Televised Game," The Pro Football Hall of Fame. www.profootballhof.com/history/decades/1930s/first_televised_game.aspx, accessed December 5, 2012.
40. Paul Patskou, "Hockey Night in Canada," *Canadian Communication Foundation,* August 1, 2007, www.broadcasting-history.ca/index3.html?url=http%3A//www.broadcasting-history.ca/sportsonradioandtv/HNIC_TV.html, accessed November 30, 2012.
41. "This Day in NY Sports History: February 28," *Long Island Newsday*, February 27, 2011. www.newsday.com/sports/college/college-basketball/ny-sports-history-feb-28–1940–1.2718167?qr=1, accessed December 6, 2012.
42. "1941: NFL on Pearl Harbor Day," The Pro Football Hall of Fame. www.profootballhof.com/history/decades/1940s/pearl_harbor.aspx, accessed December 3, 2012.
43. Frank Fitzpatrick, "A Look Back at the First TV Broadcasts of World Series in 1947" *Philadelphia Inquirer*, October 20, 2012. http://articles.philly.com/2012–10–21/sports/34607837_1_tv-sets-tv-station-press-box, accessed December 1, 2012.

44. Schultz, *Sports Broadcasting*, 8–10.
45. Catsis, *Sports Broadcasting*, 29.
46. "Sports and Television."
47. Catsis, *Sports Broadcasting*, 31–32.
48. Schultz, *Sports Broadcasting*, 9.
49. Richard Sandomir, "The Shot Heard 'round the World: A Call is Born, Saved by Mom," *New York Times*, October 1, 2001. www.nytimes.com/2001/10/01/sports/the-shot-heard-round-the-world-a-call-is-born-and-saved-by-a-mom.html?ref=bobby_thompson, accessed November 30, 2012.
50. Schultz, *Sports Broadcasting*, 10.
51. Ibid., 5.
52. "Sports and Television."
53. "Ampex: History," Ampex. www.ampex.com/news/history.html?start=30, accessed November 23, 2012.
54. Joyce Jones, "Sports Wouldn't be the Same Without the View from the Blimp," *New York Times*, October 24, 1991. www.nytimes.com/1993/10/24/nyregion/sports-wouldn-t-be-the-same-without-the-view-from-a-blimp.html?pagewanted=all&src=pm, accessed December 10, 2012.
55. "Squaw Valley 1960," Olympic.org. www.olympic.org/squaw-valley-1960-winter-olympics, accessed December 4, 2012.
56. Catsis, *Sports Broadcasting*, 33.
57. Schultz, *Sports Broadcasting*, 12–13.
58. Adam Mann, "TelStar 1: The Little Satellite That Created the Modern World 50 Years Ago," *Wired,* July 10, 2012. www.wired.com/wiredscience/2012/07/50th-anniversary-telstar-1/?pid=, accessed November 15, 2012.
59. Tom Hoffarth, "Army–Navy, Instant Replay, Tony Verna, 45 Years Later," *Farther off The Wall*, December 5, 2008. www.insidesocal.com/tomhoffarth/2008/12/05/army-navy-insta, accessed December 10, 2012.
60. "Super Bowl I Recap," NFL.com. www.nfl.com/superbowl/history/recap/sbi, accessed November 30, 2012.
61. Larry Harnisch, "The *Heidi* Game Remembered, November 17, 1968," *Los Angeles Times,* November 18, 2008. http://latimesblogs.latimes.com/thedailymirror/2008/11/the-heidi-game.html, accessed, November 28, 2012.
62. John Vrooman, "The Economic Structure of the NFL," in *The Economics of the National Football League*, ed. Kevin G. Quinn (New York: Springer, 2012), 12.
63. Schultz, *Sports Broadcasting*, 12.
64. "Munich 1972," Olympic.org. www.olympic.org/munich-1972-summer-olympics, accessed December 1, 2012.
65. Bob Raissman, "Glickman Helped HBO Click," *New York Daily News*, February 23, 1997. http://articles.nydailynews.com/1997–02–23/entertainment/18039844_1_hbo-president-championship-boxing-hockey-game, accessed December 13, 2012.
66. "Behind the Scenes: Our History," TBS. http://static.tbs.com/about_us/PR/mile.htm, accessed December 10, 2012.

67. Geraldine Fabrikant, "The Media Business: NBC and Cablevision Plan Join Programming Venture," *New York Times*, December 23, 1988. www.nytimes.com/1988/12/23/business/the-media-business-nbc-and-cablevision-plan-joint-programming-venture.html?src=pm, accessed November 10, 2012.

68. Sam Donnellson, "PRISM, SportsChannel on Way Out?" *The Philadelphia Inquirer*, March 20, 1996. http://articles.philly.com/1996–03–20/news/25636426_1_prism-comcast-acquisition-brian-l-roberts, accessed November 30, 2012.

69. Karl Taro Greenfield, "ESPN: Everywhere Profit Sports Network," Businessweek.com, August 30, 2012. www.businessweek.com/articles/2012–08–30/espn-everywhere-sports-profit-network, accessed January 12, 2013. Link now expired.

70. "WGN Station History," WGNTV. www.wgntv.com/about/station/stationhistory, accessed December 13, 2012.

71. Kevin Allen, "College Kids Perform Olympic Miracle," ESPN.com, December 23, 1997. http://espn.go.com/classic/s/miracle_ice_1980.html, accessed December 3, 2012.

72. Bill Gorman, "Super Bowl Ratings Do Not Decline in the 4th Quarter; And More Facts you didn't Already Know," *TV by the Numbers*, January 26, 2011. http://tvbythenumbers.zap2it.com/2011/01/26/super-bowl-tv-ratings-do-not-decline-in-the-4th-quarter-and-more-facts-you-didnt-already-know/80390/, accessed December 1, 2012.

73. *NCAA* vs. *Board of Reagents Univ. of Okla.*, 468 US. 85 (1984). http://caselaw.lp.findlaw.com/scripts/getcase.pl?court=us&vol=468&invol=85, accessed November 14, 2012.

74. "Sports and Television."

75. David Hinkley, "Sports Radio Pioneer Art Rust Dies at 82," *New York Daily News*, January 14, 2012. http://articles.nydailynews.com/2010–01–14/sports/17944739_1_radio-talk-art-rust, accessed November 24, 2012.

76. Neil Best, "First Time, Long Time for Bill Mazer," *New York Daily News*, June 16, 2011. www.newsday.com/sports/columnists/neil-best/first-time-long-time-for-bill-mazer-1.2962262, accessed November 25, 2012.

77. Alex French and Howie Kahn, "The Sound and the Fury," ESPN.com, July 10, 2012. www.grantland.com/story/_/id/8016912/don-imus-mike-mad-dog-fall-rise-first-all-sports-talk-station-wfan, accessed November 25, 2012.

78. Andy Bloom, "The History of WIP by Operations Manager Andy Bloom," June 14, 2012. http://philadelphia.cbslocal.com/2012/06/14/test-3, accessed December 10, 2012.

79. Schultz, *Sports Broadcasting*, 7.

80. Catsis, *Sports Broacasting*, 87–88.

81. Ibid., 44.

82. "History," NHK. www.nhk.or.jp/digital/en/HDTV/07_history.html, accessed November 12, 2012,

83. Larry Stewart "A Consumer's Guide to the Best and Worst of Sports Media and Merchandise," August 14, 2000. http://articles.latimes.com/2000/aug/14/sports/sp-4070, accessed December 3, 2012.

84. "Simulcast," WXYC. www.wxyc.org/about/simulcast, accessed November 10, 2012.

85. "NBA Technology History," NBA.com. http://hoopedia.nba.com/index.php?title=NBA_Technology_History, accessed November 12, 2012.

86. "Fox, Cablevision Revamp Sports Deal," *The Street*, February 22, 2005. www.thestreet.com/_googlen/stocks/media/10209873.html?cm_ven=GOOGLEN&cm_cat=FREE&cm_ite=NA, accessed November 30, 2012.

87. Michael L. Rozansky, "Comcast Deal Isn't the End of PRISM It Could Benefit Both Firms to Leave TV Rights as is," March 24, 1996. http://articles.philly.com/1996-03-24/business/25636634_1_comcast-executive-comcast-chairman-ralph-roberts-comcast-deal, accessed November 30, 2012.

88. "First HDTV Baseball Game," YouTube Video, 6:33, posted by tjlivy, December 6, 2009, http://www.youtube.com/watch?v=9Dcu_2J2904.

89. Michael Sandler, *Kurt Warner and the St. Louis Rams: Super Bowl XXXIV (Super Bowl Superstar)* (New York: Bearport Publishing, 2007), 19.

90. "History of NASCAR," Nascar.com, July 17, 2008. www.nascar.com/news/features/history, accessed November 10, 2012.

91. "World Series Averages Record Low Television Ratings," Associated Press, October 29, 2012. http://msn.foxsports.com/mlb/story/Rating-for-World-Series-opener-drops-to-record-low-82295310, accessed November 30, 2012.

92. "MLB.tv Celebrates Ten Years of Live Game Streaming," Sports Video Group, August 28, 2012. http://sportsvideo.org/main/blog/2012/08/28/mlb-tv-celebrates-ten-years-of-live-game-streaming, accessed December 1, 2012.

93. Ben Hammersley, "Audible Revolution," February 11, 2004. www.guardian.co.uk/media/2004/feb/12/broadcasting.digitalmedia, accessed November 15, 2012.

94. "Big Ten Network to Officially Launch August 30," BigTen.org, July 2, 2007. www.bigten.org/genrel/070207aaa.html, accessed November 29, 2012.

95. Erick Smith, "Eyes of Texas are not on the Longhorn Network when it Launches," *USA Today*, August 27, 2011. http://content.usatoday.com/communities/campusrivalry/post/2011/08/longhorn-network-launch-high-school-highlights/1, accessed November 29, 2012.

96. Michael McCarthy, "Versus set to Become NBC Sports Network," *USA Today*, August 1, 2011. http://usatoday30.usatoday.com/sports/columnist/mccarthy/2011-07-31-versus-nbc-sports-network_n.htm, accessed November 30, 2012.

97. John Ourand and Tripp Mickle, "Will Fox Launch All-Sports Network?" *Sports Business Daily*, April 2, 2012. www.sportsbusinessdaily.com/Journal/Issues/2012/04/02/Media/Fox-channel.aspx, accessed December 2, 2012.

Chapter 2

THE PRODUCTION PLAN

WE LOVE TO WATCH

In terms of audience, nothing is more diverse than the universe of people who watch, follow, root, cheer, and listen to sports. The reasons are not hard to understand. First, fandom is a shared experience that families, friends, and even strangers in bars can get together and cheer. All the connection takes is someone in a similar jersey, or maybe even a clap or yell at that particular moment of a game where your team is scoring, causing a turnover, breaking your heart, or hoisting the trophy. Second, every team begins each season anew, with a chance to win. Granted, some teams seem to inherently have a better chance than others due to resources, players, or recruiting. Every team begins with a spotless record, and the story of their season is written in real time for all to see.

While most of us would love to be season ticket holders sitting in the stands or luxury boxes to root for our team, often we must follow our team from afar. The public relies on an army of professionals who cover the games and provide information about everything in the world of sports. This might be the game in the middle of an August pennant race, or maybe the press conference of the Hall-of-Famer retiring after a long career, or perhaps the young draft pick holding up his jersey for the first time. These moments are captured for the world to see, listen, or read.

How do these moments get from the field, court, arena, or studio to the fans and viewers? What is this overall process? From the on-air talent to the producer, director, and the technical crew, the production of sports is a complicated dance of many moving parts. The overall goal is always to tell a story. Often, the story being told is a mix of many plotlines that are woven over time. Some angles might reflect the strategies of how the game is being won or lost, others might have nothing to do with the outcome itself and instead highlight the human drama inherent in the event, with sports merely serving as a backdrop.

In this chapter, we will look at how this process works, who works on the shows, and briefly discuss the different types of shows that are typically produced. Throughout the rest of this textbook, we will go into more detail of each of these positions and productions.

TELLING STORIES . . .

It's the top of the hour. We fade from black to a wide shot of the field and we hear an announcer set up the game we are about to see. Often, the language is epic and dramatic and pits two teams or individuals against one another in a struggle to win the contest. Over the next few minutes, we learn about each team and probably highlight one or two points about each squad, how they are doing in the current season, perhaps some things to pay particular attention to.

Then the game starts. The coverage is augmented by camera angles that show us how a certain play succeeded, hearing the roar of the crowd, the thud of a hit, a coach in the huddle talking about adjustments to be made, an announcer giving insight into the call on the field or what is happening next, and graphics that show the score, key stats, the up-to-the-minute playoff situation, and some replays and highlight packages that show the big moments in dramatic slow motion. At the end of the broadcast, all these elements work in concert to tell the story of the game, the team, the participants, and often the other players in and around the game.

That is what the viewer sees at home. Behind the scenes, many people are working very hard to bring all this to light. For most of this chapter, we are focusing on production of live, unscripted sporting events, although we will also briefly cover scripted shows as well.

PLANNING, PREPARING

The biggest challenge of covering any event is not knowing exactly what will happen. The results are not known beforehand, and some of the greatest moments in sports were born from events that no one predicted were going to be interesting. Even in a studio or scripted environment, some of the elements of production can be unpredictable, from electrical or equipment issues, to a myriad of things that can pop up and create situations that folks will have to deal with at a moment's notice.

With this in mind, the best piece of advice comes in two parts, planning and preparing. While these might seem like the same thing, they have some key differences. To highlight this difference, allow us to introduce a phrase:

Plan for what you can, prepare for what you can't.

Sample Rundown

Page	Slug	Source	OC	TRT	Show Time
1	Open/Tease	Tape Machine	Music Sting	:30	:30/:30
2	Hello & Welcome	Bob Announcer On-camera		:15	:45/:45
3	Standings	Full Screen Graphic		:15	1:00/1:00

A rundown is a simple plan of events for the talent and crew to know the order of elements for a segment of a show. This is a very simple version of a rundown. Many producers will develop their own version with more or less information. For this basic rundown, we include page number, slug, source, out cue (OC), total run time (TRT), and the segment and show time.

A **page number** is a simple identifier for each element of the show. A producer or director can use these to quickly note what element they want to see, rehearse, move or delete. In conjunction with the page number, a producer will include a **slug** or a short three or four word description of the element. Again, this allows for quickly identifying an element of the show. For example, they might say, "let's take a look at page 3, standings…" In this example, this would alert the talent, director, graphics, audio, and camera that we are going to see a full-page graphic.

The **source** is a quick notation for where this element is coming from. This could be a camera, a tape element, graphics machine, or some other source. Often, this is assigned by a director, and they will mark up their personal copy of a rundown with their own notations to keep track of each element's source.

The **out-cue** (OC) and **total run-time** (TRT) are used to let people know about when a particular element is finished. An outcue would be very useful at the end of a taped piece and is typically the last few words of a sentence or music sting. The **show time** of a show is simply a tally of the total time elapsed in a show. During live shows, whether scripted or a sporting event, the channel that is showing the event has a very specific time the show must start and end. The producer will be particularly interested in how the actual show matches up with the estimated show time. If the show is running long or short, then the producer will need to make adjustments to different elements of the show. How do they do this quickly? They are able to quickly adjust the flow of a rundown because of the built in ease of adjusting elements. For example, we are moving page 3 to the next segment and going to break right after page 2. In a few short words, everyone knows what is happening.

For some parts of your show, you will know exactly what is going to happen. These are the moments you develop a solid *plan*. If you have five minutes before the opening tip of your basketball game, then you can *plan* for every second of those five minutes. If you have a 30-minute studio show, you can *plan* for what is going to be seen the entire show without surprise. Planning means you spend time before the show writing it down and sharing the plan with everyone who needs to know so no one is surprised, and everyone can accomplish their task in concert with everyone else. The plan is the roadmap, the guide, the rundown of events.

A rundown lists the elements of the show. Each element will often have a number to distinguish that piece of the show from everything else. The slug will give a brief, three- or four-word at most description of that piece. Then the rundown will often include the source, length, and run-time of the piece. Depending on who you are and where you are working on the show, the rundown provides key pieces of information so that everyone can literally be on the same page at the same time. A director will need to know what element is coming next, an audio technician will need to know where the next source of audio is coming from, talent will need to know what they are voicing over or talking about next, the tape room would need to know what element to cue up and play next, camera operators will need to know what is their next shot, and graphics will use that information to let them know what graphic is next. This plan allows for predictability.

When you are dealing with a live sporting event, other than how many rounds, periods, or players on the field or court, or the general rules of play, you will not be able to reliably predict what is going to happen. You will need to diligently *prepare* for what you cannot definitively predict. This relates to everyone on the crew. Preparing means you try your best to think of likely scenarios and the possible courses of action. Let's look at a few examples to see what this might mean.

Let's say you are covering a football game. And let's assume that at some point, one of the teams will score a touchdown. How can we *prepare* for this situation from the different crew positions? If you are the announcer, you might have practiced a new way to announce a touchdown, including the name of the team, who scored, and what the current score is before the extra point. If you are the graphics coordinator and graphics operator, you might need to have shells built for whoever scored and give some key stats about the player's season. Perhaps there is a player who is approaching a record number of points scored and you will need to be ready to know the significance of the touchdown. If you are the director, you have set up your camera operators to get you various shots. You want to see a hero shot—in other words, a close-up image of the player who scored—on two of your cameras, another camera is responsible for getting the head coach, two other cameras are getting crowd shots, and the game camera is getting ready for the extra point. As a camera operator, you need to harken back to the meeting you had with the director before the show started where she explained what was expected. In the tape room, the operators are looking for replays and getting ready to roll out to the commercial with good angles of the score and a player reaction. The audio booth is mixing in the crowd that is going nuts with the announcers' excited calls and remembering the cannon that is about to go off in the end zone. And, as we go to break, roll some music to button up the segment.

That is just one of numerous situations that everyone has to be ready to handle. And while we are suggesting to *plan* for all that you can and to *prepare* for as much as you can, you also need to steel yourself that this is essentially impossible! "What?" you ask, "I can't plan or prepare for everything?" Well, we don't mean to scare you, but no, you can't! Things happen that you can't even imagine: a tornado hits in the mountains, the star player suddenly retires five minutes before the game, a massive sit-in erupts at center court, who knows what it might be? No matter what position you are working, you will need to troubleshoot as best you can and make the best of whatever happens. In the end, you will have plenty of time after the show to reflect and add that crazy situation to your repertoire of circumstances you will be ready to handle!

THE CREW

Bringing any production to life requires a team of people who bring both creative and technical skills to the production. These people form a crew that in some cases has just met for the first time that morning, yet in a matter of hours must set-up and get ready to work as a well-oiled machine to collaborate and produce a sporting event. Throughout this book, we will go into great detail to discuss each of the crew member's roles in the production. As you consider your career choices, remember that while you might strongly identify with only one of these jobs, understanding how all these roles fit together in the big picture will provide you with a greater understanding of your role and ultimately help you succeed no matter which job you perform. In addition, you might go into your career thinking you want to head in one direction, but might end up in a totally different area. Part of your success will, of course, be your proficiency in performing your job function. However, understanding how you fit into the overall operation, which includes having some understanding of the big picture, will make you more effective in not only doing your job, but getting help from the numerous people you are working with on the crew. No production happens overall with just one person, but many productions, in the moment-to-moment progression of a sportscast, have been saved or ruined by individuals.

Here we offer a summary of the positions you will encounter.

On-Air Talent

On-air talent are the face of the production. They could be play-by-play, color analysts, reporters, anchors, or other special guests. These special guests could be anyone from former players to league officials to a coach or manager being interviewed during the game to provide insight as events unfold. These roles have a wide range of job functions, and later in this text we look at many strategies to help you navigate these roles.

On-air talent has the job of explaining the action and leading the viewer or listener towards key moments, statistics, storylines, and people involved with the sportscast. Talent must be prepared with as much information as possible, including player names, backgrounds, strengths, weaknesses, and key stats. In addition, the best on-air talent has the ability to roll with situations as they unfold. Much like a news anchor that has to decipher a situation and analyze on the fly, so too must on-air talent be able to observe and process a massive amount of information happening in front of them and often with the voice of the producer and/or director in their ear. The task of calling a game or anchoring a studio show can be quite daunting, but an increased comfort level often comes with experience.

Throughout this book, we delve into the many different facets of the performance of on-air talent. While the audience sees their final performance, the work done behind the scenes to prepare for the camera lens, microphone, and the glare of lights is an important trip to take and understand. For example, you must take a close look at your performance and find productive ways to practice and get feedback on your work. In addition, the different skills needed to be a reporter, anchor, play-by-play, or color analyst are all different in the intricacies they require you to master. Before you hit the air, the preparation you will do, whether it's the research you perform or the relationships you make with sports information directors or athletes or other sources, will all require a thoughtful and coordinated plan . . . and perhaps some luck to be in the right place at the right time. However, as we have discussed, planning and preparation can greatly increase your chances of not needing luck and instead being able to rely on hard work. We feature in-depth information on these facets and more throughout the book.

The on-air talent might be the face and voice that the audience sees and hears, but they are the tip of the iceberg in terms of the crew working diligently to bring the show to life.

The Producer

The term "producer" can be confusing. What exactly does this person produce? What is the difference between an executive producer, a coordinating producer, and a show producer? In essence, anyone with the title of producer is responsible for content. An executive producer is ultimately responsible for the content on the channel. At times, they might be an executive producer for a single show, but often they oversee entire networks or several shows. A coordinating producer manages several producers, oversees their work, and keeps tabs on the overall branding of a channel. A show producer is essentially in charge of the production on-site or in the studio. They will answer to and seek advice and feedback from the coordinating and executive producers.

Show producers have prepared the content for the show, and might have had a large hand in selecting the crew, prepping the talent, booking facilities, and handling media relations as it pertains to integrating the televised event with the actual event. A producer delivers this plan to a variety of people who take their ideas and put them into action. These people include the director, graphics designer, audio mixer, tape operator, master control engineer, the facility manager of where the event is taking place, and other technical crew. In addition, the producer is responsible for making sure sponsored elements make it into the show. In the end, the producer has the final say on content and coverage. This might involve such various decisions as making a call on an angle being used, whether to include a potentially inflammatory sound bite from a player or coach, to where the crew is allowed to park or eat lunch.

On many shows, a producer has people to help them with the process of getting a show ready for air. These people include associate producer, production assistants, and possibly production interns. We discuss the role of a producer and their crew in greater detail in Chapter 10. While they are involved with many decisions, to make the show come to life and the production plan to work, a key partner for producers are the show's directors.

The Director

A close ally of the producer of a sportscast is the director. The director is often the person who takes the producer's ideas and comes up with the strategies to implement them. The director is often the link between producer and crew, and has responsibilities to work through technical challenges before and during the show. A director's main tool is his or her voice. Everyone on the crew takes their cues from the director. Similar to an orchestra conductor, the director calls for certain things to happen. This might be a camera move or cut, a graphic coming on the screen, music to play, or a tape rolling. A director will defer to the producer for some decisions, for example, when to run a promo, where to lead the announcers for a certain story, or which replay angle to use.

In other situations, the director is on their own and must make decisions based on conversations that probably happened several hours or days before the show. For example, the producer might want to highlight a particular player or coach, or there may be a league or channel-mandated storyline that they need to cover. In addition to all of these decisions, the aesthetics of the show are often under the guidance of the director. For example, how tight is a good angle of the goalie, how long do we see a graphic, when do we cut from a dejected player, and many other decisions that need to be made in a split second and cannot be discussed and debated.

A producer and director need to be in sync with the goals of the production. This allows the plan that the producer has made to be clear to the entire crew. With so many different positions and personalities, being a good director often means being part technical wizard and part human resources expert.

A director also needs folks who can help them keep the show in line. Assistant directors can do tasks such as keeping track of time for various elements such as commercials and packages as well as handling some pre-production. The technical director (TD) is often the crew chief who makes sure people are in place when and where they need to be. The TD usually handles the technical details to make sure all equipment is in working order and ready to go. The process of the crew going through and checking that everything is in working order is called a "fax." The technical director will make sure that cameras, graphics, and replay sources are in working order as well as a variety of other checks. For example, a few items that a TD might check are that the monitor wall in the front of production has the correct sources and that the camera operators can hear program audio.

Camera

As the eyes of the production, camera operators are responsible for composing the images of an event. This might include shots of athletes, coaches, fans, or general shots of the ambiance of an arena. Camera operators have the challenge of wearing several hats throughout the course of a day of work. First, they must be technically proficient with the buttons and menus of a camera and make sure technical standards are met. Next, camera operators are artists who can capture the action in aesthetically pleasing ways. They might begin with the traditional wide shot, but perhaps they will add an interesting perspective to show the flight of the ball, or the perspective of a player of a certain aspect of the game, or even follow the instinct to stay with a player and not follow the ball leaving their hand. In addition, a camera operator needs to have the skill of being able to make moves, pans, zooms, tilts, and rack focus with confidence and reliability. As we will say often with many if not all of the positions around a sportscast, practice is a key element for camera operators to gain and improve their skills.

Audio

Without sound, many of the key moments of a sporting event would lose their punch. While a picture may say a thousand words, the swell of a crowd, the unforgettable call from an announcer of the game-winning play, or the swelling music at the beginning or end of a show are important elements of a sportscast. The main sound mixer, or A1 (yes, like the steak sauce), controls the overall sound mix of the show. This includes a myriad of elements including the announcers and other on-air talent, crowd and effect microphones, music, sound effects from graphics and other elements, as well as tape playback and in some cases commercials.

The primary assistant to the A1 is an A2. On bigger shows, the number of A2s grows. Together, the audio department lays out the plan for placing microphones, setting up the announcer location, and checking that everything is working properly.

During the show, the A1 will mix these various audio sources together. They will be responsible for following the format of the show and taking cues from the producer and director about when to insert music, track tape machines, or play back other audio elements.

Graphics

The graphics department consists of people who are responsible for creating and presenting various graphic elements for the show. A graphics coordinator, often an associate producer, will handle most of the preparation for what graphics and elements are needed for the show. A graphics operator will handle the technical building of these elements. Depending on the size of the show, there might also be a score bug operator and a statistician working to keep track of key pieces of information about the event. The "stats" position might also give some of these numbers to the on-air talent to use during the sportscast.

The flow of building these graphics begins before anyone arrives at the truck or control room. Using a variety of sources, including team notes and league information, as well as figuring out some interesting connections on their own, a producer and their associate producer will generate a list of items for the show. This could be as basic as a player name, jersey number, and position or their statistics for the year. In addition, the show might have sponsored elements that will need to be included.

Once they arrive at the event's location, the graphics coordinator and graphics operator will begin building the show. Each item will have a specific location in the graphics machine and having a good system to be able to call these graphics up becomes a key strategy for an efficient graphics team.

Increasingly, the graphics operator needs to have sophisticated computer skills. Often the linking of data streams from league sources or the scoreboard need to be integrated into the graphics machine. For example, the show might want to use stats for a particular basketball player that shows the points, rebounds, and fouls for the current game. Rather than have to look up their stats and try to type those numbers in very quickly, a data stream can have those numbers plugged into a graphic shell automatically. If that player is fouled and is heading to the free throw line, the lower third graphic can be ready in an instant.

Tape

To call this position tape is more and more frequently becoming an inaccurate description. Tape, as in physical cassettes containing some form of tape stock, are increasingly disappearing. The norm is now non-linear recording devices and hard drives to playback, edit and store footage. While many production facilities and trucks still have tape decks to play back older footage, soon they will disappear in the same way that reel-to-reel tape machines used to be a staple of production and now exist in museums only.

In spite of the lack of actual tape machines, people still refer to this area as the tape room. In this area, operators are tasked with playing back various elements during a show. During a live event, the primary function is to show replays of key moments and edit short highlight packages. These packages are often rapidly produced within seconds of a play ending. As machines have become more versatile, these packages can manipulate sound effects and music as well as add effects to the video.

On larger shows, a tape room will have one or more tape producers assigned to help keep track of all the elements of a show as well as key moments during the event. At the end of the show, the tape room will "melt down" the key moments and packages of a show for a producer to take with them. These melts will be used in future productions. By only saving the key moments, this allows for more efficient storage. One of the challenges facing productions today is how to effectively manage all the data generated from events.

SPORTSCASTING EVENTS

The types of events that sportscasting covers generally fall into the broad categories of either live events or scripted shows. As we have discussed earlier in the chapter, no matter what is being produced, these events are all telling stories. For each type of event, the crew can be very small, with one person wearing several hats. For example, the producer might also be the director and technical director and, after the show, might exchange those hats for that of editor. On a larger show, the technical crew can resemble a small broadcast production station that assembles for a few days to produce an event, and then disperses to different shows across the globe. However, no matter what the show, the production of any event is, at its best, a wonderful choreography of many different people all pulling together to do their jobs to the best of their abilities to produce a compelling product.

Live Events

From a high school game to the Super Bowl, more sporting events are covered today than ever before in history. Leagues and teams are eager to get their product not just on the fields of play, but also onto the screens of their fans. These screens might be traditional television screens, but, as we will discuss Chapter 19, the Web, tablets, and mobile devices are increasingly being used to watch and follow teams.

The live event is often done after rights are paid to a league, organization, or, in some cases, directly to the teams. They can cover a single game or an entire season. The decision to cover a live event will immediately have an economic impact on many levels. For one, the cost of producing the event as a sportscast comes with costs associated with facilities and crew in addition to the rights fees. Often, the producing entity will sell advertising sponsorships for the sportscast to either reduce the cost of production or, hopefully, turn a profit for the channel. In some cases, a channel or network will pay for the rights to a product knowing they will lose money. They do this because the marketing and promotion their channel will receive as a result of covering the games is worth the investment. We will cover this in more detail in Chapter 18.

The logistics of producing the event will often start with a site survey. This inspection of the venue and surrounding area will give the production team an idea about everything from where to park the truck and crew parking, to camera and microphone placements, the location of the booth and, hopefully, any potential challenges associated with covering the event. Visiting the site before the production can also show whether there is any special equipment the crew will need in order to produce a game. For example, if a football game is being produced at a high school, the producers are likely to need to rent equipment to allow cameras to get high enough to effectively cover the action. In addition, a venue that does not normally host sportscasts might require an external source of power in the form of a generator truck.

Some sports leagues will have broadcast standards that a production must follow. For example, they might need instant replay for the officials, and this would require a certain number of cameras and integration with the field to be able to show several angles to a referee who would then make a decision. Other league mandates might include rates for the technical crew, rules about where the coverage can and cannot go (for example into locker rooms or huddles), and minimum standards for equipment.

Often, the technical crew members working on live events are more freelance than fulltime staff. However, the producer, associate producer, and some of the production assistants are more often fulltime staff with the channel or production company responsible for putting on the show.

Scripted Shows

Unlike a live event, a scripted show is usually a more controlled setting. Often, a producer is able to create a rundown of a show that can account for every second of the entire show. These would include sports highlight shows such as ESPN's *SportsCenter*, or magazine shows that feature several pre-produced packages. The variations on these shows might be in the delivery of the on-air talent but, in the end, a producer has much more control of a scripted show than a live event.

For many channels, the folks working these shows might be totally staff, although in some cases a large part of the technical crew are daily hires. This may differ based on the size of the show or channel.

Sometimes these shows are very news oriented and are intended to provide as objective a view as possible. Other times, the shows are more about marketing the team or league.

POINTS FOR DISCUSSION

POINTS FOR DISCUSSION 2

1. What is the most exciting or significant sporting event you have seen live on television? How did the picture and sound tell the story? What technical and creative elements were used?
2. How important are stories in covering live events?
3. What are the most common live events you watch? Compare two of those events and try to reverse engineer the following information:
   a. How many announcers?
   b. How many cameras?
   c. Which specific parts of the show were planned in advance?
   d. Which parts of the show were only determined as events unfolded live?
   e. Were there any parts of the show that seemed to flow well?
   f. What part of the show seemed less prepared?
   g. Research one of the positions introduced in this chapter. Find two people who do that job for a living and ask about their career path, salary, and the positive and negative aspects of their job.
4. How do the technical and creative elements of a show work together to create a sportscast?

5. Envision covering a live event. What would be areas of your event that you could *plan*? Why could you *plan* for these? What would be some parts that you could *prepare*? Why would you have to *prepare* and not *plan* for some events and not others?

6. Think about the different crew positions. What are some traits that you think would be beneficial for each of the crew to have in order to be successful? For example, if someone was on-air talent, they should be able to speak well and have the ability to think on their feet. What are some traits for other positions? What position do you think suits your personality the most? The least?

7. How would producing a scripted show be different than producing a live event?

8. Many people compare live sporting events to reality television? How are they similar? How are they different?

9. If you had a three-minute opening segment before your favorite sports team's next game, how would you open the show? Produce a mock rundown that demonstrates what you would show. What would be key information for each member of the crew to know? How could they discern this information from your rundown? What extra information might they need to get either from you or on their own?

Chapter 3

RESEARCH AND RELATIONSHIPS

Trust is defined by the dictionary as the "reliance on the integrity, strength, ability, surety, etc., of a person or thing; confidence." As a sportscaster or producer, you have to be confident in the resources and people that purport to supply you with the facts necessary to get your job done. Conversely, those folks need to develop a trust in *you*. From play-by-play to reporting, from anchoring to sports talk, from producing to directing, the trust factor is pervasive.

Getting people to trust you as a sportscaster is no different than it is getting people to trust you as an individual. Doing the right thing by the athletes, coaches, and administrators you deal with will go a long way towards engendering their trust in you. That includes—to borrow the Fox News phrase—fair and balanced reporting. It also includes correctly utilizing or *not* utilizing information that's given to you "off the record" (more on that later in this chapter). It means dealing with whomever you encounter in the same way that you would have them deal with you, in other words, the golden rule.

Cultivating a sense of trust in information sources often comes with time, experience, and a sense of discipline; checking yourself to be sure you know something is right before you put it on the air. That's not always easy considering the constant pressure of deadlines. The myriad of available resources tantalizingly beckon you, presenting themselves as quick and easy founts full of "facts." That's why you need to ask yourself the "trust question" before you use anything. *Can I trust this publication, website, or news account? Can I trust this person is telling me the truth?*

Determining what resources you can trust will ultimately allow viewers and listeners to trust *you*. Diligently doing your research and vetting the resources you rely on will go a long way toward cementing that relationship. Looking and sounding the part purely from a performance standpoint is good, but your true credibility as a sportscaster will also play a big part in determining your ultimate success.

We'll have more on what and who to trust later in the chapter. First, let's talk about where sportscasters can go in order to do their jobs.

AVAILABLE RESOURCES

Some of the sources of information available to sportscasters include the following:

You

■ To quote the late newsman Walter Cronkite from the 1950s CBS news program of the same name, no source of information is more reliable than when *You Are There*. It could be a game or practice. It could be your own shooting or note-taking during an event, practice, or interview. There's nothing like a first-person account. Don't rely on others if you don't have to. See it and hear it for yourself. There's also the additional benefit of team or school personnel seeing you at the event, yet another way to gain *their* trust in you

The Team, School, or League

■ **News release:** A printed or electronic document containing news on a trade, a hiring or firing, an event or promotion, or perhaps a statement in response to an issue in the news
■ **News conference:** A staged event formally announcing or promoting any of the issues that might be presented in a news release. The principals involved in this are normally made available for interviews from a podium and later in smaller, informal groups or one-on-one
■ **Game notes:** Formulated and issued by the media relations or sports information department of a team, league, or school, they contain stories, statistics, and other background information on players, coaches, teams, and the league. Game notes are supposed to contain up-to-date information and are normally issued before a team's game. They can be made available online or in printed form
■ **Media guides:** Also available online or in printed form, these are typically annual publications that give deeper information, statistics, and history about a particular team, its players, or a league
■ **Websites:** A compendium of some or all of what media guides have to offer plus other fan-friendly items such as ticket availability, promotions, the broadcast schedule, etc. A team will often "cover" its own news stories on its website and even issue breaking news there as well

The Media

■ **Television and radio:** Certainly one of the primary ways to monitor a player, team, or league you cover on a regular or one-time-only basis. You can follow them through the events they participate in or the news they make

■ **Newspapers:** Both the printed and electronic versions that cover sports on a regular or occasional basis. Typically a newspaper's beat writers can be among the more well-informed about the particular team or sport they follow

■ **News agencies:** Also referred to as wire services, these organizations supply news to broadcasters as well as other media outlets

■ **Magazines:** Both the printed and electronic versions that cover sports on a regular basis

■ **The Internet:** On a daily basis, this spawns an increasing number and substantial variety of websites, blogs, and podcasts that can feature a particular sport, team, or player. They range from the pure black-and-white of statistics and reference material to the colorful (off-color?) opinions and commentary of the authors to the streaming of the actual games themselves

■ **Social media:** Including but certainly not limited to Twitter, Facebook, Instagram, and Tumblr, as well as various other forums and chat rooms where fans occasionally interact with team personnel as well as with each other. Sportscasters follow teams, schools, and players via social media and will get news and quotes from there

■ **Books:** Published material that may contain important background information on a topic you are covering

■ **Films/movies:** Any feature film, documentary or short that has information that may be useful to you

The People

■ **Media relations director or sports information director:** The chief liaison between the team or school and the sports media. They are normally in charge of producing news conferences, issuing news releases, arranging for credentials, scheduling interviews, and generally being available at most times to answer questions or clarify issues

■ **Team personnel such as players, coaches, general managers, athletic directors, and others in the front office:** Depending on individual team and league guidelines, these people can be made available for interviews before or after games and practices as well as during news conferences and other special events. As mentioned, special arrangements can be made through the media relations or sports information director to do interviews at other times

■ **Your counterparts:** Fellow media members you might encounter while covering a team or an event.

GATHERING INFORMATION: WHO DOES WHAT AND WHY

Before seeking answers to your questions about a game, team, player, or other issue, you need to ask a few questions of yourself:

■ Will you be properly credentialed in order to have access to the game or news conference so that you can get the video and audio you need?

■ If it's a feature story that you are originating, do you know what you're going to shoot or record, who needs to be interviewed, and will you have access to everything you need?

■ Are you familiar with the teams, the players, the coaches, as well as the short and long-term meaning of a game?

■ Do you understand the significance of the news conference you're about to cover?

■ For a feature, do you have an idea of the different story angles that need to be told?

■ Do you have deep, reliable background information on the principals or issues involved?

Any sportscaster attending a game, news conference or other event will often need to be properly credentialed through the media relations or sports information department. This also includes coordinating seating during the event, interviews as well as access to certain parts of the venue. If you're doing a feature story outside the auspices of a particular school or team, you'll need to coordinate logistics with the principals involved. Try to schedule as much as possible in advance including where and what time to meet, where you can shoot or record, etc.

Sportscasters should *always* be doing their homework. That is, always be aware of what's happening through the resources and sources available to you, so that when you're ready

■ No Cheering in the Press Box

Jerome Holtzman was a sportswriter who was elected to the writer's wing of the National Baseball Hall of Fame in 1989. Holtzman, who died in 2008, wrote a book entitled *No Cheering in the Press Box* where he profiled 18 prominent sportswriters.[1]

"No cheering in the press box" should be the credo of any sportscaster who covers an event. It is, quite simply, unprofessional to do so. Even if you harbor a secret rooting interest, you need to comport yourself in a way that never reveals this. Simply keep it to yourself.

Another doctrine to keep in mind is *no autographs*. Again, unprofessional—it's simply not the reason you are there. You might have long idolized the player or coach you're about the interview, but again, keep it to yourself.

to broadcast, you can do so with a sense of purpose and perspective. That said, here are a few more specific points about preparation.

Reporters

Do your homework so that you're familiar with what's at stake, whether it's a game, feature story, or the theme of a news conference. Be prepared with questions and angles, although you should also be prepared if there's an unexpected turn of events.

Brian Feldman is a sports reporter, anchor and videographer for KMOV-TV in St. Louis. His primary sources are team or school-supplied.

> "Just about everybody, and it doesn't matter what level you're looking at, has a team (or school) website. When you get up to higher levels you have media guides—although lower level minor league teams and colleges often have media guides as well. That's the ultimate resource for me. Whenever a season starts, a team will put out a media guide, so make sure (sports reporters) get one of those things and have it with you at all times. Have some sort of bag or briefcase and throw that media guide in there because that will have more information than you'll ever know what to do with."

One more thing: be sure your equipment is in good working order, that cameras or recorders are operational, all batteries are charged, all microphones and lights are working, and that you have spare parts as well!

Anchors

As stated, sportscasters should *always* be doing homework and that's particularly true of sports anchors. They are asked to report on a myriad of stories every night, not just local but national and worldwide as well. Because of the nature of the position, anchors might become tied to the studio and closed-off to the outside world. Periodically getting out to games or practices and also covering stories as a reporter helps bring anchors closer to what they're covering from the inside. Constantly checking on resources and other sources they may have culled over time helps give the anchor perspective when writing and ultimately, delivering the story.

Sideline

It is especially important for sideline reporters to manage logistics with the media relations or sports information director, given their need to report during a game or event. Advance planning should be done as it relates to seating, standups during play or timeouts, access to dugouts and benches, as well as coach or player interviews.

Sideline reporters should come prepared with a number of "evergreen" storylines (in other words, feature stories that are not time-sensitive), but should also be prepared to report on any late-breaking news or developments during the broadcast.

As we will detail in Chapter 6, sideline reporters will sometimes draw a close relationship with the league or teams they are covering. In covering football for example, a good part of the week could involve telephone or in-person meetings with coaches and players going over storylines and strategy.

Once you've done your research, there are a number of ways to organize it. Longtime sideline reporter Craig Sager of Turner Sports says he's decidedly old school.

> "I always have these index cards. I write everything down. Basically it's an "open book test." [On each card] I have information on every player—not just height, weight and scoring average but other things that are pertinent to him; things like how many games he may have missed because of an injury, so if he suffers the same injury, for example, there's no speculation. I also have cards for every individual team."

Television Host

Preparation for hosting a show that bookends a live event or that simply stands alone can take many forms. A list on a notepad or electronic tablet of key topics to be discussed or facts that need to be referenced is a solid plan. Exactly how that is laid out and subsequently referenced is something that evolves over time depending on the demands of the show and the personal preferences of the host.

That said, like other disciplines of sportscasting, the host has to be ready—within reason and the restrictions of the format of course—to allow the show to head in different directions.

"You have to listen because preparation only gets you so far," says Russ Thaler, the host of Major League Soccer coverage on the NBC Sports Network.

> "Preparation gets you to the starting block. You have an idea of how this whole thing is going to play out, but if you're not listening, you can end up looking like an idiot because you're not following up when something interesting is said. Instead, you've just moved onto your next topic point."

> "I used to host the show *NBC Sports Talk* and that was more of a free-flowing conversation. When you're hosting a live game event like I do with Major

League Soccer, we have a pretty tight time frame to get everything in, so your preparation tends to be a little more scripted, so to speak."

Talk Show Host

Talk show hosts will often come ready with a number of issues or storylines to be delivered off the top of the show as potential topics of discussion. Other times, one overriding story will be offered. In any case, talk show hosts need to be prepared so they can offer informed opinions, answer listener/viewer questions and ask pertinent questions of guests on the show.

"I'm a little bit different than other talk show hosts," says John Gambadoro, a sports talk co-host on KTAR radio in Phoenix. "I chart every game I watch, so I always have a notebook in front of me for every game. That way I can talk about any play, no matter when it happened in the game. I also search the Internet and read all the major newspapers. And I do all of my research at night in preparation for the next day."

Play-by-Play

Play-by-play announcers need to come prepared with many of the nuts and bolts necessary to bring the viewer or listener into the game such as basic roster information and pertinent statistics. Coaching strategies and stories about the participants also help to make a well-rounded presentation, although like many of the other sportscasting disciplines, play-by-play announcers need to be prepared to alter their presentation depending on how the game is being played out.

Play-by-play announcers will often do their homework on cards or boards that they can refer to during the broadcast. Preparing and organizing this material differs from sport to sport and from broadcaster to broadcaster.

Wes Durham is the play-by-play voice of the NFL's Atlanta Falcons as well as college football and basketball on Fox Sports South. He says leading up to the start of a season, he'll keep track of each team through the newspapers.

"Once the season begins and I start with individual game preparation, I begin with the game notes for core information that I use throughout the year. I will also reference the cumulative statistics of the

Wes Durham, courtesy of Jimmy Cribb, Atlanta Falcons

teams as well as the box scores from the game before. Then I'll take the depth chart and start to lay out a board. It's a process that can begin Sunday night—or Saturday night for a college game—in preparation for the next game a week later."

"I also create a four-by-six index card. I put the depth chart of an offense on one side and the depth chart for the defense on the other side. I then try to memorize all of the names and numbers on the depth chart."

Mike Emrick is hockey's preeminent voice as the lead NHL play-by-play announcer on NBC. He says preparing for a single game is quite literally a day's work.

"It's about an eight-hour preparation," says Emrick, given the 2008 Foster Hewitt Award by the Hockey Hall of Fame, the highest accolade bestowed by the Hall to a broadcaster.

"Usually the night before, I write the statistics for each team on the right side of my scorecard that I've developed over the years. That part takes time, but entering it by hand allows me to write it in different colors where I can designate team leaders and so forth. Biographical information is also gathered the night before."

"Game day is about four hours, including the practices I attend. I also get the game notes that are printed by each team. I then transfer certain pieces of information to my card because the act of rewriting the information also helps to put it in your mind. For me, writing down the stats and any specific notes saves me in two ways. One, it puts it into my mind before the game and, two, if a goal is scored by a player and I have a note on him, it keeps me from having to rifle through page after page of notes."

Producers and Directors

A key factor behind the scenes is the relationship of the producer, director, and the on-air talent. These three entities need to be in lock-step in terms of the slant of the production, interview, or mission of the sportscast. In addition, a producer will often need to develop relationships with teams, players, media relations, and others as mentioned above. In some cases, the on-air personality will not be involved in the planning of an interview or production up until the time they arrive at the venue. While this is not ideal, the producer will need to be able to quickly brief the talent on the slant of the interview and might even provide potential questions. In Chapter 10 we will elaborate further on the relationships between producers, directors, and their crews.

■ Keeping Track at the Track

Keeping track of what's happening in an event can help a play-by-play announcer deliver timely information, as well as provide perspective, as the game unfolds. To that end, the announcer should always have some sort of electronic tablet, a scorebook, or at least a notepad to track stats as well as other notable events that occur. At the college and professional level, a stats person or a small monitor featuring a "live box score" makes certain stats and other up-to-the-minute information available.

Keeping track of an event as massive as a NASCAR race certainly presents its share of challenges. Mike Joy, the principal announcer for NASCAR on Fox, says a lot has changed over the years.

"When I did radio play-by-play [of auto racing] back in 1979, we only got a scoring update from NASCAR every ten laps. Somebody on a [phone]line would call up to our booth and a woman would write down the scoring as the cars crossed the line. If we had cars three, four, five laps down, it might take eight to ten minutes to get a full rundown.

The first big advance . . . we gave the girl in the booth doing the rundowns three-part, multi-carbon forms. She'd get the lead lap cars and then hand that to us, then she'd get the "one lap down cars" and put that on the next copy and so forth. We thought that was a big advance!"

Mike Joy, courtesy of FOX Sports

"Now, because of GPS, NASCAR scoring is all computerized. We have in front of us a screen with—in order—all the drivers, all the cars, how many laps completed, how far behind the leader they are, what was their fastest lap, when that lap happened and when was the last time they made a pit stop.

In 2001 at Fox we started using a ticker to put scoring across the screen—much like a stock exchange—continuously. And at that time, a lot of people hated it. One fellow said he put duct tape across the top of the TV screen because he couldn't stand the cars going one way and the ticker going the other. But now, you can't do an auto race without "real time live" scoring. We're also supported in the booth by four other people doing statistics and historical work, and a social media manager because the teams, drivers' wives, and other key principals are tweeting constantly throughout the event."

DEVELOPING RELATIONSHIPS

Someone to tell it to is one of the fundamental needs of human beings.

Miles Franklin

Of all the available resources listed earlier in this chapter, none is more important than the people who are in some way connected with the team, the school, or the individuals you cover as a sportscaster. That includes the players, coaches, general managers, athletic directors, media relations directors, equipment managers, agents, promoters—just about anyone who draws a paycheck from sports. Resources such as websites and game notes are great for information and the latest statistics. Newspapers, magazines, blogs, and the like can provide in-depth background and interesting fodder (much of which needs to be verified!). But it's the relationships you form with the people you cover that can add a unique dimension to you as a sportscaster.

For example, a sports anchor who is tethered to the studio with minutes to go before air gets word of a rumored trade, but a quick call to the team's general manager, who he's known for years, accurately refutes the rumor. Perhaps a talk show host has a relationship with a player who tips him to the fact that the manager has told him he's going to put him in the starting lineup for the first time this year. Then there's the play-by-play announcer who is accorded a private meeting with a coach who gives him insight on what to look for in the game that night.

Forming good, long-lasting, trusting relationships is an art, an art that takes time, patience, and people skills. And while not considered mandatory by some, it is often the by-product of your physical presence at games, practices, news conferences, and other team-related functions.

Here are some views on different aspects of building relationships:

Greg Aiello, Senior Vice-President of Communications with the National Football League

"So much of our business is based on relationships and trust and that sense of trust is borne out by what the reporter reports over time. If a person feels they've been burned by a reporter, that's a problem. Those who have done it a long time have a chance to stake their reputation. Then there are people who are relatively new to the business and if you (league or team personnel) don't have a relationship with him or her, you tend to tread more carefully and see how the relationship develops. If they become good reporters and haven't burned you in any way, you learn to trust them."

Suzyn Waldman, Color Analyst for the New York Yankees

I think that comes from being there [with the Yankees] a very long time [27 years in 2013]. And it was different back when I first started, people were much more trusting. People don't trust (you as much) now because of cell phones, Twitter, and the like. So the players are much more reticent to develop the kinds of relationships we had 25 years ago. [These days], you're friendly, but you're not friends. Players tell other players whether someone can be trusted or not. So for the new players coming in, they know I'm not going to hurt anybody. I think what also has to happen is you have to know what you're talking about. Players know as soon as you open your mouth whether you should be taken seriously or not.

Mike Emrick, Lead Hockey Play-by-Play Voice for NBC

The best advice I can give when speaking to players is to remember their time is limited. They're all together after a practice or before a morning skate after the coach's meeting or when they go out on the ice. Rather than scooting around and try to get something from ten players, spend a little time with just one or two.

Tim Frank, Senior Vice-President, Basketball Communications, National Basketball Association

The most important thing for sportscasters [who don't work for the team] is to try to be honest and upfront. They also need to be accessible to players when they say something a player doesn't like. If a player confronts you about it, you have to have the ability and understanding to communicate what you said and why you said it. I think the sportscasters I respect the most are the guys who go to the locker room every day. I always believe the majority of players don't want you to kiss up to them but, instead, be honest with them. I've noticed throughout the years that the sportscasters that the players really liked and respected were the ones who were honest with them.

John Kincade, courtesy of John Kincade

John Kincade, Co-Host of the *Buck and Kincade* Sports Talk Show on 680, The Fan, Atlanta

My relationship with the athletes that I need to cover needs to be one of respect; that when I do my show, I treat them with the utmost respect. I do not personally attack them. I do not choose to get too colorful in my criticisms. I do tend to have a hard opinion about what they're doing. But I never want to be too close to an athlete so that I can't criticize them. Same thing goes for coaches and front office executives. In fact, I think the most key relationships need to be with the people that work for the teams. I've always had very solid relationships with the people who work for the teams: media relations, assistants to the general manager, people like that. I think it's most critical to have a relationship with them because they know your show, they monitor it, they understand what the coverage is like. And if they respect you and they think you give their players and their organization a fair shake, they will be your water-carriers by getting critical players and critical executives on the air with you when you need them. They know I'm not a cheap-shot artist in terms of approaching their teams or them personally. They won't always agree with your opinion—they may think you're half nuts. But they realize the value of my stage to get news out to their fans.

Chris Dachille, Executive Sports Producer, WBAL-TV, Baltimore

When I need an interview, I almost always go through the media relations or sports information director because I've gotten burned by personally going directly to players or coaches. Then the media relations person catches wind of it and we get reprimanded, so I go through the proper chain of command. Obviously if it's for a story that they [media relations or the team] don't necessarily want on the air, you have to go a different route. But if we're looking for, say, a preview of spring training or a preview of the basketball season with a local college, you go through the sports information director.

HAVING A "GO-TO PLAYER"

This is taken from the basketball term "go-to player," normally the star player who a team goes to for a basket in the game's final moments. For sportscasters, their *go-to player* is the one they would turn to in situations where a sound bite is needed and there are few places to turn because:

- the team just suffered a difficult loss and few if any player wants to comment
- there's a controversial issue involving the team or a fellow coach or player and a statement is needed
- there's a situation involving the sport (i.e., performance-enhancing drugs or a contentious new rule) and a comment is needed
- there's a national sports or news story and a local angle or reaction is desirable

Go-to players often turn out to be one of the team's stars because they are interviewed more frequently and are generally either more comfortable offering their comments or simply feel the responsibility to do so given their status. Other times, it can be someone who is simply more relaxed than most in dealing with the media. But you might also develop your own go-to player simply because you have taken the time to develop the kind of relationship with this person where they feel comfortable doing an interview with you no matter what the situation.

■ Slander, Libel, and Defamation

Attorney Charles Kelly is uniquely qualified to discuss slander, libel, and defamation. As a partner in a Philadelphia-based law firm, he specializes in such cases. But before he became a lawyer, Kelly was a newspaper reporter with a degree from Northwestern University's Medill School of Journalism. Here, he offers some advice for sportscasters:

Q: What is the general meaning of slander, libel, and defamation?

A: This is when a reporter makes a false statement about a person and that false statement has diminished the person's reputation in the community. This law actually dates back to 1776.

Q: What does a sportscaster need to understand as it relates to slander, libel, and defamation?

A: A younger reporter needs to remember the adage that they're only as good as his or her sources. You need to have a *reliable* source. That means someone who has provided you with reliable information over time or, if you haven't had the luxury of a relationship with someone, you need to try to ensure that you are dealing with someone who is in a position where they would be expected to have that kind of information. A classic example is, you're working on a crime story and you'd like to speak with a police officer who's investigating the crime. That's an example of a *reliable* source.

Also, be sure to keep your skeptical side in place, which means constantly sifting information to be sure it's inherently probable or improbable. Even if you have a reliable source, if that person suddenly starts telling you that the moon is made of cream cheese, that's a moment to stop and say "there's a problem and maybe I should check this out."

Finally, a sportscaster should keep in mind their job is to accurately report. It's not to score points or to further an agenda.

Q: How does the sportscaster's responsibility differ in live interviews versus recorded ones?

A: If an interview is live, the reporter can't edit that. What you can do is not endorse [what the person is saying] and in turn, be a good reporter and question a particular statement. If it is recorded and you have time to review what's been said, then the law starts to put duties on you to be a good reporter.

Q: What are the consequences in slander, libel, or defamation cases?

A: Typically the employer does end up being the primary source of protection for the reporter who is usually covered under the company's insurance policy. So, the reporter is often shielded from jail time, punitive damages, or legal fees. However, in some situations, the reporter's job, reputation, and general future in the profession can be at risk. That said, people who are thought of as good reporters are often sued because they frequently uncover something significant. In those cases, your company will often stand with you and protect you during the process.

TRUST

Actually defining what a *good* relationship is between a sportscaster and a member of a sports team is not always easy. It's a working relationship, but it's not all work. It's a friendly relationship, but you're not necessarily friends. Instead, there's an unspoken, unwritten *understanding* that almost imperceptibly governs the association. And the primary underpinning of this understanding is *trust,* a trust that works both ways. Can you trust that what someone is telling you is true? Are they telling you something just to further their own agenda? And what about their trust in *you*? Will you utilize the information in a way that gives it proper perspective or will you take it out of context and give it a different meaning? And if they give you something "off the record," will you use it if they tell you not to? Will you protect them if they say you can use the information without identifying them?

The same goes for the other resources available to sportscasters; the game notes, media guides, websites, newspapers, magazines, blogs, and tweets. Which ones are accurate? Which ones are not?

Who and what do you trust?

Before we try to separate the wheat from the chaff, it's important to note that no one resource or one person can be counted on to be 100 percent accurate all the time. People make mistakes. Even the most trusted resource may have an occasional error. Therefore, it's important to remember that if you have any doubts, be sure to double-check that the information is correct.

You personally can be a good source for information, including anything that you individually compile in terms of stats, information, or observation. This is especially helpful when covering sports at the high school level, where resources are sparse. Sportscasters then often speak personally with coaches and athletic directors to get any background information or statistics on the team or its players.

"My eyes are the biggest resource," says Brian Baldinger, a former NFL player who's been a football analyst on both radio and television. "I watch as much film as anybody I know in this business and I trust my eyes."

Websites, publications, and game notes that are authorized by the league, team, or school are generally reliable as outside resources that can be used for general reference. Statistics, especially at the college and professional level, are often compiled by third-party companies. Background information on the team as well as records and history are normally compiled and vetted by media relations or sports information staffs. Interviews and news conferences are also frequently available on these websites.

Other general reference publications and websites that are *not* published or produced by leagues, teams, or schools have proven themselves to be reliable over time. The "reference" series of websites (www.baseball-reference.com, www.basketball-reference.com, etc.) is an example. You'll discover more of these as you do research on your games, players, teams, and stories. Also, ask other sportscasters or media relations folks for recommendations.

In terms of any other media (television, radio, newspapers, magazines, websites, blogs, etc.) or social media always double- or in some cases, triple-check to be sure it's correct (more in Chapter 9 of this book, Social Media and the Web). Go to the source, a team spokesperson or other high-ranking official in the know. *Make sure it's correct.* At the very least, if the story is important enough for you to put on the air and validating is difficult, *attribute it to the entity that published or aired it.*

"I typically verify something that I see or hear is true by going to the player or coach," says Jason Benetti, the director of communications and play-by-play announcer for Minor League Baseball's Syracuse Chiefs. "I'll say, 'hey, I was just clicking around online and I saw this thing, is that true?' Frankly, if I see a nugget or a statistical piece of information and that's all I have, well that's not a good story anyway. This way, you can go to the source and flush out the full story. So from one interesting note, you can generate an inning's worth of material."

Jerod Smalley is the sports director at WCMH-TV in Columbus Ohio. He says:

> "We all fight that battle now with "unnamed sources." Everybody has sort of adopted that phrase because it's become an easy way to get around things. There are some stations that have policies where you don't report what other people report unless you can confirm it yourself. That said, I do understand the culture where you use someone else's story as long as you're giving them the proper credit. In many cases I think it's appropriate. But ultimately, you still have to do the work and eventually make it your story."

■ "Off the Record" and "Being First vs. Being Right"

Sandy Padwe is a professor at the Columbia University Graduate School of Journalism. He's also been a sports reporter and editor at such publications as *The New York Times* and *Sports Illustrated*, and authored three sports books.

Professor Padwe weighs in on two important topics: the pressure of being first versus the need to be right and the true meaning of the phrase "off the record."

> "Let's take the absolutist definition of "off the record" as we used to teach it here at the school when I first started 20 years ago. Off the record meant exactly that, it was off the record. You couldn't print it, you couldn't put a name to it, and you couldn't use the information in any way shape or form. In fact, in the textbook that we still have here at the school, that's how it's phrased.
>
> What that has become over the years is that each reporter seems to negotiate those grounds. Let's say, for example, there's an accident and a reporter is on the scene talking to somebody and one source will say, "OK, off the record this is what I saw." So the question becomes, what does "off the record" mean in that case? The reporter will then say, "what do you mean by off the record?" And the witness will say, "just don't use my name."
>
> What I'm saying is, "off the record" now is pretty much up for negotiation between two people. There aren't too many people who stand on the old definition of it."

The issue of being first versus being right has taken on added significance given the ability to break news not only via television, radio and websites, but also through social media. "Another horrendous turn of events in journalism that has only weakened the entire profession," laments professor Padwe.

> "Nobody checks anything anymore, or there's very little checking. The Manti Te'o case is a perfect example. I don't know how this has happened. Well, conceptually I know how

it's happened. I don't know how it continues and why nobody puts a stop to it. And until somebody does, it won't stop.

It's a product of our digital world and the so-called competition to be first. Look, I worked for wire services, you wanted to beat the other guy. When I worked for newspapers in major cities, you wanted to beat the competition. But you researched the story, you confirmed it. It wasn't that you just ran with something that somebody said and didn't even bother to check it. Today there's too much of that. Nobody cares about sourcing anymore.

What does it matter if you report something 30 seconds after somebody else?"

BE UNIQUE

The pressure of competition—even competition from unaffiliated bloggers, tweeters, and the like—is one of the main reasons for Professor Padwe's feelings. While it is important to face the competition (at least the people truly employed as sportscasters), don't be afraid to step away and stand out from what everybody else is doing. That is, try to be unique in some of the stories you cover, that you talk about or that you tell as a play-by-play announcer. Try to originate your own stories by asking questions of the media relations folks who know the teams and players best. Be a good observer of what's going on in your area and see if you can't find a story where nobody else can. This will be especially helpful if you start out working in a small market where the local angle is king.

POINTS FOR DISCUSSION

POINTS FOR
DISCUSSION
3

1. At what point would you decide you are going to trust a source? A resource?
2. Try to find what appears to be a reliable reference source that is *not* produced by a league, team, or school.
3. Choose a story you'd like to cover and discuss how you would research background information.
4. Prepare for any one of the following:
   a. Sideline for any sporting event.
   b. Host for a TV pre-game/post-game show or sports talk show.
   c. Host for a radio sports talk show.
   d. Play-by-play for any sporting event.
   e. Show how you would keep track of scoring and other significant events as the play-by-play announcer for a sport of your choosing.

5. Discuss how you would earn the trust of a player or team official and how you would learn to trust them.

6. Choose a sports story from television, radio, or the Web and discuss how you would substantiate the various elements in the story.

7. Discuss how you would treat the issue of "off the record."

8. Discuss how you would come up with your own, original sports story

ENDNOTE

1. "Jerome Holtzman, 82, 'Dean' of Sportswriters, Dies," *The New York Times*, July 22, 2008. www.nytimes.com/2008/07/22/sports/baseball/22holtzman.html?_r=0, accessed March 14, 2014.

Chapter 4

WRITING

There are fundamental differences in writing for the ear as opposed to writing for the eye. Adhering to these precepts is critical to writing good broadcast copy and we'll address that in detail later in the chapter. But style is nothing without substance. And as we detailed in Chapter 3, nothing is more substantive than the need to be accurate in your research. This has to be your first rule in writing as well. So, it tops our list of the many things to keep in mind when writing your sportscast, be it for television or radio:

- Accuracy is paramount
- The journalistic precepts of the *five Ws and the H* (who, what, where, when, why, and how)
- Attribution/direct quotes
- Correct pronunciations
- Correct grammar
- Short sentences
- Active tense
- Take an angle
- When applicable, lead with the latest
- Giving each story its own individual treatment through writing
- Give the background
- Write conversationally
- Use contractions
- Mostly simple word usage
- Write personally
- Have fun and be entertaining
- Write with the visuals in mind

- Complement the video
- Don't write redundantly into a voice-cut
- Avoid clichés
- Judicial use of numbers
- Titles come first
- Use transitions between stories
- When writing for someone else make it "reader-proof"
- Keep it professional, not personal
- KISS–keep it simple, stupid
- When in doubt, leave it out (crossing the line)
- It's sports: make it entertaining and fun!

BE RIGHT

Accuracy *is* paramount. Checking and rechecking facts is critical. Even if you're confident, look it up anyway. In Chapter 3 we covered in detail the need to be correct and the myriad of sources available to corroborate your information. Strongly consider a twist of the old joke and *do* allow the facts to get in the way of a good story.

The facts of a story should include elements known as the *five Ws and the H* (who, what, where, when, why, and how). It's Journalism 101 and it's considered mandatory for just about any story. How they are used in a story and to what degree depends on what the story is about and how it is written. In other words, when reporting on a matter of great urgency (the death of a notable sports figure or a late-breaking trade) the five Ws and the H will appear in or close to the lead, whereas a report on a game or a personality profile could reveal the five Ws and the H in varying degrees as the story unfolds.

Facts or purported facts are given additional weight by the use of attribution. For example, don't say "the Hawks baseball team will be looking to make a deal before the trade deadine" without some sort of attribution. Say "Hawks General Manager Joe McMurphy says he's looking to make a deal for some pitching help before the trade deadline" and it carries a lot more veracity. If *you* think the Hawks will be looking for pitching help, be sure to say just that in the story, indicating that it's your opinion.

Pronunciation is an important aspect of being right. Mispronouncing a name or a word can alter meanings, hurt credibility, or simply be a distraction. When in doubt, look up a word in the dictionary. Names can be checked with credible sources such as pronunciation guides, public relations folks, people who know the person whose name you're trying to pronounce or the person himself. Once you've checked out the pronunciation, write it phonetically on your script, circle it, and/or rehearse the pronunciation until you know you've got it right.

Grammar is also critical for many of the same reasons that pronunciation is important. If you aren't sure about your grammar, utilize a published or personal resource for checking your work. The news or sports director should also have a particular stylebook that governs writing and reporting in his or her own newsroom.

THE EYE VS. THE EAR

As we alluded to at the beginning of the chapter, when writing for broadcast, it comes down to the ear versus the eye. Dennis Smith, the since retired news director at WLBT-TV in Jackson, Mississippi, says good broadcast writing is "good, tight, crisp, clear, short, to the point." Peggy Phillip, news director at KSHB-TV in Kansas City, Missouri, says, "one of the things I don't like to see is when people write sentences that are too long. Remove the unnecessary words. Make sure you're not redundant. Write short, active sentences."

As a sports anchor or reporter, the audience is *listening* to your message, whereas if you're writing for a newspaper or website, your message is being *read*. So it comes down to a difference in the cognitive process between listening versus reading. For the listener, the words go by quickly and only once. A reader can read at his or her own pace and, if necessary, reread a particular passage. Your writing should reflect that difference. Instead of the passive, compound sentences for readers, writing for the ear should use short, simple sentences with an active voice. In other words, keep it as current as possible and if you feel a comma coming on, put a period instead.

Again, in the words of Kansas City news director Peggy Phillip, "short, active sentences." Consider these two choices for on-camera lead-ins:

> The Columbia Cats were in action tonight at Keane arena taking on the Springfield Sabres in what was not only the renewal of a fierce rivalry, but a battle for first place in the South Division of the Northern Hockey League . . .

It's long-winded and past tense (not to mention quite formal). Instead, consider the following . . .

> The Columbia Cats are finally in first! Their long climb to the top spot climaxing tonight at Keane arena. The rival Springfield Sabres were there. It was like a playoff game . . .

The first line is the consequence caused by the result of the game, so you're as current and active as possible. The sentences are short and to the point, allowing you to punch the important facts and create some excitement and drama.

Now, let's suppose you anticipate being very busy the night of the game—in fact *you're* the one who has to shoot and edit the highlights of the hockey game. Unless something major happens during the game (i.e., an injury to a star player, the firing of a coach, etc.) you can go with a lead that you wrote in advance. In that case, construct the story in such a way that you are using your lead to begin the build up to the game's conclusion, stating what is at stake and allowing the highlights and graphic of the final score to ultimately tell the story . . .

> Consider the rise of the Columbia Cats. First-place seemed a long shot a month ago. But they're playing superb hockey. Tonight, a chance to take the top spot at Keane arena. Could they beat their rivals, the Springfield Sabres? . . .

Short, punchy sentences. Drama. And the viewer has to stay with you through the high-lights to see who won.

Writing for radio utilizes many of the same principles of short sentences and active tense. In fact, your writing carries even more weight since there are no visual aids to tell the story, only what you have to say.

MAKE IT MEANINGFUL TO THE AUDIENCE

The lead to a story is very important in that it will get the attention of the viewer or listener. It is your chance to say, "hey, you really need to know this!" So, try to get creative with every lead you write by finding a compelling *angle* to a story. Use that angle at the top and then, give us the pertinent facts while telling the rest of the story. So don't just say, "St. Joe's hosted Colonial tonight in high school basketball," say "Two crosstown rivals took their game down to the final possession tonight. St. Joe's and Colonial!" And if you can, make your lead as current as possible. Say you're writing a lead for the game the day after, you might say "Colonial High School is all abuzz this morning following their team's win in the final seconds last night against St. Joe's."

Give every story you write its own individual treatment. As human beings, we are emotional and those emotions take quite a ride with our sports teams. Always keep your audience in mind while writing and think about how *they* will feel about the story.

Happiness, sadness, excitement, frustration, and shock are just some of the emotions fans go through.

"I think that every story has its own personality," says Fred Hickman, sports director at WVUE-TV in New Orleans. "With a lot of the electronic effects—which is nice—all of the graphics and the ability to do things with computers, like making a player look big and then make him look small, that's all great. But if you're not telling the story with your writing, then it becomes forgettable and it becomes monotonous and it becomes less real and less personal."

Be sure your writing (along with your delivery of course) reflects that.

When time allows, give some background to a particular story so the viewer and listener can understand and appreciate the story's emotive elements. The above example, where it's stated that St. Joe's and Colonial High School are "crosstown rivals," gives a quick perspective to fans who are new or simply unfamiliar with the schools. Background also helps when writing about a story that has had a fairly long shelf-life. For example, you might write a story on the local college's continuing search for a new hockey coach. Adding a line saying the latest candidate is the "fourth one to be interviewed" or a line saying the new coach would "replace Ken Jenkins who recently left the school after 15 years to take the job at State College" gives the viewer/listener a better understanding of the story.

WRITE AS YOU WOULD TALK

As we will discuss in Chapter 5, one of the goals of a sportscaster is to sound conversational. *Sounding* like you know what you're talking about instead of sounding like you're reading is one of the critical components for credibility. One way to help you speak conversationally is to *write* conversationally.

"Write how you talk," says Brian Feldman, a sports anchor and reporter for KMOV-TV in St. Louis. "That is the number one thing that was ingrained in me from day one. When you're in high school, you don't ever write for broadcast. You're always writing literary essays with a thesis statement and then you have supporting arguments and so forth. So you're supposed to write in an advanced type of way that makes you seem like you're older than you are . . . you're supposed to use big words. This is the exact opposite [of broadcast writing]. You have to write like you are talking to people who don't have the knowledge that you have."

This might sound easy, but it's actually an art that takes a little time to grasp. When you write, visualize yourself literally talking to a friend, imaging how you might tell

Brian Feldman, courtesy of Suzy Gorman

him or her the story of a game or other event. For example, you wouldn't walk into a room and say, "guys, the Peninsula Pilots took on the Herman Hurricanes tonight in a Minor League Baseball game at the stadium and, for the third straight night, won in extra innings." Instead, one might imagine you saying, "guys, it happened again! The Pilots won in extra innings. Drama for the third straight night!" Of course, you don't want to get too caught up in the vernacular. The trick is to write conversationally while at the same time staying true to all the journalistic precepts that govern good reporting. Good writing for a sportscast provides the pertinent facts spiced with a liberal mix of conversational nuance.

Using contractions will help you achieve the illusion of conversation. Simply, we speak in contractions all the time. You'd probably say "the Titans *couldn't* hold off the Hawks tonight," as opposed to "the Titans *could not* hold off the Hawks tonight." So, why not write it?

Word selection is another critical element to conversational writing. Simple, easily understood words that occur most often in the conversations we've been discussing are best. Many of us are guilty of using more complex, "thesaurus-style" words. More often than not, it's not a good idea unless a particular word or phrase is critical to the story. Use of similes and analogies is often a great way to explain something or help to put a situation into perspective. When it comes to word selection and sentence structure in general, remember KISS—*keep it simple stupid.*

If you're comfortable with it, color outside the lines, so to speak, by adding some other forms of creativity. Alliterations (*Johnson's jubilant jets*) can sometimes be pleasing to the audience. A particular idiom or phrase might also help you to connect to the viewer and oftentimes those phrases become a signature that's unique to you. But be judicious. Chris Lanni, news director at WJAR-TV in Providence cautions, "I am not a particular fan of the sports catchphrases that some sports anchors fall back on, but other stations are, so that's a personal choice."

This method of writing will naturally begin to evoke parts of your personality. Unlike delivering the news, personality is an integral part of sportscasting. Sports are often a viewer's escape hatch from the harsh reality of life. Along with that comes the sportscaster's mandate to entertain, and at the crux of that is your own personality. Personality is all of the emotion and other characteristics that make you the *unique* individual you are. As you write, imagine almost any conversation with a family member or friend, allowing your personality to come through. Sprinkle it into your writing.

WRITING TO VISUALS

Whether scripting as an anchor or a reporter, it's important at all times to *keep the visuals in mind* when writing to video. This can be when writing to a video package that has already been edited or when scripting to video that will "cover" your voice-over. As indicated in the section below on scripting a reporter package, writing should generally enhance what people can already see. That said, as we will reiterate later in this chapter, it might be necessary to write more precise descriptions of certain visual elements in order to draw the viewer's attention to something specific in the video. An example might be a critical play in a game where a close call by an official—such as whether or not a player was out of bounds—eventually helped to decide the outcome of a game.

If you're going to use copy for video highlights, you don't want to write this:

> Then at 5:35 of the period, Smith netted his 35th goal of the season for the game-winner as he took a pass from Morgan and beat the goaltender over his right shoulder. The tally placed him fourth in the league in scoring and put him on pace to set a record for goals in a season for his team . . .

Instead, use shorty, punchy lines that accentuate what people can already see.

> A little more than five minutes into the third . . . boom . . . the game-winner. Morgan the set-up. Smith goes top-shelf. His 35th of the season. He's fourth best in the league. On pace to set a team record for goals in a season . . .

More times than not, however, voicing over highlights is accomplished not through writing per se but by ad-libbing while using a "cut sheet." The cut sheet contains a brief description of the highlight and when it occurred in the game. As we'll discuss in Chapter 6, the action of the highlights package and the very nature of ad-libbing requires the anchor to change the cadence and provide a more upbeat, exciting delivery.

When writing into a sound bite, be sure to avoid being redundant. So, the last few words of your lead-in should essentially paraphrase what the person is saying in the bite.

For example, let's say a bite from the manager of the baseball teams starts like this:

> I could tell by the top of the seventh that Jones was getting a little tired. He'd lost about a foot off his fastball and he'd walked the first two hitters he'd faced . . .

Don't use this as a lead-in:

> Manager Joe Smith could tell Jones was getting tired . . .

Use that and your words will match those of the manager. Instead, paraphrase by writing this:

> After six innings, manager Joe Smith was ready to go to the bullpen . . .

Like much of what you are reading in this chapter, this is good advice when writing for radio as well as television.

By the way, if you don't have a sound bite from a person but you do have a quote, don't say "quote . . . unquote," say, "in his/her words," and then write what they had to say. And at all costs, refrain from the reporter's pet phrase "told me." It's inherent in the fact that you have the quote that it was either told directly to you or at least you were within earshot. The use of "told me" is at worst egotistical and at best unnecessary and a distraction.

A FEW MORE THINGS

Remember that working in sportscasting is a team effort. You're expected to give 110 percent. And always bring your "A" game . . .

> Team effort.

> Give 110 percent.

> Bring your "A" game.

A cliché is defined as "a trite, stereotyped expression . . . a common thought or idea that has lost originality, ingenuity, and impact by long overuse." Not a good tool for unique, ear-catching, conversational broadcast writing.

They're in the driver's seat.

It's do or die.

There's no tomorrow.

You know them when you hear them. Try to avoid using them. After all, you control your own destiny (sorry).

One tool that has gone from being a cliché to being inappropriate is the use of military terms. Phrases like "he's got plenty of weapons" or "she's getting ready to go to war" have become increasingly unsuitable.

Also, try to avoid overusing statistics and various numbers unless you can make them mean something. In other words, if you have to use a number, put it in perspective. Don't just say "that was his 32nd home run" or "she's shooting 58 percent," say "his 35th home run is second in the league" or "her 81 percent foul shooting is tops on her team." Other examples of putting statistics into perspective include phrases like "that's in the top ten", "that's well above the league average," or "that puts him on pace to set a team record." Also, some numbers are better rounded off. Instead of saying "attendance was 6,472" say "attendance was nearly 65-hundred," and add perspective by saying, "just short of a sellout."

Using graphics can help to make numbers more meaningful and palatable to the viewer. Use them to show exact numbers or create lists that—you guessed it—provide perspective. Add additional perspective by writing to the graphic in such a way that it enriches its meaning and doesn't just repeat what people can already read for themselves.

Because writing for television or radio is for the ear, titles should come first so as to indicate to the viewer or listener the significance of a person's name *before* hearing the name. Let's say a particular story includes mentioning the other team's head coach, a person you might not be too familiar with. If you write "tonight's third period was delayed 15 minutes while Marlene Foster, head coach of the Wildcats . . ." the viewer or listener might be trying to figure out who Marlene Foster is upon first hearing her name and will not pay attention to who she is. However, if you write "the third period was delayed 15 minutes as Wildcats head coach Marlene Foster . . ." the listener or viewer can immediately associate the name that follows "Wildcats head coach" as a name of some significance.

Use of transitions will create flow and continuity between stories. A good transition can actually "connect" one or more stories, even if they're seemingly unrelated. You can end a football story and go right into a basketball story with the following:

> . . . the Panther's next game will be at home against the Stingers Saturday afternoon . . .

> Afterwards, you can hang around State College's campus for the varsity *basket-ball* team's season opener. That'll be seven o'clock that night . . .

Other times, a single word can link one story to the next:

> . . . That's the third straight game the hockey team has lost by a *goal* . . .

> The *goal* of the women's lacrosse team this weekend is to . . .

Use transitions judiciously. If you use them too often, the whole presentation can become hackneyed. That said, banal transitions like, "in the NFL today" or "at the ball-park tonight" won't do anything to punch up your presentation. Challenge yourself to occasionally come up with something a little more pleasing to the ear.

Writing copy for yourself is different than writing copy for someone else. In the event you have to write for someone else, be sure the copy is "reader-proof." In other words, reader-proof copy contains little if any of the personal style and other touches that are made to fit your own personal style. Reader-proof copy tends to be cleaner, simpler, and more basic than what you would write for yourself. Determining reader-proof copy isn't foolproof, but it does help if you read it thoroughly with a critical eye before you give it to the person who's performing it.

SCRIPTING A REPORTER PACKAGE

As we covered in Chapter 3, no matter what you're reporting on, one of your first priorities is to do your homework. This dovetails with our earlier point, the top one on our list, the one that says *accuracy is paramount.* Use all of those research sources and relationships to ensure you get it right.

TAKE A UNIQUE ANGLE

After doing your homework, you'll begin to formulate a concept for a video or audio report, even before you cover the event or do the first interview. Based on your research or your general knowledge of the situation, you'll start to contemplate *taking an angle* in advance of doing the story—what you feel is the most important or compelling way to look at it. The angle can also be determined by something you encounter later in the field, perhaps a story that's told to you, a voice-cut or a particular piece of video or audio obtained during the process. The angle needs to act as "the hook" for the report, something that is going to captivate the viewer or listener and leave them craving more. Sometimes the hook will be obvious and straightforward like a game-winning touch-down pass, the signing of a big free agent, or the firing of a coach. But always be on the lookout for something unique and different. Perhaps the quarterback who threw the big pass overcame some personal issues in order to play the game, the free agent decided to sign because he rooted for the team as a kid, or you happened to learn that the coach was fired by an owner who was urged to do so by the players. Other times, you might find a gripping piece of video or audio that captures the essence of either the person or the issue you are covering.

"One of the most important things that a sportscaster can do is find the story I haven't heard before," says Paul Gluck, an associate professor of practice at Temple University's School of Communications and Theater. "The level of redundancy that is just the nature of sports coverage is mind-numbing. "Yes, there was a game tonight. Yes, somebody won and somebody lost. Yes, the winning fans were happy and the losing fans weren't." But what can you tell me about what happened that night during that game or in preparation for the game or after the game that's different the last time these two teams met? What story can you find that I haven't heard before? How do you take a particular element of what occurred in front of you and emphasize that as a way to compliment the full story?"

Of course, if the lead of the story is obvious, be careful not to bury it. On the other hand, always try to challenge yourself to take a more distinctive slant and don't necessarily fall back on the obvious. Whatever your angle turns out to be, it is ultimately put into context through the storytelling process known as scripting.

PUTTING ELEMENTS ON THE SHELF

Once you have decided on the angle, you need to figuratively layout the "elements" you'll need to help you to tell the story. Primary among these elements are the different aspects of the story you want to convey, perhaps listed in bullet-points, along with the viable sources of information as support. Have these aspects listed in order of most to least important, often referred to as the "inverted pyramid." The other elements are the tools available to you that help to convey the story. They can include, but are not necessarily limited to, any combination of video, video with natural sound, sound bites, standups, graphics, music, and, of course, eventually your own words. Audio reporters create the same outline of points you want to cover in your story along with the supporting material, bites, natural sound, and other elements available to you.

It helps to know what your elements are *before* putting your words on paper. That's because you need to write with those elements in mind so that the words and elements eventually complement one another.

SOUND THINKING

Choosing sound bites often occurs once the interviews are complete. Sound bites are similar to quotes; short statements from your interviewees that help to facilitate the story. Bites should help to advance the story or provide additional credibility to points you want to make in the piece. You will need to select "ins" and "outs" for bites—in other words, the first few words that start the bite and the last few that end it. Generally speaking—and this is often dictated by the length of your piece—bites will often run from five seconds to around 15 to 20 seconds or so. The length of sound bites and how many you use will be determined by a number of factors, including the information in the bite, the articulacy of your interviewee, and the length and tenor of your report. Good reporters will make written or mental notes of "good bites" as they hear them during the interview or news conference. Remember, you can even use a sound bite as the "hook" for your report, another reason to be a good listener during an interview. When possible, bites should be selected in such a way that they stand alone as statements and do not sound like the person is getting ready to say more (although sometimes this just isn't possible).

Once you have chosen sound bites, store them on your "shelf".

STANDUPS

A reporter standup is another important element to a video story that is bound to end up on your "shelf." Standups allow you to put your personal imprint on a story. They should be used judiciously. Rarely do you start a sports report with a standup.

Instead, your on-camera appearance is normally used somewhere in the body of the report to:

- link one aspect of the story to another
- act as a tool to emphasize an important issue
- explain a part of the story where visuals are not available

Or at the end of the report to:

- encapsulate the context of the narrative
- present any future ramifications the story may have

OTHER ELEMENTS

Music is great for video montages or during certain segments to create emotion or mood. Remember, using certain kinds of music is prohibited unless you pay a rights fee. There are private companies that produce generic music beds (sound effects as well) that convey all sorts of moods and emotions, which can be purchased and used accordingly.

Graphics are excellent visual tools, especially when numbers are being used to prove a point, indicate a trend, or make a comparison. Again, when possible, allow your writing to enhance the graphic—writing specifically to the video only when an important point needs to be hammered home. Graphics can also be used when reporting person's specific quote that happens to be a big part of the story. In this case, you would probably repeat the exact words of the quote in your voiceover so that you and the viewer can read together. And remember to keep your graphic up long enough to allow the audience the time to read it. Try to avoid graphics that are too busy to comprehend in a relatively short period of time.

INVERTED PYRAMID

With your elements on your shelf, start to pull them down and use them for your storytelling. After the angle, you need to "pay it off" by telling how that angle is germane to the story. Then you are off and running. The scripting process essentially utilizes the various elements in a way that makes sense, telling the story journalistically with proper supporting visuals, all the while transitioning smoothly between the different elements. Scripting can be slow at first, trying to combine that storytelling with the accompanying visuals and other elements. Again, be sure you don't write without keeping the video in mind. At times, you might need to be more specific in your writing when, for example, you are showing a critical play in a game and want the viewer to take special note of something. Otherwise, while you certainly want your writing to be factual and informative, let it add a dimension to video. Ultimately, while "getting in" all of the visuals you want to get into your report, you have to be sure you journalistically include everything that is deemed important to the story. This is certainly not easy at first.

Radio reporters should know that, while they're obviously not writing to video, natural sound that is mixed underneath and is relevant to what they are writing can be an effective tool.

SCRIPTING NUANCES

At times, two or more bites can be edited together to make one thought or two thoughts that might naturally follow one another. Depending on the style dictated by your employer, the bites can be covered by footage or a reporter cutaway (more on that below). Also, a video effect or simply allowing a "jump cut" to air might also be permissible, again, depending on what your employer dictates.

As we stated earlier in this chapter, when scripting into a sound bite, do not repeat what the person is about to say, but rather paraphrase what their quote is about, allowing the bite to effectively finish or expand on your lead-in.

When you script after a bite, you might want to occasionally pick up on a key word or two from that bite, using it to transition to the next element. Transitions are an important part of scripting. They help to quickly and smoothly steer the viewer or listener toward new angles of the story. Natural sound can also be a good way to efficiently and effectively introduce a new angle or element of a story, either by cutting directly to that sound hit or by allowing the audio to "leak" under your previous video for a second or two first, then doing a so-called dissolve or "split edit." Quick sound bites are also good for transitions. Video effects can also be used, but be judicious. You want to use a video effect for a specific reason in the storytelling process, not make it look like a cheap car commercial!

Video footage will not only be used to cover the reporter's voiceover, but it might also be used to cover some or all of a sound bite if it is important and helps to do so. The natural sound that accompanies the footage should be mixed in with the sound bite or the voiceover. And while you're editing, feel free to use the various angles of something you shot in order to enhance the visuals and advance the storytelling.

In certain interviews—particularly those for features—"cutaways" can be used. A cutaway is a shot of the reporter listening as the interviewee is speaking or it can be the reporter asking a question. The former can be an effective way of covering two sound bites that are "butted together" to avoid so-called "jump cuts" (other times, a video effect can be used between jump cuts or, if your policy allows, simply leave the jump cut in). When a good follow-up question is asked, video showing the reporter asking the question can be used. Both the listening cutaway and the restating of a question is often recorded after the interview is complete, with the reporter simply restating the question, either shooting over the interviewee's shoulder or utilizing a close-up of the reporter, where the interview subject could already have left the room.

COME FULL CIRCLE

Ending your story is important too. You can use the end to pay off the angle you used in the beginning, especially with a reporter standup. If not, use footage with accompanying voiceover or someone's sound bite to hopefully tie a perfect bow around the package, thus encapsulating the main point or points of the piece.

Ron Harig, news director at KOTV-TV in Tulsa, Oklahoma, sums up his idea of a good reporter package this way:

> Good, strong storytelling. Leads that are conversational and interesting. Good characters—it's always been true and it's true today that if you can tell a story through somebody's experience, it makes for a better story. I think a lot of it is just peeling back layers. So many reporters tend to be superficial in their reporting—they just cover the surface and they don't drill down deeply enough to get the backstory or that little nugget in the story that would make it interesting.

EXERCISES—FOR BOTH TELEVISION AND RADIO UNLESS OTHERWISE INDICATED

EXERCISES
4

1. Make a list of the steps you would need to go through to ensure that a story or certain facts in a story were correct.
2. Make a list of ten hard-to-pronounce names or places and rewrite them in a way that would allow you to pronounce them correctly.
3. Pick a sports story and write it for broadcast three different ways, each time using a different angle.
4. Write a sports story once for print and a second time for broadcast.
5. Edit a video package and then write a corresponding voiceover for it.
6. Write a story for broadcast two different ways, once with a more serious tone, the second trying to be as funny and entertaining as possible.

7. Write a story for broadcast two different ways, once for your own personal style and the other as "reader-proof."

8. Write a sportscast with at least five stories that contains a "connecting" transition between each story.

9. Practice choosing sound bites from raw footage.

10. Script a 90-second to two-minute reporter package utilizing your research, footage, and other elements that you have gathered.

Chapter 5

PERFORMANCE THEORY

It is not so much the content of what one says as the way in which one says it. However important the thing you say, what's the good of it if not heard or, being heard, not felt.
Sylvia Ashton Warner, New Zealand writer

At an elementary level, this is the essence of what you will do as a performer in sportscasting. You are the source. You will then convey the message. You hope it will be received by the audience in the way you intended.

However, a lot can go wrong. Forget all that can interfere technically or the limitations of the medium itself. Every individual in the audience will color his or her interpretation of what they think you meant based on their own selective perception. That's just the way it is.

But generally speaking, here's what you can do to help convey your message with the precise feeling and impact you are looking for:

- Know your subject
- Good writing
- Credibility through performance

Bob Costas, a sportscaster for some 40 years, including more than 30 years at NBC, says there are certain essentials to being a good broadcast performer.

"While there are more styles and approaches than you can count, the constants should be preparation and understanding of narrative. At a live event, there may be individual pieces, but there's always an overview. There should be a journalistic aspect to it. There also has to be an element of entertainment. That's why people tune in."

"What you want is a blend of reliable information, good use of language, some sense of entertainment and humor, some sense of history, all tied together in a narrative that has some texture to it."

Marc Ernay is sports director and morning drive sports anchor for 1010 WINS Radio, NYC, and an adjunct professor of mass communications at St. John's University. He says: "A good broadcast performer has to be entertaining, authoritative and knowledgeable. I actually have an acronym for it, I call SPEAK: Sports Performing Entertainment Authoritative and Knowledgeable."

First and foremost, substance should triumph over style. In other words, the best way to know what you are talking about is to really *know what you are talking about.* You can never do too much homework on a particular subject. As you may recall in Chapter 3 of this book, talking to athletes, coaches, administrators, media relations folks, and other media members helps to build knowledge and, hence, credibility. Research through accurate, reliable resources is also extremely important.

Writing, as we saw in the previous chapter, is also vital. Accurate information written with short, active sentences and in a clean, conversational tone can greatly enhance the ability of a sportscaster to perform—indeed to communicate.

Actually transmitting the message, however, is accomplished through your performance. This is where you need to *look and sound* credible. Sounding credible is imperative on radio, where you and your voice are the primary conveyors of the message. Television sportscasters can look the part by being well dressed, groomed, and properly made-up, but they also need to have that reliable look and sound of comfort and confidence, the underpinnings of a good performer.

SPEAK!

Knowing how to speak is important for both radio and television aspirants. Broadcast performers often need to speak:

■ conversationally, with authority and conviction
■ clearly, with little or no stumbling
■ without a distracting impediment or accent
■ with the right tone and cadence appropriate to the situation
■ while using correct grammar

For play-by-play folks, there are other issues that we'll cover in greater detail in Chapter 7, such as:

- announcing versus talking
- the difference in cadence between different sports
- the right level of excitement

For everyone, there's the matter of your overall sports broadcasting persona—in a manner of speaking, finding your own voice; that way of performing which is truly your own unique style and no one else's.

Developing that broadcast persona is something that will evolve over time and continue to develop as long as you're a sportscaster, no matter your role. It's something you will "find" through trial and error as well as the natural evolution that comes with experience and the course of time. Your broadcast persona thus becomes a combination of:

- who you are as a person
- the styles of others you incorporate along the way
- the criticism you get from those who matter
- the vagaries presented by life itself

NBC's Costas says the greatest cliché in almost any walk of life is to *act naturally.* "It's easier said than done," says Costas, who has done both studio hosting and play-by-play. "I think you see a lot of people on air now who are trying to be characters. They think personality should be measured in decibel levels. You have to grasp the distinction between bombast and wit, between irreverence and mean-spiritedness. If you're naturally outgoing, it makes sense to be that way on the air. But there are a lot of [sportscasters] out there now who have decided on a *shtick.* I think you want to have a style, not a *shtick.* If you have a style and a little bit of personality and you get comfortable enough with the craft so that you have the nuts and bolts of it down, then you can get to the point where you're relaxed and at ease enough [to present] at least some authentic version of yourself. You then hope [viewers and listeners] get comfortable with that over time."

THE DRIVING RANGE

Golfers who want to work on their game have probably been to a driving range at least once. For a few bucks, one can buy a bucket containing several dozen golf balls, allowing them to hit shot after shot after shot.

This constant repetition (or "reps" as they say in football) is how golfers marry the intricacies of the swing itself to one's "muscle memory." In other words, teaching the brain to "memorize" the swing so that you don't have to consciously think about the swing while on the course, effectively allowing you to just "play the game."

Getting these reps is the first step toward developing a natural, conversational tone for sportscasting. This can be done by reading literally *anything* out loud including:

■ Internet pages
■ newspapers
■ magazines
■ billboards
■ textbooks
■ cereal boxes
■ your own copy (of course!)

Simply take a digital recorder and start to read. Afterwards, listen critically to the recording. Have a trusted mentor or experienced broadcast performer listen as well and ask the following questions:

■ Are you comfortable and relaxed?
■ Do you have a discernible, potentially distracting accent?
■ Are you breathing in the right places?
■ Are you speaking diaphragmatically or from the nose and throat?
■ Are you projecting appropriately or do you sound too soft or too loud?
■ Do you sound like you are conversational or like you are reading?

VOICING CONCERNS

The voice itself often cuts to the heart of the matter for many sportscasters. Frequently, they will be judged on whether they have "good pipes." Often times, that's a matter of genetics and whether you are bestowed with a deep bass or baritone or perhaps the higher range of tenor. Some voices are naturally scratchy while others are more nasal.

If you don't think you have those great pipes, don't sweat it. There are many sportscasters who have adapted their style to the voice they've been given. Listen to those who you think have a voice quality similar to yours or who don't have the "classic" tone and get ideas from them. What do they do to "sound" good? Personality and good writing will help accentuate who you are. Over time, you'll develop a delivery and broadcast persona that fit the range of your voice.

"No matter the pitch of your voice, an absolute must for sportscasters is good vocal energy," says Dr. Ann S. Utterback, a broadcast voice specialist and the author of *Broadcast Voice Handbook* and *Broadcaster's Survival Guide*. "Most of what goes on in sports is high energy. You also have to have a lot of various intonations (pitches, inflections), especially when you're doing something like a scoreboard show where you have to have a good handle on intonation to make it interesting."

Dr. Utterback has been addressing the voice questions of broadcasters for some 40 years. These are her thoughts on a number of matters concerning the voice.

Dr. Ann Utterback, reprinted with permission from the *Broadcast Voice Handbook, fifth edition*

BREATH CONTROL

"You need strong muscles to control how much air you let in and let out. We have to control our muscles to contain the air in order to talk a long time on one breath. For men, the diaphragm is the second strongest muscle in the body (the uterus is second strongest for women). You use your abdominal muscles to control the diaphragmatic muscle. That, in turn, allows us to let the air out slowly as we talk."

"If you run out of air while broadcasting, you're not breathing correctly or you're trying to say too much on one breath. A good exercise to build breath support is simply to take a deep breath, exhale the sound "ah" and time yourself while doing it. Try to build up to 20, 25 seconds or longer."

PROJECTION VS. VOLUME

"It's important for sportscasters to use *projection* while broadcasting as opposed to a louder "volume." *Volume* is like a flashlight in a dark room, it throws light all over the room, but the light is not very strong anywhere. *Projection* is like a laser beam. You should imagine trying to produce a solid, tight sound wave that projects in a straight line. If you use a louder volume you won't be heard as well because the sound will dissipate. You can project by simply visualizing that laser beam and directly projecting right into the head of the microphone. You'll be heard better by projecting."

REGIONAL ACCENTS

"Accents come from changes made in something called a phoneme, which is a single sound in a language. You literally have to retrain your brain and alter the way you say certain phonemes. "General American dialect" is considered standard for broadcasters. That's pretty much down the central part of the United States, say around Denver, Colorado. Those with an accent should strive for that."

■ Mile High Pie

Dr. Ann S. Utterback speaks in the pleasant, clear tone you might expect from someone in her line of work. She also has no discernible accent, much different from the way she spoke as a youngster growing up in Memphis, Tennessee. In order to rid herself of her Southern style of speech, Dr. Utterback became her own first client.

"I grew up with a really severe southern accent. I used to say *raht nahs braht naht* (right nice bright night). And I thought my name was *Ayen* (Ann) and my brother was *Jeem* (Jim). And that's what got me into voice work, trying to get rid of my accent.

When I was in college, I went to visit my boyfriend—who's been my husband for 43 years now—and he was at Cornell. All of his fraternity brothers stood around and said "oh, talk for us, you're so cute." I was furious because I had almost finished my bachelor's (degree) and I was going to get a master's and my PhD, and I thought "how can they think I'm this southern simple?" And it was because there were three or four sounds that I didn't know how to make correctly. One of those sounds was "eye." I grew up saying "aah." So what I had to do—and it took me about a year—is I had to teach myself how to say "eye." So I would walk around the University of Memphis every day going to classes and under my breath I was saying "mile high pie . . . mile high pie . . ." I would say the sound over and over like that until I literally retrained my brain. Eventually the neurons got a different message and they began to fire differently, moving my muscles differently. After about a year I could say "eye" instead of "aah." "

BEING CONVERSATIONAL

"Sounding conversational can be helped by marking scripts, especially when it comes to emphasizing certain words. But that doesn't always work, especially during live shots when you don't have a script. The old broadcaster's device of imagining that you're "talking to somebody" helps. In other words, visualize a real live person you know well who you can imagine reacting to what you're broadcasting. It could be a friend, relative, whomever."

VOICE CARE

Voice care, while often taken for granted, is paramount. Here is a general synopsis for voice care gleaned from Dr. Utterback and other experts in the field:

- No smoking—a no-brainer
- Good hydration—half your body weight in ounces of water or other decaffeinated, non-alcoholic fluid per day
- Eating enough—especially when you are on the air; enough protein to give you the energy you need, especially when you're on the air for several hours; limit dairy and other foods that affect mucus viscosity
- Limit coughing or throat clearing; if you must clear, try swallowing or clearing the throat gently
- Don't scream—especially for long periods of time. This could lead to vocal nodules that could threaten your career
- Stretch and/or walk around if you're covering a long event
- Exercise for at least 30 minutes a day
- Plan a period or two of relaxation every day
- Get adequate sleep and elevate the head while sleeping
- Use a cool mist humidifier all year round if available

Get more information on Dr. Utterback at http://onlinevoicecoaching.com.

THINK THE THOUGHT

One overriding concept to remember, whether reading, ad-libbing or doing play-by-play: don't forget to "think the thought." "Think the thought" might sound a little ridiculous, but if you really stop to, uh, *think* about it, it actually makes sense. Have you ever read two or three pages of a book when suddenly it occurs to you that you have no idea what you had just read? The same applies to "think the thought." At times, sportscasters can get lost in their copy, their ad-libs or their play-by-play call and have little conscious thought about they're actually saying. These moments of ennui can be detrimental, where a performance might be delivered without the appropriate emphasis or feeling, getting back to the quote from Sylvia Ashton Warner that began this chapter.

Like the golfer, aspiring sportscasters should "hit bucket after bucket." Getting all the reps you possibly can should begin to help you sound less like you are reading and more authoritative, comfortable, and conversational. You will be able to read over certain words and syllable combinations in a style that is smoother as opposed to the stilted and affected sound of someone who is obviously reading.

And remember, be critical of what you hear and what you need to do in order to improve. Take to heart the criticism of experienced professionals, college professors and others.

RELAX, RELATE, CONCENTRATE

Another concept to keep in mind while performing in any realm of sportscasting is this little phrase: "Relax, relate, concentrate."

Relaxing is imperative when performing in any situation, from sportscasting to athletics to a business meeting. Tight muscles can constrict your voice. Being tight mentally can inhibit the clear, quick thinking you need to perform.

Relate, while performing, to the situation as a whole. Relate to your copy and its real meaning so you can perform it with feeling. Relate to a story and whether it's happy, sad, dramatic, etc. Relate to any situation or story angle and get in touch with the unique emotion that it invokes. Relate to a broadcast partner, if you have one, and try to develop the kind of chemistry that will make the two (or more) of you a good team.

Concentrate. It sounds simple but again, like anything else, a lack of concentration can cause mistakes, mispronunciations, and other issues. If you find your concentration waning, you have to mentally find a way to bring yourself back into the moment and "perform."

YOU ARE A RIVER

The authors are not geneticists, biologists, or philosophers, but it is reasonable to postulate that you are not just *you* through happenstance. In other words, who you are as a person is a confluence of many factors having to do with your family history, your friends, and others with whom you associate.

To that end, as strange as it might seem, think of yourself for a moment as a river. A river starts as mere rivulets in the mountains. Eventually it is fed by smaller rivers and streams along the way, getting wider with each mile. Now, think of yourself, an aspiring sportscaster, in those same terms. You have your own, nascent style. But along the way you are "fed" or influenced by others, those whom you spent time admiring or simply grew up listening to or watching.

Athletes, musicians, actors, and actresses are invariably influenced by their "idols" during their formative years and sportscasters are often times no different. Marv Albert's distinctive "Yes" or Chris Berman's "He could . . . go . . . all . . . the . . . way" are often imitated, be it their signature phrases or their overall styles.

When trying to find your own "voice," that is your own, unique broadcasting style, it is important to delineate between *imitate* and *influence.* If you try to imitate another sportscaster, you are bound to come off as a parody. Chances are, a prospective employer (let alone your audience) will see through it and it will not be to your benefit.

But if you happen to admire someone's on-air style, you can certainly allow their style to *influence* yours. Returning to the river metaphor again, accept their influence as a tributary into your own personal flow. It is bound to be just one of a substantial number of small streams that you intersect with along the way. Eventually, they will all "feed" into you, adding to your river, to a point where that particular quality that you like is indiscernibly mixed with an overall style that will eventually be uniquely *you.*

Geoff Arnold, courtesy of Geoff Arnold

"By listening to other broadcasters," says Geoff Arnold, who has been both a radio play-by-play broadcaster and a studio host, "it helps you figure out 'oh, that's the side of my personality that once I'm on the air, I'd like to bring out a little bit.' But even before I started worrying about personality and style, I was really more concerned with learning the basics. So I'd listen to other broadcasters for that as well."

In 2014, Los Angeles Dodgers voice Vin Scully marked his 65th consecutive season with the ball club. Scully is acknowledged by many to be the greatest sportscaster ever. He says for announcers just starting out, the faster you identify your own broadcasting persona, the better.

> Red Barber [a member of the broadcasters wing of the Baseball Hall of Fame] once told me not to listen to other announcers because you bring something into the booth that no one else does. And I was overwhelmed by that statement. He said "you bring yourself because there's no one else in this world quite like you. So, hold onto that." And I've tried to do that ever since.

AD LIBITUM

Ad libitum is Latin for "at one's pleasure." Yet many sportscasters think of anything but pleasure when faced with the need to *ad-lib*, the abbreviated form of the word. Ad-libbing is often considered the sportscaster's equivalent to walking the tightrope without a net. You have to perform extemporaneously—live or taped—without the security of notes, a teleprompter, or script of any kind.

Actors do it. Comedians do it. Jazz musicians revel in it.

Play-by-play announcers ad-lib as a matter of course, yet much of what they do comes as part of a certain rhythm or cadence. It includes a certain percentage of set descriptions or phrases that become a regular, repeated part of their lexicon.

Anchors frequently ad-lib highlights and scores, by choice when reading their copy or when forced to if the teleprompter fails. Reporters will ad-lib during live or taped standups from the field or court. Studio hosts and panelists will ad-lib large portions of their show while sports talk hosts will generally perform for an entire shift with perhaps a page or two of notes.

"In this day and age, if you can't ad-lib and think on your feet and do a good live shot without referring to notes, then you should be a producer or writer or something else," says Ed Kilgore, a sportscaster for some 40 years and member of the Buffalo Broadcasting Hall of Fame. "Ad-libbing is one of the single most important skills of being a television sportscaster in this day and time."

"I have to be honest with you," says David Schuster, a sports reporter and talk show host at Chicago's WSCR 670 The Score. "[Early in my career] I was a little nervous ad-libbing. But it takes time. Most of it is just knowing your subject and being able to communicate. If you know what you're talking about you can pretty much ad-lib almost anything."

Overall prerequisites to becoming good at ad-libbing include:

■ Thinking the thought
■ Relax, relate, concentrate
■ Thorough knowledge of your subject
■ Practice, practice, practice

When producing a short standup that's to be taped in the field, keep the two or three points you want to include in that standup in your mind and just connect the dots by using complete sentences. Longer live shots often come as answers to predetermined or open-ended questions from an anchor. In that case, use the same principle as shorter taped standup, only be ready to ad-lib perhaps 30 to 45 seconds or more, writing the important points on a notepad and/or rehearsing it beforehand helps. Just remember that you'll be live so even if you make a mistake or stumble, keep going.

"The important thing," says Jerod Smalley, a television sports director in Columbus, Ohio, "is to keep it simple. Then you'll perform better around the most important facts that people need to know. If you make it so complex that you try to get in too much in a short period of time, you're just not going to perform it very well. You'll stumble around and maybe get some things wrong."

The key is, don't be afraid to ad-lib. Be sure to practice whenever you can. Reps, as we've stated before, are key. Do it whenever you have time, as much as you can. Simply jot down several key points to an imaginary story on a notepad, stand there with a microphone or some sort of prop, and do it again and again.

THE LOOK

Chris Lanni is the news director at WJAR-TV in Providence. He says those who can combine a good *look* along with sound have the total package.

> "It [comes down to] the ability to engage the viewer through the camera. So it has to do with voice, eye contact, facial expression—having a visual and verbal exuberance for what you're talking about or reporting on. A lot of that is natural ability. But there are also some tricks of the trade that can help make the viewer connection through the lens. You need to include the viewer through body language, leaning forward, hand gestures and by making the presentation conversational as opposed to confrontational."

Russ Thaler is the host of Major League Soccer coverage on the NBC Sports Network. A former sports anchor and reporter, he says that engaging the viewer through a camera lens is the hardest thing he's done in his career.

> "The goal is to be yourself as much as you can. If you fake it, that comes across on TV. Now where it gets tricky is, it's hard to "be yourself" when you don't have a great idea of who *you are*. At the age of 21, 22, you may not know who you are as a person—you're still developing. As you go on and do it more and more you become more comfortable being "you" on camera. And if you do get hired because you're being someone other than you, you're putting yourself in a really tricky spot because then you have to be that character."

AND RADIO . . .

The ability to "reach through the radio" is something Marc Ernay relishes. He's the sports director and morning sports anchor at 1010 WINS Radio in New York City. He says you can be credible and entertaining without "sounding like the big-voiced radio guy of the past."

> "I think one of the things that has gotten me to this point [in my career] is the fact that I'm an "active listener." I'm a member of my audience. In other words, I want to be entertained, so I entertain the listener. I try to deliver the information with some sort of originality, with an entertaining twist, with a delivery you're going to pay attention to. And another thing—I get the names right. I make sure that the pronunciations are as accurate as possible."

HOW YOU CAN LOOK YOUR BEST (AESTHETICALLY SPEAKING)

I'm not ugly, but my beauty is a total creation.

Tyra Banks

Tyra Banks started modeling when she was a teenager, no doubt due in large measure to a certain amount of natural-born beauty. But you might infer from her quote that much of what was done to promote her image was done, shall we say, with a certain amount of creativity.

Looking good on camera comes down to two things: looking as aesthetically pleasing as possible along with the ability to visually and orally communicate with comfort and confidence.

The part of looking good aesthetically *is* a big part of being on television. After all, television is a visual medium, so good looks matter to some extent. It's not necessarily the be-all and end-all, but it can come into play. And so news directors and others who hire talent do consider someone's appearance. Try not to be offended or put off by this, it's just the way it is. Some of those who hire people to be on-camera have inherent criteria for how they feel a sportscaster "should look." While not a necessity, a full head of hair, a proportionate nose, clear skin, and other similar attributes are generally all deemed desirable. Women are judged similarly in terms of their looks. In television, beauty is not necessarily always skin deep.

"If I had to rate the importance of [good looks] one through ten," says Bridget Lovelle, news director at KSPR-TV in Springfield, Missouri, "I'd probably say seven or eight."

Many go to great lengths to create or enhance beauty with procedures such as hair transplants, plastic surgery, and the like. For many the suggestion here is to build on what you've been born with—to make the best of it in order to enhance your appearance on-camera.

Carie Brescia is a celebrity make-up artist and beauty expert. She says:

Carie Brescia, courtesy of Christopher Gabel

> "If somebody wants to get into the business, make-up is a key part of a person's on-air image. Like it or not, we are all judged on our image. To get started, you can go to a general cosmetics counter and get a pressed powder one shade darker than your natural skin color. You don't have to wear a lot of make-up, but you don't want someone being distracted by your shiny forehead and not hearing the words that are coming out of your mouth. Your hair needs to be groomed. Men who are losing their hair, I say, "bald is beautiful. Cut it short." For women, hair should be no longer than shoulder length."

Brescia also says that men who are reluctant to use make-up need to get over it. "For some men it's like, 'I'm too macho or I don't want to be seen as wimpy.' It's essentially out of their comfort zone. But in order to succeed in broadcasting, you have to let yourself be out of your comfort zone. You don't want to see anything that's kind of shiny or dark."

"To me," says news director Lovelle, "[I ask myself] 'is there anything distracting about this person's appearance?' Is there something that distracts from what they're saying? If so, it's going to count against them."

Among women sportscasters, says make-up artist Brescia, there's the issue of grooming yourself to work in what is essentially a man's world.

> "What I feel a lot of women struggle with is having that balance of being a woman reporting on men's sports. You can't dress too sexy or feminine, but you shouldn't try to be one of the guys either. In my opinion, I think that tailored outfits [are good]. If you're on the field somewhere reporting, I think a polo shirt is fine. Neat and tidy hair—and not too long, I can't stress that enough. I find in the sports world you want to have it shoulder length. I like to call it "university hair," that long hair young women have. I like to cut about a foot off of the average woman once they graduate college. It's time [after graduation] to be

professional. People want to listen to your smart words and look at your smart appearance. They don't want to see you flipping around your hair. It's going to take away from your credibility."

"The way people dress is so important," says Peggy Phillip, news director at KSHB-TV in Kansas City, Missouri. "It's the colors they choose that really pop out. So if somebody has a résumé tape of themselves dressed in dark slacks and a white shirt, it's not going to be that impressive. I look for color. Even if you're in a small market and you buy your clothes at Kmart, figure out a way to go down to the tailor and get it fitted. It makes all the difference in the world. You're making an impression and if it doesn't fit right, it looks bad, especially in high-definition."

"Once you have your clothes, hair, and make-up together," Phillip says, "It's often your talent that can ultimately win out. There are a lot of pretty people on TV. Somebody who's good-looking is easy. But I always say 'passion trumps pretty.' And so I look for people who I feel are engaged and plugged in."

The passion that Phillip is talking about should be one of the main reasons for tackling any vocation, especially sportscasting. Always allow this to come through anything you do in the business. As a performer, the audience will perceive your passion and will often embrace it.

But Phillip is also alluding to the uncanny ability of some performers to figuratively "reach" through the camera; to engage with and communicate to an audience as if the performer was in a room with just the viewer. Not easy when staring into a lens with a teleprompter in front of it.

How to be visually comfortable, communicative, engaging, and entertaining often comes down to:

- a thorough, working knowledge of the story, enabling you to look and sound authoritative
- visualizing a friend or other familiar person on the other side of the camera
- performing with the side of your personality that is upbeat and energized, with a comfort level and a conversational style that is truly and uniquely yours
- "thinking the thought" and remembering to "relax, relate, concentrate" while performing
- giving each story the individual treatment (happy, sad, suspenseful) it deserves through your performance and your writing

"Whatever you want to say about looks, it still goes back to the presentation," says news director Lovelle. "If someone's average looking but they have a lot of energy and their presence just comes across the screen and they're very conversational with me, I would consider them above somebody who's maybe better looking but doesn't have as much personality. If [the good looking person] is boring, I'm going with the average-looking person."

NERVES

Racehorses experience it. We'll see it on occasion right before a race, when they're getting pushed into a starting gate. They buck, jump, and carry on.

Because they're nervous.

They're nervous because they know what's coming. Their adrenaline is pumping, preparing them to perform, but they have no place to go. All they can do is wait for the bell and the swinging of the doors, releasing them to race. Being stuck inside the unfriendly confines of a starting gate can be constricting and disconcerting.

You, the sportscaster, are in a similar situation. You're preparing against the clock; perhaps some combination of researching, interviewing, writing, editing, and rehearsing. Then as you get closer and closer to going on . . . live . . . you're waiting there . . . breathing . . . heavily . . . waiting for the red light . . .

You are not alone in this feeling. In fact, most sportscasters—most live performers in almost any genre—are feeling the same thing. It's only natural. Even those of us in the business for years—decades—experience some form of nervousness before going live, on the air.

Think of it this way: *nerves are the body's way of getting you ready to be a success.* Like the racehorse, you've been trained and you are ready. You've prepared your work and now your body is preparing you for that state of awareness, of acute concentration, which requires you to perform on that figurative tightrope without a net; that live situation where you need to execute the first time, indeed the *only* time you have a shot at doing it. But your time to perform hasn't quite arrived, yet your mind/body knows what's coming, feeding you the adrenaline rush you need to succeed. Except you can't take the steps to succeed because airtime is still moments away. Hence, the case of nerves.

Dr. Stacey Woelfel is news director at KOMU-TV, Columbia, Missouri, and an associate professor at the University of Missouri School of Journalism. "When people get

Stacey Woelfel, courtesy of Stacey Woelfel, Missouri School of Journalism

nervous," he says, "they're imagining that when it goes badly it will be viewed more badly than it actually will. So putting some things into perspective is important."

CBS's Jim Nantz is a five-time National Sportscaster of the Year, who has covered virtually every sport since joining the network in 1985. He says he had to combat nerves early in his career. "I was 26 years old and CBS trusted me with everything, from working the Masters to hosting the Final Four. I mean I was nervous! People used to say to me all the time, 'how come you're not nervous? You look so calm.' And I said, 'wow, I've got them fooled.'"

Learning how to handle nerves comes with time and experience. For some, it's a matter of certain relaxation techniques they may have learned over time. For others, there are triggers they can implement that help them reach a state of calm quickly. Often times, nerves will simply dissipate once a performance has started. Simply, the more you do this, the more you will learn to handle that adrenaline rush and subsequent case of nerves.

OOPS!

I'm chasing perfection

Kobe Bryant, Los Angeles Lakers

As great as Kobe Bryant is, he knows perfection is an illusion. Nonetheless he and many others—sportscasters included—continue their "relentless pursuit of perfection," as the Lexus commercials used to say. Acknowledging the obvious, that nobody is perfect, will hopefully help calm the nerves and allow you to go on when you make the inevitable mistake. Of course good preparation will help to prevent mistakes before they happen, but we all know our very humanity ensures that's not foolproof. So you also need to be prepared, in essence to have the right mindset, when you mess up.

The Dodgers' Vin Scully says you have to work your way through it if you make a mistake. "That's no way to go on the air," he says. "It's like a ball player—he can't go up to the plate thinking 'I hope I don't strike out.' He's got to be walking up there thinking 'I'm going to hit this ball ten miles.' Well, the same with a broadcaster. And once you break through that fear of failure and that fear that you're going to make a mistake, you begin to relax."

"I don't get hung up on making a mistake," says CBS's Nantz. "That's where I see most sportscasters, what really flusters them, is they memorize what they're going to say so much that when they miss or stumble over a word—and people do speak that way—the train is off the tracks and they have a hard time getting back on the rails again. It's no big deal. Don't fear the little verbal bobble. It happens."

And when you make the inevitable mistake?

"You should acknowledge it," says Scully. "I think you make a mistake if you gloss over it. If you say 'I'm sorry, I messed up—I didn't mean to say that,' I think the listener will say 'well I've done that myself' and will accept it. If you try to just smooth it over and ignore it and keep on going . . . if it's rather important, *that* would be a *big* mistake, not the one you actually make."

"Fix it," says Russ Thaler, the host of Major League Soccer coverage on NBC. "People make mistakes and I think people watching TV understand that you're not perfect and you're not a machine. Fix it, don't make a big deal about it."

When mistakes come from others involved with the production, the on-air talent is the first line of defense when covering up. If a piece of video, a graphic, or some other element is not ready or there's some other problem that requires you to stretch your on-camera segment, you'd better be prepared to do so. This is where the ability to ad-lib is critical. Teleprompters do, occasionally, fail. Would you be able to ad-lib your way through a sportscast or other segment if that happened? Knowing the subject of your standups or sportscast thoroughly will help you to do this.

Certainly it can be disconcerting when you have to deviate in order to help protect somebody else's mistake. But for anchors and reporters, this is your job! Blaming somebody else, especially on the air, is counterproductive. This is when you need to take one for the team. If you can't do it, and do it with a certain amount of aplomb and grace, you don't belong in a situation where you are live on the air.

Other times you go off script should be a little more controlled, such as the time before or after your sportscast when you may be asked to banter with the news anchor and/or weather person. This requires a different sort of mindset as a performer, where you have to help in the transition from news to sports and back again. Therefore, being familiar with not only the format of the show but also the news (or weather) in general can be helpful.

■ Jack-of-all-Trades . . . Master them all

Shortly after he started working in his first job in television, Rudy Mezzy tweeted a very important message to his friends at Temple University in Philadelphia, his alma mater.

"This was the first time I had to be a 'one-man band,'" says Mezzy, "I hadn't done it in college. I had somebody shoot for me [at Temple] every time. So when I shot my own standup for the first time, I tweeted, 'if you haven't done this yet, it should be the next thing you do.' I told them 'if you're [shooting yourself] for the first time, make sure it's in college.'"

In college and not at KOLN/KGIN-TV in Grand Island Nebraska, the nation's 105th market, where there's little Mezzy doesn't do. He is a living example of what aspiring sportscasters need to do: be

Rudy Mezzy, courtesy of Patrick Rosenbaum

prepared to produce, shoot, edit, write, do graphics, and even do the news.

"Most of the time I do news three days during the week and I anchor the sports on the weekend. I produce the sports myself. At first it was very overwhelming. Sometimes in life there are things you react poorly to because you don't think you can handle them and I did that at first. But as I've gone on it's gotten easier and easier. Technology helps to make it easier."

Technology that you need to be familiar with even if you eventually want to become the next Bob Costas or Joe Buck.

■ Never Say Anything in Front of an Open Mike

One night while working at the now defunct PRISM-TV in Philadelphia, co-author Marc Zumoff was the anchor for a sports update show that was being recorded for playback later that night. Keep in mind these were the days of *videotape* recording.

At one point during the recording, the editor who was in charge of playing back highlights failed to play those highlights at the right time, so the recording had to be stopped. Actually, while the performance itself was stopped, the videotape machine continued to record the proceedings. And so it recorded Zumoff, sitting at the anchor desk, waiting to resume the show. While waiting, he jokingly referred to the editor who had made the mistake in terms that—shall we say—would not be appropriate for the air. Eventually, the videotape was rewound and the recording was resumed from the point of the show where the mistake was made, but Zumoff's joke about the editor remained on the tape. Everyone then went home.

As it turned out, the person responsible for playing back the show on the air forgot to stop the machine when the show was over. As this person attended to other things, the tape continued to play until it got to the point where Zumoff was sitting at the anchor desk, waiting to resume recording and, yes, viewers heard and saw him saying those inappropriate things to that editor. It was a major embarrassment for him and something that could have led to Zumoff being fired.

This was a case where Zumoff thought he was in a situation that was foolproof—recording a program that was to air later and was not live on the air per se. His mistake, though, was one of broadcasting's cardinal sins: *never say anything at any time around an open mike that you would not want to have said over the air.* You may think you're in a benign situation such as he did. But always beware. Either through someone's unwitting error or because someone is trying to intentionally hurt you, what seems like an innocent or harmless situation could come back to bite you, all because you thought you were "off the air."

EXERCISES—TO BE DONE ON CAMERA OR AUDIO ONLY

EXERCISES
5

1. Read *anything* aloud and play it back. Ask yourself:
   a. Do I sound and/or look conversational and credible? If not, what changes do I have to make in order to correct that?
   b. Are my facial expressions natural and appropriate?
   c. Are other gestures, such as using hands, appropriate or necessary?
   d. Can I smile naturally?
2. Practice some voice and breath exercises including:
   a. Being comfortable and relaxed.
   b. Working on any accent that might be evident.
   c. Breathing in "natural" places.
   d. Speaking from the diaphragm as opposed to through the nose or throat.
   e. Projecting appropriately and not sounding too soft or too loud.
3. Explain what you think is meant by:
   a. Think the thought.
   b. Relax, relate, concentrate.
4. Watch and/or listen to other sportscasters you admire and try to pinpoint what it is that you like about their performance style and how you might incorporate that into your own personal style

5. Ad-lib at different intervals (15, 30, 45, 60 seconds):

   a. A pre-planned standup with specific talking points.

   b. About any subject that is given to you seconds before you're supposed to talk.

6. Do a standup as if you are a reporter in the field and you are answering questions from an anchor in the studio.

7. Television only: critically think about and solicit feedback on your look, especially in the areas of:

   a. Hair.

   b. Complexion.

   c. Dress.

8. Are you nervous before performing? If so, think critically about why you think you're nervous and how best to handle it.

Chapter 6

REPORTER, ANCHOR, SIDELINE, HOST, SPORTS TALK

REPORTING

Reporters are generally responsible for heading into the field and covering games, news conferences or generating feature and personality pieces. Whatever the story happens to be, there are some common principles to good sports reporting that are universal to both video and audio.

"A good sports reporter is curious," says Ron Harig, news director at KOTV-TV in Tulsa, Oklahoma. "It's somebody who's really interested in what's going on around them. Curious about the layers of a story, finding more than what presents itself on the surface. Somebody who keeps asking questions and doesn't necessarily take things at face value." "You should also read a lot. So often these days, people come in not being well grounded, not knowing what's going on in the [sports] world. So I'm always telling reporters that you're going to be a better writer, a better reporter, a better journalist if you read a lot."

As we covered in Chapter 3, no matter what you're reporting on, one of your first priorities is to do your homework. Then, you need to work with the media relations folks on logistics such as credentials, where and what you can shoot, and access to interviewees. In some cases, these and other issues are resolved directly with the principals you'll be covering.

After doing your homework, as we covered in Chapter 4, there's the concept of *taking an angle* to your story. Again, you begin to develop this angle or "hook" as soon as you begin your research and it may continue to evolve through the interview process, scripting, and editing.

INTERVIEWS

Interviews are often an essential part of a sports report or, for that matter, a studio show or sports talk show. Generally speaking, there are some good precepts to keep in mind for conducting interviews no matter where or when they take place.

Players and coaches are often available before a game, in formal or informal settings. After the game, a coach or manager is frequently made available in a news conference while the players might do interviews in smaller groups or one-on-ones in front of their dressing area. Sometimes, following the news conferences, the principals will break off into smaller groups or even one-on-ones, where you can ask your own questions. In feature stories, you'll often have the opportunity to "stage" the interview in a studio or on location, whether utilizing a shot of the two of you or a single, static shot of the subject.

WARM 'EM UP

Pre-interviews in one-on-one situations are sometimes an acceptable way to develop a rapport with a possibly reluctant interviewee. This might help to elicit a better response to your questions. Veteran coaches and players might not require this, although a little "warm-up," especially if you're interviewing this person for the first time, can help. Pre-interviews or warm-ups are also useful with younger players or those who are microphone or camera-shy. In that case, a quick gloss over the handful of questions you have in mind—say for a feature or, perhaps even more importantly, before a live shot where your interviewee might have a case of nerves—might make sense.

Russ Kilgore is the news director at WINK-TV in Fort Meyers, Florida. He says, "Primarily [in an interview situation] it comes down to good people skills. You just want [the interviewee] to feel comfortable: comfortable with you, comfortable with the fact that there's a camera there. You just want to put them at ease as much as you can. There isn't any of that with locker room interviews. There isn't any of that when you're chasing somebody down for some sort of a story about conflict where you're in "aggressive mode." There's not much you can do to make those people feel comfortable because you're coming after them!"

LISTEN WELL

The most important part of being a good interviewer is to be a good listener. Theoretically, you can go into any interview with one question and if the interviewee says something that is intriguing and/or requires a follow-up, then that becomes your next question. You can do an entire interview this way, following up by going down different roads. Of course you want your report to be comprehensive, so if there are other aspects of the story that need to be addressed, then other types of questions are required. Having a few questions prepared for your interviewee is fine, but constantly referring to them from a notepad or simply reading can be disconcerting. In a long-format interview, where you are talking at length with someone as part of a feature, it's generally acceptable to have a pad with some prepared questions. Still, even in this mode of questioning, good listening is a key.

BE NATURALLY CURIOUS

If you're asking yourself a question about a particular sports story or an individual event or player, chances are members of your audience are wondering the same thing. As a multi-Emmy award-winning host for NBC, Bob Costas has asked perhaps tens of thousands of questions.

"Any question that might be of interest to the audience and that isn't considered inappropriate is a good question," says Costas. "Actually determining what *is* of legitimate public interest is constantly blurred and there are many people who do not adhere to my definition of [what's appropriate]. But if the question is of legitimate interest and would be something that your audience would be curious about, it's a good question."

ASK OPEN-ENDED QUESTIONS

A reporter who has done their homework and is armed with good background information can be a good thing. But sometimes, reporters will stuff so much information into a question that the subject is left with little choice but to agree or disagree, answering with a simple "yes" or "no" to a question that has somehow morphed into an outright *statement.* Include brief background information in a question if

Bob Costas, courtesy of NBC Sports

you must in order to place it into proper perspective. But ask the question in such a way that it elicits (you hope) a thoughtful and deep response.

If a respondent does give you a short answer, be prepared with a follow-up. For example, you might ask "what did player X bring to the team before he was traded?", the response might be "a lot." Then, you have to be ready to reply "like what? Give me an example."

KEEP QUESTIONS BRIEF

Also, try to keep your questions relatively brief. At times, some elaboration is required in order to put a question into perspective or to remind the interviewee (or the listener/viewer in a live interview) of some important contextual information. However, too many interviewers try to show how knowledgeable they are with a pedantic display of questioning that is often too long and tedious. Shorter questions may actually get a more honest and revealing response as opposed to those long questions where interviewees would have a chance to formulate an answer.

THE STUPID QUESTION

Is there such a thing? "Yes, and you hope you don't ask it," laughs NBC's Costas. "There are any number of [stupid] questions. One of the worst—say after a home run or shot to win a game—'how does it feel?' Or a lot of people pose the question this way: 'talk about the third quarter' or 'talk about what happened in the second half.' That's not a question. I think we all can do better than that."

DON'T RELATE, JUST FACILITATE

There is a tendency for some interviewers to include themselves in the conversation during or immediately following the interviewee's answers. Sometimes during the answer, the reporter can be heard affirming either agreement or comprehension by saying "uh-huh," "right," or something to that effect. Some are inclined to affirm the answer with a "that's fantastic" or "I agree," while still others will paraphrase or nearly word-for-word repeat the interviewee's answer. Remember, you as the reporter are not there to necessarily relate (although a host might be called on to react differently in the context of a longer format interview show), but rather to *facilitate*. In other words, you are simply there to get the interviewee to respond to your questions, nothing more.

CUTAWAYS

As we discussed in Chapter 4, "cutaways" can be used in certain interviews, particularly for features. Again, the cutaway is a shot of the reporter listening as the interviewee is speaking or it's of the reporter asking a question. Both the listening cutaway and the restating of a question is often recorded after the interview is complete, with the reporter simply restating the question, either shooting over the interviewee's shoulder or utilizing a close-up of the reporter when the interview subject could already have left the room.

MR. MICROPHONE

Good microphone technique is important. Many news conferences provide direct audio "feeds" where you can connect to a box that distributes audio from the podium directly into your camera or recorder. If you're doing interviews with a "stick microphone," be sure not to place it too close to your mouth or to that of your subject (we once saw a reporter smash a coach in his teeth!). Doing that could "over modulate" or distort the audio. When asking a question, wait until you are finished the question before swinging the mike over for the answer and vice versa. Proper use of a clip-on or boom microphone is covered more extensively in Chapter 9.

STANDUPS

Reporter standups are both live and recorded. Recorded standups allow you to put your personal imprint on a story. They should be used judiciously. Rarely do you start a sports report with a standup, live shots being an obvious exception. Instead, your on-camera appearance is normally used somewhere in the body or at the end of the report to:

- link one aspect of the story to another
- act as a tool to emphasize an important issue
- explain a part of the story where visuals are not available
- encapsulate the context of the narrative
- present any future ramifications the story may have

Standups can vary in length for many of the same reasons as sound bites. It is obviously a staged event, so visual appeal and context is important. For example, a story on a particular baseball player might feature a standup with that player in the background taking batting practice. A report on the construction of a new arena might show the reporter in a hard hat with workers in the background. A story on hot dog vendors might indeed show the reporter in the stands hawking same. Much of this depends on the tenor of the report and the creative demands or limitations of your news or sports director.

When using a "stick" microphone during your standup, remember the best placement is at the "breast plate." In other words, holding your mike in that general area will make for the best combination of fidelity and aesthetics (keeping the mike away from your face).

Conceptualizing a standup is part of the duality of being a good sports reporter. While covering the game, the news conference, or the feature story, you are in two modes—while gathering the information you are also thinking about how to structure it. Since the standup is crucial to this process, you'll have to be thinking about that too. So after interviewing the hockey team's goaltender, when he goes back to stopping shots at practice, you're going to have to swing into action quickly and stage that standup with him in the background before he leaves the ice for good. And remember, that standup can't be done willy-nilly. It has to have context as it relates to your script.

YOU'RE LIVE

Performing a *live* standup might be a part of your sports report as well, especially if you're at a big game or news conference. As we said earlier in Chapter 5, this will require you to ad-lib 30 to 45 seconds or more, either in response to a generic toss from the anchor or answering a specific (perhaps predetermined) question. Again, you may want to write the important points of your standup on a notepad and/or rehearse beforehand. You also might want to include a sound bite in your standup that you lead into and then "tag." If you also happen to have an interviewee with you in the live shot, this is where the pre-interview helps immensely. Let your subject know what's going to happen, that you are taking a toss from the anchor, that you're going to ask him or her a question or two and that you will toss back to the studio at the end of the standup. In some circumstances, it might help the interviewee to let them know the questions beforehand, while others will need no such prompting. Be sure to let your interviewee know not to leave the location until you say it is OK—that is when you're off the air. And above all, remind your subject that you are *live* so that they fully understand the circumstances. Again, if your interviewee or you make a mistake or stumble, just keep going. Unless it's a crucial aspect to the event and needs correction in order to impart the story accurately, simply let it go.

ANCHORING

A sportscaster can make a good career out of being a great reporter. But for many, *anchoring* is considered one of the plum jobs of the business. The pay is usually better, while the visibility is certainly greater.

Good sports anchors are said to have a certain "presence." They look good. They sound good. Over time, they build credibility in almost any situation and control over almost any moment. They inform and they entertain with blessed amounts of talent and energy.

THE TELEPROMPTER

Reading off of a teleprompter, if you haven't done it before, might take some getting used to. There's always the issue of *sounding* conversational while *reading*, something we covered earlier in Chapter 5. But there's also the matter of looking natural while seeing your copy scrolling in front of you. Certainly all of the tips we just referred to about knowing your story, visualizing a friend on the other side of the camera, "thinking the thought," etc. will help. Constant repetition will also help you to get used to it. After anchoring a show with a prompter—even if it's just for practice—be sure to record it and watch yourself afterwards. Hopefully it will help to convince you that the viewers don't "see the words" you are seeing, nor do they see you reading.

When first breaking into the business, you may have to run the teleprompter yourself. Later, others will do this for you. But no matter who's running it, remember *the prompter is following you* and not the other way around. It will go as quickly or as slowly as you do. If you stop to ad-lib, it will wait for you.

All of this said, good sports anchors should treat the teleprompter as an aid, not a crutch, according to Kevin Finch, news director at WRTV-TV in Indianapolis.

"The sports anchor should already know the script," says Finch. "The anchor, hopefully, writes his or her own material, so you can't be more intimately familiar with [the script] than when you've written it yourself. So that when it comes up on the teleprompter, that's just a nice little guide for you."

"And always keep your hard copy with you. Teleprompters die, computers die, power goes out. You can't let [the teleprompter] be a crutch. It has to be an aid."

LET'S GO TO THE HIGHLIGHTS

As we discussed in Chapter 4, the anchor will more often than not ad-lib to a highlights package using a "cut sheet." This cut sheet contains a brief description of the highlight, allowing the anchor the freedom to ad lib, injecting his or her own brand of personality and excitement. Here, the cadence of the anchor often shifts, ebbing and flowing with the importance of the highlight and what it might mean to the fan at home. Many anchors adapt almost a "play-by-play" style as they give deeper meaning and emotion to what the audience can already see.

One important note to remember on highlights that are used from sources other than your own channel. Be sure to consult with the news director, sports director or your immediate supervisor about the policies governing use of these highlights. In some cases, footage or audio from certain events is not allowed to be used at all. In other circumstances, highlight use is limited to certain programs or events at your channel or station. Different leagues, teams, schools, or media outlets have set procedures that will allow use of their highlights, depending on the contracts they have in place. A "courtesy" is often used to acknowledge use of someone else's footage and it's important that you credit the correct entity and do so according to your company's policy or style.

OTHER PERFORMANCE ISSUES

Once you're comfortable with the prompter, you'll be able to incorporate other aspects of performance. Smiling, frowning, or other facial expressions that come naturally and at the appropriate time can help to truly communicate the emotion and tenor of a story. Some will use hand or other physical gestures to make a point. Whatever you do physically to communicate should be done only if it's within your own comfort zone and it's considered appropriate by your employer.

"Personality is certainly an important characteristic," says Jerod Smalley, sports director at WCMH-TV in Columbus, Ohio. "And I don't mean someone who's 'the greatest person on earth.' I mean somebody who is approachable, likeable, and witty. I say witty as opposed to telling people to be funny. To me, wit shows intelligence and gives some credence to who you are and what you're doing."

There is also the time that you're off-camera and either reading over B-roll or voicing highlights. Maintain the same appropriate treatment and emotion off-camera that you were trying to generate on-camera. Highlights can be scripted or, frequently, the anchor will ad-lib off of a sheet that might be as simple as a list of the edited highlights, in order, with a brief description of each. Ad-libbing is actually encouraged, allowing the anchor to perceptibly shift into a different gear. Voicing-over highlights then becomes some combination of witticism, commentary, unique phrases, or even some virtual play-by-play.

A FEW MORE THINGS

When multiple cameras are being used, you may be asked to end one story and switch to another camera for the next. The best way to soften the transition is to give a brief look down at your copy when ending a story—say on camera one—then complete the change by looking up into the assigned camera two. In larger markets, a floor director will also be helping you with the transition.

In the smaller television markets, you would likely produce your own show, be it in the field or in the studio. This will require you to handle all of the logistics necessary for taking your sportscast from concept to air. What stories you cover will all be determined by available equipment, coordinating logistics, the amount of airtime you have, and what you sense the viewer needs to see most. Grasping, indeed embracing the necessary skills of a good producer is paramount to making a good sportscast happen.

In larger markets, you may then work with a sports producer. Angst between talent and producer, small or large market, is as old as the business itself. Chris Dachille is the executive sports producer at WBAL-TV in Baltimore. He says:

"I always feel that I have an open line to [the anchor] and likewise back to me. At times we will have a very free-flowing discussion where we can get very

Chris Dachille, courtesy of Jed Gamber

upset at each other. Often people who work in this business have very strong opinions. I've always found the way to get through any problem is with communication. It's funny, we're in the communication business and communication isn't always on the top of someone's agenda."

The producer plays a vital part when leading an anchor or reporter, live on the air, into some sort of video package. In this case, the talent will have a producer in their ear counting them down to the first frame of video in highlights package, a sound bite, or a report. While many anchors and reporters would be just as happy never hearing from a producer while they are live, this sort of coordination is a necessary part of live television. Ultimately the ability to keep on doing what you're doing, no matter what is going on around you, is critical for both sports anchors and reporters.

■ Radio days

Marc Ernay loves radio, and it shows. Actually, it doesn't show since you can only *hear* him. But Ernay has embraced the medium to its fullest, evidenced by his rise to sports director and morning sports anchor at 1010 WINS Radio in New York City. He's also teaches his craft as an adjunct professor of mass communications at St. John's University. Ernay says being a good radio sportscaster requires a lot more than just reading the scores, something people can readily receive online or via their mobile device.

"So, you have to give people more. You want to give the story behind the game. One of the things I was brought up believing was that you're telling a story no matter what [the subject matter] is. For example, something happened in that game that's going to cause people to talk about the game. Otherwise, it's just a game. There's something in that game—perhaps that someone has never seen before—and that's what you want to focus on."

Ernay has a pleasant voice, but certainly not the stereotypical baritone that many feel is a radio prerequisite. To reiterate his words from Chapter 5:

"I don't sound like the big-voiced radio guy of the past. I think one of the things that has gotten me to this point (in my career) is the fact that I'm an "active listener." I'm a member of my audience. In other words, I want to be entertained, so I entertain the listener. I try to deliver the information with some sort of originality, with an entertaining twist, with a delivery you're going to pay attention to. And another thing—I get the names right. I make sure that the pronunciations are as accurate as possible."

But when it really comes right down to it, Ernay says it's not the voice or the style as much as it is the writing.

You have to know how to get the message to people. Remember, I have to get people who are busy running around every morning doing something else—nobody sits around anymore and just listens to the radio—so I have to give you a reason to sort of pause and pay attention. And the way I describe [that process] is I'm grabbing you out of the speakers and shaking you by the shoulders saying, "I have something important to say, please make sure you're paying attention." And you do that by popping out of the speakers. You have to give them energy [along with] a well-written, thoughtful and informative presentation.

SIDELINE

In September 1972, 11 Israeli athletes and coaches were killed by terrorists at the Olympic Games in Munich.[1] The idea for having a sideline reporter may have grown out of this terrible tragedy. At least that's according to sportscaster Jim Lampley:

> *In Lampley's telling, the job [of sideline reporter] grew out of the wreckage of the 1972 Munich Olympics, where new wireless technology was put to such vital use in ABC's quicksilver coverage of the Israeli hostage crisis and the subsequent massacre. Says Lampley: "Months later, they asked, 'What else could we do? Would it work in a football stadium? Could we put someone on the sidelines?'"[2]*

Two years later, the article continues, Lampley became "the first officially designated sideline reporter (along with another reporter, Don Tollefson)."[3]

Here's more from the article, giving pause to anyone aspiring to be a sideline reporter. This was Lampley's response to how he regards sideline reporting today.

> *"I'd get rid of it entirely," says Lampley, ABC's former "golden boy," in the words of* Sports Illustrated, *who was once regarded as the presumptive heir to Jim McKay. Lampley is now known mainly for his work on the Olympics and HBO's boxing broadcasts. "All the injury-related information, all the other sideline stuff, you can do that just by having somebody on the sideline who's not on the air, reporting directly to the production truck. I just don't see what it adds. Unless I felt my viewership was going to go up because somebody was really good-looking, so dramatically, amazingly, dynamically good-looking. But that doesn't make any sense at all to me."[4]*

WHAT CAN I ADD?

Despite the feelings expressed by Jim Lampley, a good sideline reporter *can* be an asset to a live event sportscast. Fresh and unique storylines provided by the sideline reporter are welcome additions. But other aspects such as up-to-the-minute updates on strategy and injuries—updates that the announcers might not get as quickly, or at all, while tethered to their broadcast locations—might be deemed critical to a broadcast's success.

Larra Overton's résumé includes sideline reporting for the Big Ten Network:

> "You have to have 20 storylines going into the event. But at the same time, you have to be able to think on your feet and be adaptable. Many times you can't plan. You have to be prepared to do something quick on some guy and then suddenly if there's a turnover, you might have to do something else instead. You have to change in a moment."

> "And when you do get on the air, you have to be concise."

YOUR OWN PERSONAL GAME PLAN

While sideline duties will vary from sport to sport and from telecast to telecast, this glimpse onto Overton's preparation for a Saturday football telecast serves as a good template:

> "You start about a week out for a football game. There might be a telephone call with the producer and the talent on Monday. Tuesday, Wednesday, and Thursday will offer some combination of research and conference calls with competing coaches, at least the head coach and a coordinator from each team. You then gather storylines from that. You're looking at every potential major contributor to the game and all along you're making notes. Friday morning can be an all-day affair talking with sports information directors, other coaches, and players. If you're lucky, you have a Friday night dinner with your broadcast team where you can compare notes and, hopefully, create chemistry."

Overton's homework regimen demonstrates the preparation needed to be a good sideline reporter. Nearly two-dozen storylines plus the necessary overall knowledge to—pardon the expression—punt in case something unexpected happens. And if a celebrity or notable politician surprisingly appears at the game and you are asked to do the interview, you have to have the broadcast savvy and flexibility to do that as well.

Craig Sager says his regimen for preparation is the key for him. Sager has been working the sidelines for Turner Sports since 1980.

"I'm old school," says Sager. "I have index cards. I write everything down. It's an open-book test. I keep a file on every team and every player and update them through the season. When it comes time for me to cover that team or that player, I'm ready."

A FEW MORE THINGS

Ad-libbing is a must, especially with a fast-breaking storyline where you've had time to jot down a few notes and then—bam!—you're on the air. "Being able to ad-lib is key," says Sager. "I try at all times to write things down which, in turn, helps me to memorize it easily. Knowing your facts helps too."

Sticking to the facts and not speculating, says Sager, is paramount. Good sideline reporters, like good play-by-play and color analysts, should tread carefully, particularly when it involves an injury to a player.

"You don't want to speculate," says Sager. "I get very upset when sideline reporters speculate. They'll say, 'oh, that looks like a torn ACL.' Well, no, you don't know if it's a torn ACL. You say he's holding his knee. Well, it could be a number of things. So I tend to say just the facts: 'The doctors are looking at his knee, he'll be evaluated later.' Then you get the information later from the head athletic trainer or the coach. At major events, you will learn who to go to for injury information beforehand."

As we covered in Chapter 3, good reporters with solid relationships can bring timely, breaking information to a telecast, including insightful nuggets of information and perhaps, if the ground rules allow, late-game strategy. Developing those solid relationships days, weeks, months in advance of the game you're covering can be very valuable.

■ What's fair game?

In 1999, Major League Baseball unveiled its All-Century team, which included Pete Rose. Ten years earlier, Rose had been banned from baseball amid allegations he had bet on games during his playing and managing career with the Cincinnati Reds. Despite the ban, Rose was permitted to participate in ceremonies honoring the All-Century team before Game 2 of the World Series at Atlanta's Turner Field. During the live telecast, NBC Sports reporter Jim Gray interviewed Rose and, to the surprise of many, asked Rose if he was ready to admit that he bet on baseball. Rose declined to make any admission to Gray, but the reporter continued to go after Rose who, at one point, described the interview as a "prosecutor's brief." Ultimately, Gray's decision to seize this particular time to ask those kinds of questions elicited a shower of criticism, commentary, and debate.

Craig Sager was part of the NBC reporting team that night and was a few feet away from the controversial interview. We asked Sager if athletes and coaches are always fair game.

"They are fair game, but just to a certain point. The situation with Jim Gray and Pete Rose, that was just so off-target, it was tough for me to be a part of it.

They had talked to Pete Rose [beforehand] and they basically talked him into doing the interview. They told him—quote—they had information that would be vital to him being reinstated back into baseball. Apparently what Jim was getting at—I don't want to speak for him—was that if he could get Pete to admit he bet on baseball, they would be more willing to reinstate him. So that was Jim's premise and he wasn't going to stop until he got the answer that he wanted.

I was standing with Hank Aaron getting ready to interview him. While listening to Gray's interview with Rose, I turned to Hank and I said, "you're not going to believe where this interview is going. [Rose] has already answered him once, twice, three times and Jim won't let up." The crew kept asking Jim, "hey Jim, lighten up."

Afterwards I saw Jim and he said, "I did the right thing." I said, "well, OK, that's what you believe." And he still believes to this day that he did the right thing. But that's just a difference between us. I just thought that was one case where [coaches and athletes] are fair game, but in that case, he went too far.

I think [when trying to decide when a coach or athlete is fair game in a live situation] you use common sense. You have to use common sense in terms of what you're dealing with and what the consequences are going to be. It's one thing to make news, but it's another thing to make news at somebody's expense, especially when they don't deserve it.

There are certain times—when you're dealing with injuries and people's emotions—[when you should] step back. There's a time to go after the hard news and get your questions answered, but once you [ask the question], you move on. You can't just keep on going after them. You have to have a certain etiquette and a certain respect for people."

Sandy Padwe is a professor and special lecturer at the Columbia Journalism School. He was a special consultant to ESPN for 19 years and worked as a sports reporter and editor for a number of major, metropolitan publications including *The New York Times*. He says:

"I don't think there should be any restrictions or strictures on questions that need to be asked. If there's going to be a news conference or big media availability, everything should be fair game at that point. When I say fair game, I think the reporter should be thinking ethically and intelligently, but I don't think there should be any restrictions on them.

That said, I just don't think Gray handled himself very well. I didn't like his whole approach to it. He should have been more "journalistic" about it. I just don't think it was the right setting. I think both parties were set up to fail at that point. I don't think Gray did anything wrong, in a sense, because he was trying to get an answer to a question. I don't think he did anything unethical. He just pushed [Pete Rose] very hard—I don't want to say in a non-professional way—he just pushed it too hard."

Jim Gray, currently a freelance sportscaster based in Los Angeles, was contacted but elected not to comment.

SPORTS TALK RADIO

Listen, everyone is entitled to my opinion.

Madonna

Many sports fans are, you'll pardon the expression, in concert with Madonna. They are passionate about their sports and their teams. Many love to discuss, banter, and, yes, argue their opinions about the day's sports developments down to the nub. Their forum for doing this is often sports talk radio.

Sports talk has done much to help radio remain a viable medium. New York City's WFAN (formerly WNBC) became the first radio station dedicated completely to sports talk and play-by-play on July 1, 1987. A quarter-century later, the sports talk format has grown significantly, up an estimated 65% over the past decade and currently encompassing more than 700 stations throughout the United States. In 2012, NBC and CBS each started their own sports talk radio networks.

Facilitating all of this is the sports talk host, who all at once is reporter, fan, critic, and entertainer. They serve up the best sports topics of the day, give their slant on those headlines and, at times, further debate them with callers. They conduct interviews with players, coaches, and front office personnel to both enlighten and enrage the fan. They also might be in a position to break sports news stories on their shows as well (see more in Chapter 3).

PREPARE TO BE DIFFERENT . . . AND GREAT

Owen Murphy is a veteran sports talk show host, producer (for, among others, Dan Patrick), and consultant at both the network and major market levels. He's heard a lot of sports talk in his career and he thinks much of it is . . .

"Boring. I've listened to sports talk all over the country, big markets, small markets, and it just strikes me that everyone does the bare minimum to get by. They don't go that extra step to make sure that everything they're doing is the best it can possibly be."

And so in Murphy's opinion, what does make a good sports talk show host?

"The guys I like," says Murphy, now producing *The John Curley Show* on KIRO-FM in Seattle, "are the ones who try and take a subject they care about or that their audience cares about and make it huge. Good use of sound, have a great opinion, take you inside the story in a way that is unexpected. When I was a program director, I gave my [sports

Owen Murphy, courtesy of Josh Kerns

talk] hosts a simple job description, 'be entertaining and insightful while building great conversations.' The hosts that are able to do that are the ones who I think are great."

As seen in Chapter 3, there are a number of ways to prepare for a sports talk show. This is especially important for interviews. But according to sports talker John Kincade, good preparation helps you to become a good *facilitator* of sports talk, and not become the entire show.

"I go with the 80–20 rule," says Kincade, who co-hosts a show on WCNN, 680 The Fan in Atlanta. "There's never going to be less than 80 percent (from) my guest. Secondly, I always believe that I never use an interview with a guest to affirm my opinion. The guests are not there to affirm or go against your opinion. Leave it open-ended. Let [the guest] present their opinion without having to react to yours."

EXPRESS YOURSELF, TO A POINT

That said, John Gambadoro, a co-host on Phoenix's KTAR, Arizona Sports 620, says having an opinion is at the crux of what he does. "The key to sports radio has been and will always be your opinion. People want to know what you think, not what you know. It's important to know things, but it's more important to have an opinion on those things."

Fans, of course, have their opinions. Kincade says when treating callers, it's best not to take it personally and err on the lighter side. "If a caller is personally attacking me, they open the door for me to personally attack them back," he says with a laugh. "But you have to try to keep it to some level of fun. I always love it when someone will be attacking me or calling me a moron, I always try to end the call with something that will make people laugh. Like I'll add a certain element that's self-effacing. I'll be like, 'you know, I *am* an idiot. But I'm not an idiot on this point.' Do something where you say, 'OK, let the caller get a few jabs in, but it's going to be a split decision in your favor.'"

In terms of criticizing a team or a player without letting it become personal, we give the final opinion to sports producer Murphy.

> "I think you start by assuming that the people you are talking about have some general idea about what they're doing. So the general manager has some idea about building a team. If you go at it from that point of view, even if you're being critical, at least then you're being fair. And I personally believe in fairness because I think it makes better conversation. You can disagree with the moves [a general manager] makes, there's nothing wrong with that. But I don't believe in getting personal. [Admittedly,] getting personal *can* be entertaining I suppose, but are you being insightful?"

HOSTING

Sports talk has also proliferated into television, including straight-out debate shows. Add to that the myriad pre-game/half-time/post-game shows as well as shows that are issues-oriented and/or investigative. Regulating the pace and tenor of these programs is the job of a show host.

"First and foremost [a good sports show host] has to have the mechanics down," says NBC's Costas, who has won more than a dozen Emmy awards for his hosting.

> "The best make it look easy. A lot of people would be surprised at how many moving parts there are, how much the host has to juggle and the input that [the host] gets simultaneously from the producer. So there's a little bit of keeping a bunch of plates twirling in the air."

> "Once you have the mechanics of it down, then the other elements are the ability to listen to what others [on the set] are saying, the ability to think on your feet

because while there is a format and there is a script, you never know what might happen, so you have to be able to ad-lib. You also have to be knowledgeable about the subject matter because you want to set up [the people on the set with you] and let them shine."

Ultimately, a good host will drive a show, keep it interesting and on time. A good host does not necessarily have to dominate (although they might have to), but rather, facilitate.

As Costas alluded to, the host has to be in synch with the producer. The producer has a format to which he or she has to adhere. That format is normally divided into segments, with each one having its own specific tone, subject matter, guests, and timing. The producer has a list of elements that is designed to enhance that segment and it's up to the host, mostly in response to the producer talking in his or her ear, to help implement those elements or, in some cases, skip them because of time or other issues.

Preparing to host a show is done in concert with the producer. Sometimes the producer will take input from the host on what the format looks like while producers will be married to a concept or idea and will simply tell the host to make it happen. Whatever the case may be, the host needs to internalize the vision of the producer through a pre-show meeting so he or she has a feel for what the show needs to look and sound like. At the same time, the host has to be able to shift gears on the fly and change/add/subtract at the whim of the producer, often during the show or right before it.

The host has his or her own responsibilities independent of the producer, including research on the issues to be discussed or on the guests who are appearing. Much of this research needs to be laid out in such a way so that the host can refer to it on an as-needed basis.

Once the show begins, a lot of the host's responsibility revolves around transitioning to and from various segments. Typically, the host might voiceover a recorded open, then a live welcome to the show with a wide shot of the set. A close-up could come next, with the host introducing him or herself and either reading off of a teleprompter or ad-libbing what is coming up on the show (graphics and/or video might also be used in this segment). Then, an introduction of the guests would probably ensue.

From there, it's the host's job to get and keep the show moving by introducing topics, adding commentary to spur conversation or debate, regulating a debate between two or more guests or transitioning to a graphic, taped segment or any other element the producer may want.

"In short," says Russ Thaler, the host of NBC's coverage of Major League Soccer, "you need to be in the moment and stay in control, especially when things are threatening to get out of hand."

Thaler adds, "Sometimes people come in with agendas, especially when it's a straight interview with a newsmaker. You have to be ready to ask a pointed question that gets you to the point that you're trying to get answered, as opposed to allowing someone to simply state their agenda."

REPORTER EXERCISES—FOR TELEVISION AND (WHERE APPLICABLE) RADIO

1. Pull a list of stories that have already been packaged for television or radio or already written for a website or newspaper. Challenge yourself to come up with a different angle or lead for that story.
2. Do a minimum five-minute video or audio interview of a classmate on any subject of interest. Do this spontaneously, without doing any research. Could you comfortably sustain the interview for the entire five minutes? What were the challenges in doing the interview? What was the key to keeping the interview going?
3. After the interview, record some cutaway questions and reactions on video. What are some of the challenges in doing these?
4. Practice short, eight- to 15-second standups by doing the following:
    a. Conceptualize each standup using bullet points.
    b. Perform the standups in the field and critique.
    c. Conceptualize three different standups for a single story. One standup should be used as a "bridge" in the middle of a story, another at the end of a story and a third as a "tease" to be used during a newscast.
5. Conceptualize a single standup for a story that can be used either as a "bridge" in the middle or as a "tease" and perform this standup three different ways.
6. Practice a longer standup of at least 30 to 45 seconds as if you were on the scene of a breaking story and were reporting live in a Q&A with a studio anchor.

    Extra credit: do this in the field with your instructor *one time only.*
7. Research, shoot, script, and edit a video or audio reporter package.

ANCHORING EXERCISES—FOR TELEVISION AND (WHERE APPLICABLE) RADIO

1. Script and perform a 90-second sportscast.
    a. For television:
        i.   One script word-for-word with the teleprompter.
        ii. One script ad-libbed around bullet points.

      iii. Highlights, voiceover video, and sound bites if available.

      iv. Use a "cut sheet" for highlights.

  b. For radio:

      i. One script word-for-word.

      ii. One script ad-libbed around bullet points.

      iii. Voice-cuts and play-by-play highlights if available.

2. For television only, same as the exercise described in question 1, only with a producer in the anchor's ear counting down to packages.

3. Allow your instructor to "sabotage" your "live" television or radio broadcast where something goes wrong and you are forced to keep the broadcast going.

SIDELINE EXERCISES—FOR TELEVISION AND (WHERE APPLICABLE) RADIO

1. Prepare for an event at your school or for a local team as if you were going to be on the sideline, courtside, or rinkside, including:

  a. General homework on the teams, strategies, personalities, and other storylines of the game.

  b. Three or four "feature-oriented" standups.

2. If possible, perform these elements as part of a broadcast or "off-line" including all of the above along with any situational standups (i.e., injuries, etc.) as well as pre-game, intermission or post-game interviews.

SPORTS RADIO EXERCISES

1. Debate a sports topic with a classmate. Each of you gets a 20-second response over two minutes. Then, each of you take the *opposite* point of view and debate that topic again, using the same format. What did you learn from this exercise?

2. Prepare the following elements as if you were going to host a sports talk radio program:

  a. Opening monologue on the topic or topics you are going to cover (:90).

  b. Background information on these topics.

  c. Schedule and prepare questions for an interviewee.

3. Produce and host (solo or with a co-host) a one-hour sports talk show, including callers (i.e., arrange those call-ins with your friends for a particular time) and an interview. Schedule time at your school's radio station (live or off-line), utilize an Internet site, or produce it on your laptop. Feel free to be as creative as you want, including the addition of pre-produced elements such as a show introduction, music bumps to break, a sports update, etc.

HOST EXERCISES

1. Prepare to host a sports program on television or radio. This can be a pre-game, half-time, between period, post-game, or other stand-alone, half-hour show. Design the format, make a list of guests, and the topics to be covered.
2. Produce this on video or audio. Coordinate the crew and other elements such as booking guests and additional video or audio elements as needed.

ENDNOTES

ENDNOTES
6

1. Francie Grace, "Munich Massacre Remembered," CBSNEWS.com, February 11, 2009. www.cbsnews.com/stories/2002/09/05/world/main520865.shtml, accessed February 1, 2013.
2. Tommy Craggs, "The First Sideline Reporter: 'All of this was just Nonsense,'" Deadspin.com, July 28, 2009. http://deadspin.com/5323838/the-first-sideline-reporter-all-of-this-was-just-nonsense, accessed February 1, 2012.
3. Ibid.
4. Ibid.

Chapter 7

PLAY-BY-PLAY AND ANALYST

PLAY-BY-PLAY

Anchoring or reporting the sports or participating in the broadcast of a live sporting event—as a performer or on the technical side—can be immensely satisfying. But no position in sportscasting brings a non-participant closer to the action than that of the play-by-play announcer. He or she is overlooking the arena or the field, vividly describing all that goes into an unscripted passion play as it happens. As they do this they are in direct, immediate contact with the people most interested in the outcome of the proceedings, the fans.

Baseball Hall-of-Famer Vin Scully, in his 65th consecutive year as the play-by-play voice of the Los Angeles Dodgers, sums up the credentials of a good play-by-play announcer as "basically accuracy, preparation, information, and entertainment all wrapped up into one."

Mike Breen is ABC's play-by-play announcer for the NBA Finals. He also broadcasts NBA playoff and regular season games on ESPN as well as the New York Knicks on MSG. "I think if you asked the viewer who's watching at home, 'this guy who's calling the game, does he sound excited, does he sound enthusiastic, does he sound informed and prepared, and does he make me wish I was at that game sitting alongside him?' If you can accomplish those goals, I think that's a good play-by-play announcer."

Like all artists, play-by-play announcers prepare and perform in their own unique styles. A certain amount of that is dictated by the medium in which they are performing and the sport they are covering. That said, many issues concerning performance and preparation for play-by-play announcers are consistent across the board, no matter what.

Jim Nantz has been a broadcaster for CBS sports since 1985 and has covered, among other sports, the Masters, NFL football, and NCAA basketball. He says: "It always gets back to preparation, because we're storytellers above all. We're there to observe and tell people what we see and then combine that with information in the hopes that you have something fresh and unique."

DO YOUR HOMEWORK

Play-by-play announcers who feel they can simply "open their mike and broadcast the game," are doing a disservice to the fans and the broadcast itself. Good preparation adds depth and breadth to any broadcast. How best to "do your homework" for the game and the resources available is detailed in Chapter 3.

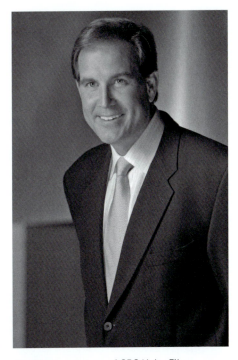

Jim Nantz, courtesy of CBS/John Filo

As you gather this information, pertinent facts are normally arranged in the announcer's personal style, perhaps using some sort of chart, card, or flipcards that can be referred to during the event. While some in the business hand-write a new chart for each game, many have taken to using a computer program of their choice. Using some sort of electronic spreadsheet or software saves time, particularly when covering the same team where much of the basic information changes little from game-to-game.

Once you build your charts, the first thing to consider is becoming familiar with player identification. Number memorization is mandatory in hockey and soccer. In football, it's important to at least know the numbers of the skill position players while perhaps relying on a spotter for tackling and blocking identification. Baseball's slower pace makes number memorization a little less important, although your chart needs to help identify players in position on the field. In basketball, number memorization helps, although it may not be mandatory given that players may be more readily identifiable through their physical characteristics.

While charts do vary from individual to individual and from sport to sport, each will have a number of things in common:

- Complete rosters with numbers and correct name pronunciations
- General individual team information
- Certain statistics and other facts that could be used during the broadcast

Understand the operative word here, *could* be used. The fact of the matter is, most of the information you prepare for a game will *not* be used. Judiciously using your material will be discussed later in the chapter.

There's no correct way to write out or arrange this information on your chart. Laying it out vertically or horizontally with the use of various font styles and colors will be a matter of personal choice. But chances are, given the limited room, the information you obtain may have to be abbreviated or written in such a way that perhaps only you will understand it. Getting ideas or taking a look at the charts of other, more experienced announcers is always helpful. Still, expect your chart to continue to evolve as you find out what works and what doesn't.

Vin Scully, courtesy of Fox Sports West

▪ Vin Scully

"Hi everybody and a very pleasant good afternoon to you, wherever you may be . . ."

That is the signature line that calls all of southern California to attention. The line belongs to Los Angeles Dodgers' play-by-play voice Vin Scully, acknowledged by most as the greatest play-by-play announcer ever. Not just in the history of baseball where he's made his greatest impact, but in the history of the business.

At the top of Scully's stunning résumé is his longevity. In August 2013, he announced he would return in 2014 for his 65th consecutive season with the ball club. When he started with the then Brooklyn Dodgers in 1950, gasoline cost 27 cents a gallon, a postage stamp was just three cents, and the minimum wage was only 75 cents per hour.

Scully is a member of a number of Halls of Fame, including his 1982 induction into the Broadcaster's wing of the National Baseball Hall of Fame as the Ford C. Frick Award recipient. In 2001, the press box at Dodger Stadium was named in his honor. In 2005, the book *Voices of Summer* by Curt Smith named him baseball's all-time best broadcaster based on "longevity, continuity, network coverage, kudos, language, popularity, persona, voice knowledge and miscellany." In 2009, the American Sportscasters Association selected Scully as the Top Sportscaster of All-Time.

Scully was interviewed on August 27, 2013, just a row from his usual spot, behind home plate, in the Dodger Stadium press box.

Q: Are you still learning?

A: Oh absolutely. There are things that you take for granted and then suddenly you can't reach for it and get it when you need it. That always pops up. Also in baseball—and that's the only sport I do now—there's plenty of time to hang yourself [laughing]. So, you have to be very careful. It's a high-wire act at all times so you try very hard to be careful.

Q: Do you have to like that element, being on a high-wire without a net?

A: I would think so. I think you have to enjoy the challenge. And of course, I love baseball, I love the game itself and I assume anyone who's heading in that direction has the same feeling. I don't know how you can do nine innings in three hours and dislike what you're looking at.

Q: What is it about broadcasting that you still love?

A: Part of it is the roar of the crowd. The roar of the crowd excited me when I was eight years old, crawling under a big four-legged radio and I would hear the roar of the crowd and I would get goose bumps and I would wish that I were there. A Tennessee–Alabama football game and there's a kid in New York City listening to it because of the roar. I think the crowd more than anything gives me a lift. There are days, naturally, when you come to the ballpark and maybe you'd rather be home doing something else. But once that crowd begins, it just seems to lift me up and away we go.

KNOW THE RULES

An integral part of doing your homework is also knowing the rules. This is a fluid process, meaning that it's something you'll always be doing because there are many rules and they are always changing. Here's how to learn the rules and keep up with them all season long:

- Obtain a rulebook from a team or the league (printed or online)
- Seek out other support materials
- Talk to game officials and league supervisors
- Keep the rulebook with you
- Bookmark certain rules for easy reference
- If you don't know the rule, just ask!

MAKING THE CALL

Of course, actually calling the action is the real joy. Put it in the context of an opera, where the play-by-play announcer is certainly performing and in a way, singing. The song does not contain musical notes per se, but there is a rhythm to it. And like opera, there are acts, plot lines, a climax, and a denouement.

As characters and plotlines are developed in the game, the play-by-play announcer conveys the importance and emotion of it all. This is done with some of the same individual styling, phrasing, and passion of the opera singer; sometimes solo and other times with accompaniment. Play-by-play broadcasters are said to announce with a certain cadence, that is with a certain tempo or pulse to their delivery. This cadence is a by-product of an announcer's personal style, the sport that's being broadcast, and the medium on which the event is being broadcast.

Personal style is developed in at least two ways, as discussed in Chapter 5:

■ "Going to the driving range" begets style development through repetition, which can be as easy as going to a sporting event and doing play-by-play into a digital recorder
■ "You are a river" is when you visualize yourself being "fed" or influenced by announcers you admire and other external factors

As your play-by-play conveys the ebb and flow of the action, "it's important for sportscasters to use 'projection' as opposed to a louder 'volume,'" as broadcast voice specialist Ann Utterback explained earlier. She says "projecting is important when stressing the emotion of the moment or the intensity of the action." Changes in your cadence will also occur in these situations as well.

ON THE RADIO

The differences between the play-by-play description on the radio versus television is inherent. In radio, the announcer is virtually the entire show. In television, you are a central part of the show, but a *part* nonetheless.

"Naturally on radio, you paint the full canvas," says the Scully. "As far as television is concerned, it's already there—you put captions to the pictures. So I think it's totally different."

Radio play-by-play announcers are effectively their own producers and directors. While there is a specific format indicating when certain announcements are to be made or commercial breaks played, the radio announcer pretty much lords over the content. He or she alone decides what's important along with when and how to convey the information. But whatever conveyance is being made, from describing the action to relating the look in the eyes of an angry coach, it must be done in such a way that the listener at home can visualize the situation as if they were seeing it themselves. That means the radio play-by-play person must always remember:

- that the listener cannot see, making detail critical
- vivid descriptions such as *left side*, *right side*, *near side*, and *far side*
- specific indicators and locations that are intrinsic to the individual sport, such as *in the lane*, *at the blue line*, *at midfield*, and *deep to left field*
- other basics like what is happening, who is initiating the action, and the consequences of the play
- brief re-descriptions of the important plays
- that your voice is *everything*

GIVE THE SCORE!

Announcers will often forget that radio listeners (and television viewers) tune in and out all the time. Because of that, they often don't remember to give the most essential piece of information often enough: the score! In basketball and hockey it's *time and score*. In football it's *down and distance* along with *time and score*. And in baseball it's *the count*, *the base running situation*, and *inning and score*. Baseball announcer Red Barber, whose Major League career spanned three teams and four decades, would be reminded to give the score whenever his three-minute egg-timer ran out.

TV

Television play-by-play announcers often don't require an egg-timer. Normally a score bug displayed on the screen provides time or inning and score throughout the game. This is, in microcosm, illustrative of the TV play-by-play announcer's mandate. Unlike his radio counterpart, who must always remember that *the listener can't see anything*, the TV play-by-play person must always keep in mind that *the viewer can see almost everything!* Thus, one of the biggest issues for television play-by-play announcers is "what can I do to enhance what people can already see?"

Mike Breen of ABC, ESPN, and the New York Knicks says in terms of career development, it's best to transition from radio to TV and not the other way around.

"I think radio to TV is easier than TV to radio," says Breen, who was the radio voice of the New York Knicks before becoming their lead television voice as well. "The key to moving from radio to TV is to simply talk less, to be much more concise and also to make sure the analyst takes a much stronger role, realizing it's more important to explain why as opposed to what. It's also important to supply more background and personal information [on players and coaches]. Radio is very nuts and bolts—you're just the eyes, it's what's happening, what's the score, what's the time. With TV you can get involved with much more and that's why having the ability to work with an analyst on TV is so much more important."

Calling the action on television does not require the rapid-fire, ultra-description of radio. Instead, TV play-by-play needs to be a step removed. It's OK to allow the game and its sounds to simply "come through" the telecast, especially when the action might be deemed inconsequential: in baseball between pitches; in basketball while a team is slowly dribbling the ball up the court; in soccer during a build-up at midfield. When the play is more consequential, then the TV play-by-play announcer can hone in and be more descriptive.

The late sportscaster Ray Scott was one of the early advocates of a minimalist style for television. Sportscasting historian John Lewis once described Scott's style this way:

> "Starr . . . to Dowler . . . Touchdown" was a call Green Bay Packer fans heard Scott say many times during their dynasty. The three word description poignantly defined Ray Scott's style; simple but oh so effective. He believed in minimizing chatter, and choosing words carefully, allowing the action to speak for itself. The result was powerful. With Scott, the game breathed. His reverent, commanding tones embodied the National Football League. Former Green Bay sportswriter Lee Remmel described his voice saying, "Everything he said sounded like it was chiseled in stone." Marv Albert, a young voice of New York Sports when Scott was at his height, recalled being moved by Scott's work. From his autobiography *I'd Love to but I Have a Game*, Albert said, "He had a spare, simple elegance that still held tingles.[1]

Descriptions on radio or television will often lend themselves to an individual announcer's unique phrases. When a team was having great success in a game, the late Red Barber would say that club is "Sittin' in the catbird seat." Marv Albert's "downtown" has become synonymous with basketball's three-point shot. Hockey's Mike Emrick uses a liberal sprinkling of metaphors, highlighting a frenetic sport's finer points. That said, Emrick's TV call, like that of most hockey announcers, is a little more descriptive given the nature of the game (small puck and many hard to discern players going in and out of the game).

"Occasionally people have asked 'where does that particular phrase come from?' and I cannot say," says Emrick, who has announced both the Stanley Cup Finals as well as the Olympics. "I don't conspire to use a certain word to describe an event, it's just the translation of what I see with my eyes into whatever words I have. It helps probably to have more verbs than adverbs and things like that at your command so you can mix it up a little bit. When I was first starting to do this, one of the IHL [International Hockey League] announcers said "if you can come up with different ways to say the same thing, that will help an awful lot." That's because if you use the same word to describe the same action, well, how many times does the puck get dumped in from center ice? If you use "dumped" every time you're going to drive people nuts."

Emrick's style of unique phrasing helps to meet the mandate of augmenting what the viewer can already see. This also goes for other visuals on a telecast such as graphics. As we detailed in Chapter 4, ad-libbing to enhance what is already visible to the viewer is often the preferred style. One notable exception is when reading a graphic containing someone's quote. In that case, the viewer is reading too so it generally helps to read along. But for example, if there's a graphic showing how a football player averaged 3.4 yards per carry his first year, 4.1 yards his second season, and 4.6 yards his third, all you have to add is simply: "He's improved his yards per carry every year he's been in the league."

Speaking of numbers, allow the graphics to handle some of the more minute details such as decimal points. Instead of saying "he's averaging 15.6 points and 9.3 rebounds per game" round it off to say "he's averaging just under 16 points and just over nine rebounds per game." It's a little easier for the viewer or listener to grasp.

AND IF YOU'RE JUST TUNING IN . . .

In fact, that is *always* the case. That is, people tune in and out of a broadcast all the time. Play-by-play announcers need to be especially mindful of this. Even if it ruffles the feathers of those who've been with you since the first pitch or kickoff, feel free to repeat at occasional intervals the main storylines of the game, including a quick synopsis of what has happened in the contest to that point and a repeat of the overarching storyline (i.e., a fight for first place, a grudge match against a long-time rival, etc.). To avoid feeling like you're repeating yourself (and annoying those who've been with you the entire broadcast), feel free to preface your recap with a phrase such as "if you're just joining us," but often that's not necessary.

TRY TO AVOID CLICHÉS

In order to avoid using clichés, sportscasters should:

- Look themselves in the mirror
- Circle the wagons
- Imitate the Bob Costas of the world
- Give 110 percent

For play-by-play announcers, analysts, anchors, reporters and hosts alike, staying away from clichés—you'll pardon the expression—is easier said than done. Bob Costas, who has done play-by-play and hosted for NBC Sports since the early 1980s, says you hope you have enough facility with the language that you don't have to rely on them.

"Even the best broadcasters will occasionally use phrases which could be called clichés," says Costas, who is into his fifth decade as a sportscaster, most of it at the network level. "There are only so many ways to describe a ground ball to second base or a jump shot. But what you hope is that you don't think in clichés, that you're not offering the same, standard take on everything. Better to say this happens 'rarely' than to say 'this happens once in a blue moon.'"

CALLING THE BIG PLAY

Let's get back to our opera metaphor for a second. Often a sporting event has storylines similar to that of an opera or, for that matter, any dramatic play. And while that first inning three-run home run or those three touchdowns in the second quarter might often be the difference in winning, the real drama will often occur late in the game. That brings up an important concept for the play-by-play announcer to bear in mind. While you will certainly want to show excitement and emotion when describing that bicycle kick goal or that alley-oop slam dunk, you have to consider when this play occurs. If it comes relatively early in the contest, make sure you keep that very thing in mind. In other words, always keep "something in reserve" so that if there is a game-turning or game-winning play late in a game, you are ready to signify—with your call—that *this* is the most important moment of the contest.

When it comes to making that big call, let it be spontaneous. Scripting or planning a call takes away the human element, the real excitement, the spontaneity of it all. Relax, relate, concentrate . . . and make the call! You'll be the better for it.

Most big or game-winning moments on television are often followed by the play-by-play announcer "laying out" and not saying anything. This allows the director and producer to expound on the event with a live video and audio montage of celebration and/or dejection featuring players, coaches, and fans. In this case, the sheer sensation of the moment is conveyed best in just pictures and sounds. Words would only get in the way. On radio, it's not a bad thing to consider a similar practice, with a layout and a "crowd swell" after a big play. "They are on their feet here at the stadium after that three-run walk off home run by John Smith . . ." *after* a five- to eight-second pause might work well, really allowing the listener to feel the moment.

GOOD CHEMISTRY

After you make the call and the excitement from the big play starts to recede, look to your left or right. You may have a color analyst with you, perhaps champing at the bit to give his or her take on what just happened.

When broadcasting in college, the analyst will often be just another student. But as you move up in the commercial ranks, most analysts will be former players or coaches. Some will be more polished than others as performers. Some you will like personally more than others. But it's incumbent upon you to at least do your part to develop a good, professional, on-air relationship that connotes "good chemistry."

Good chemistry between play-by-play announcer and analyst is much the same as the good chemistry between players on a sports team. When there's good chemistry:

■ individuals embrace their roles
■ each of you has the opportunity to exhibit what they do best
■ there's an air of mutual respect and comfort
■ egos are subjugated for the common good

NBC's Costas on chemistry: "Sometimes you can just feel it right away. You hope that you get along with the person and that the person trusts you, that you want *him* to do well and that the whole broadcast matters."

Chemistry can only come by investing the time to work together on the air. A good, honest dialogue between play-by-play and analyst before and after games greatly facilitates the process. During a sort of "pre-game show" between the two of you, you can discuss what each of you plans to bring to the broadcast. This is especially valuable for the play-by-play person, who can then use this information to "set-up" the analyst during the game. This timely advice of setting up the analyst was once relayed by the late Jack Brickhouse, who was a play-by-play voice for the Chicago Cubs through five different decades. He once told a gathering of young play-by-play announcers at an American Sportscasters Association seminar to "play your color analyst like a fiddle." Some liken his advice to that of a good basketball point guard, in this case the play-by-play, making good passes to his primary scorer, the analyst.

Costas says: "You sort of work [the broadcast out] intuitively. You don't need a 'now it's my turn, now it's your turn.' You kind of just figure out which moments call for a little more of one guy than the other, which moments should be shared and which moments should be exclusively one guy or the other. It becomes kind of a dance that doesn't need to be plotted out step-by-step."

■ Work hard, use 10 percent

All that homework you do for a game? If you use 10 percent of it, it's a good night. More importantly, if you use 10 percent of it in the right way, it's a great night.

Yes, you want to use some of that background information to augment the broadcast. But you want to use those facts at the appropriate time. For example, let's say the analyst shared before the game that the home team felt it had an advantage by using running plays behind their 6–7, 340-pound left tackle. So, after Jenkins the running back scampers for 25 yards and a first down over left tackle, that's your cue to say something like "the home team executed its game plan to perfection on that play." Hopefully the analyst will take the cue and, pardon the expression, run with it.

Generally speaking, telling a story or using other nuggets or stats just to "get them in" is gratuitous and does little to enhance a player, coach, or a particular moment. But if you can peg a story or a big stat to a significant event in the game, your research takes on that much more meaning. For example, your listener/viewer doesn't need to know a particular player is his club's all-time leader in grand slams after he hits a single. But to let me know while he's trotting the bases after a grand slam that "that's Fleming's tenth career grand slam, tops in club history . . ." certainly makes it a lot more momentous.

Holding off on certain stories or facts until a suitable time takes discipline. The inclination is to want to use your homework since you went to the trouble of doing it in the first place. So, think of it in terms of quality versus quantity. Even if you use less than 10 percent of your research on a broadcast, but all of it was interesting, *timely* stuff, you've done a good job.

Knowing when to tell stories and *color* your broadcast is dependent not only on good timing but the sport and the medium as well. Baseball naturally lends itself more to storytelling because of the time between pitches, while a sport like hockey requires you to frequently wait until there is a stoppage in play. That said, hockey on the radio demands more of that type of thinking than hockey on television. Doing television hockey, the play-by-play person can at least interject here and there while the action is going on. Radio too, but much more sparingly.

The opportunity to tell stories varies, depending on the medium and the sport. Generally speaking, there's a little more room on television for stories because the viewer can already see what's happening. So, if a story overlaps a bit into a play, you can still keep up with the action. In radio, any play that's not described because a story's being told is going to be missed. In terms of sport, baseball has always lent itself to stories, with announcers sometimes covering an entire at-bat or two with a good yarn. Football has natural spots (between plays) as does basketball (free throws and other pauses). Announcers for more continuous sports like hockey and soccer have to pick their spots.

Vin Scully is acknowledged to be perhaps the greatest storyteller in sportscasting history. He was asked how he knows a story is a *good* story.

"I don't necessarily rate them good, bad or indifferent," says Scully. "I just tell whatever I had in mind and let it go at that. Sometimes, it (a story) fits better than others. I think the biggest thing you have to watch out for is to get wrapped up in a story and have play interrupt or run out of time when you have to go into commercial. Over the years you know the pitfalls, but even then you stumble every once in a while."

YOU ARE ALSO PART OF A TEAM

There are other differences dictated by the nature of radio versus television. As we alluded to earlier, in radio the announcer is also the broadcast's virtual producer and director. He or she can control when a story is told as long as the action isn't forsaken. But in television, the play-by-play announcer is bound by the structure of the telecast. He or she will frequently tailor commentary to what's being shown on the screen at a particular moment. And so when not peering out at the field, court, or ice, the announcer has to be looking at the program monitor to see what the viewer is seeing at home. That might be a particular graphic, replay, or a "color" shot of a player, coach, or fan. Most times, the producer will warn the play-by-play announcer that a particular shot or graphic is coming and to prepare to comment on it. Sometimes, it just happens or is part of the director's pattern of shots, and the announcer has to be ready to comment (although often visuals don't require any comment—a topic for producer and announcer to iron out and the announcer to get a feel for over time). And still other times, the play-by-play will make mention of something and the producer and director will follow the announcer with the appropriate supporting visual. Ideally, the announcer will attempt to give a heads up to the producer through the talk-back system that a particular shot is needed so that a comment can be made on it, but with the spontaneity of sports, that isn't always possible.

This spirit of cooperation and coordination between the announcer, producer, director, and crew is the key to making a good television sportscast. This starts with the moment everyone begins preparing for the telecast and continues until game coverage ends.

In particular, play-by-play and producer need to be in lockstep. Often both will be involved in establishing the main storyline or storylines for the game. Those storylines help to determine the format or the on-air look of the telecast, including the:

■ Game tease—typically a 30-second to one-minute video that uses some combination of video, music, graphics, and voiceover to "tease" or compel the viewer to watch the upcoming telecast
■ Telecast open—typically some combination of on-camera appearances by the announcers as well as the use of video, graphics, music, and other elements to further embellish on the main themes such as the strong and weak points of the teams or individual players, what the contest means in the standings, the history between the opponents, and so forth
■ Graphics
■ Video roll-ins and other elements

Being on the same page with these issues will allow the play-by-play announcer and producer to work in tandem throughout the telecast, like a great double play combination. Together, they can continue to weave the night's themes in and out of the telecast, as determined by the way the game is played out. Bringing storylines in and out helps to "bridge" the telecast from beginning to end while also acknowledging that fans (and this certainly goes for radio too) tune in and out all night long as well.

The play-by-play announcer hosts the open—playing a sort of traffic cop role—with the producer and director dictating the pace for timing purposes. Play-by-play will:

■ lead the color analyst and sideline reporter into their comments
■ help to transition to other elements, such as video roll-ins and graphics

In this role, the play-by-play announcer plays to the camera in various ways. Looking straight into the camera if the shot is just on him or her is fine. But when interacting with the color analyst, play-by-play announcers are often at a loss as to where to look and when. In the case of a two-shot, the announcer should spend most of his time looking at the analyst while he is talking, but occasionally glancing at the camera to acknowledge the viewers' presence as well.

The role of traffic cop for television play-by-play announcers continues during the game as well. The ability to multitask is key as the play-by-play:

■ calls the action
■ brings in the analyst

- reads promotional or commercial announcements
- refers to replays or graphics

Much like their call of the action, television play-by-play announcers should pick their spots when it comes to referring to a particular shot or graphic. For example, if there's a shot of a baseball manager, instead of saying "there's a shot of so-and-so," perhaps a quick anecdote or some other comment that includes the manager in the conversation would be appropriate. In terms of graphics, instead of saying "as you can see, he has 25 goals on the season" you might instead say "that goal total is third in the league."

Of course, all of this coordination comes at the behest of the producer who, at times, is talking in the announcer's headset during the telecast. Some producers talk more than others, and because an ill-timed directive or comment can disrupt an announcer's flow, there has to be some sort of tacit agreement on when the producer should and should not talk. If you're new to television, this whole process will take some getting used to, but after a while it's not normally a problem.

Like the sports anchor, the play-by-play announcer needs to be poised under pressure and have everyone's back. If there are technical and other issues, it's incumbent upon the play-by-play person to keep cool and do what he or she can to cover up whatever issue is afflicting the telecast. Throwing the producer, director, or another member of the crew "under the bus" might give play-by-play announcers a chance to disassociate themselves from the problem, but it will do nothing to endear him to the people who, on another night, might be in a position to save him or her from an embarrassing situation.

ROOT, ROOT, ROOT?

The play-by-play announcer often walks a fine line when it comes the exact nature of their role on the broadcast:

- Are they partial to one team or impartial?
- Do they become so partial to one team that they are deemed so-called "homers"?
- What is their role in criticizing and second-guessing players and coaches?

Partiality or being a homer is often a function of who is employing you and your own personal style. No matter the level—be it high school, college, or professional—if you are employed by the team, you will certainly tell the story of the game from the perspective of that team. The same goes if you work for a radio or TV station that regularly covers the team. That's because oftentimes both the team and the station are in partnership, so it's probably in your best interest to portray a positive image of players, coaches, and the team in general. In terms of how much of a homer you may turn out to be, that is probably more of your own personal style and how well that style is accepted by your listeners or viewers.

CRITICISM

Criticism and how much you use it depends on a number of factors. Criticism of amateur players such as high school or college is generally left out of the broadcast, although their paid coaches are sometimes left open to second-guessing. Professional players are the ones who are criticized the most because they are getting paid for what they do. The latitude to criticize may be tied to tenure and general acceptability on the part of the station and the team. The play-by-play announcer might have some liberty to criticize or second-guess, so long as it's considered appropriate and not vitriolic, chronic, or personal. The color analyst, on the other hand, has a little more leeway on this and we'll review that later in the chapter.

In 2005, Suzyn Waldman became the first woman to hold a full-time position as a Major League broadcaster, signing as the color analyst for the New York Yankees. She says the late George Steinbrenner would insist on criticizing players, at one point calling her on the phone and asking "why are you protecting this guy [a Yankees' player], he stunk last night!" While acknowledging that the attitude of the Yankees' front office is the exception, she cautions that criticism in general is often perceived by "the way you say it . . . players just don't like it when the criticism is unfair or it's personal."

Criticizing officials or umpires is often done with much more vigor. And when the replay bears out the fact that the official made the incorrect call, play-by-play announcers will often tee off on them. But discretion is advised. If there's too much criticism, announcers will often appear to be cartoonish, simply railing the officials on an almost game-by-game basis, which in turn can take some of the significance away from their comments. Criticize if you feel it's justified, but be judicious.

BLOWOUT THEATER

As you get experience, you'll find as a play-by-play announcer it's easy and fun to call the close, exciting games. Where you really earn your money is when you reach the final stages of a blowout. This can be especially tough on radio play-by-play announcers who still must describe the action, although you can weave stories and other facts in more liberally (careful not to sacrifice time and score!) knowing the game is not in doubt. On television, this is where stories and other "deep" homework can be used to (hopefully!)

keep the viewer engaged. Be careful, however, not to poke fun at the team that is losing badly. Respecting a team that's getting trounced will earn you respect, and it will not hurt you if, say, you actually end up applying for a job with that team in the future!

NBC's Costas adds: "I did a Major League playoff game with Jim Kaat and at one point in the sixth inning it was 8–0 [St. Louis] Cardinals. We told some stories and talked about some general baseball situations in a way that we wouldn't have had the game been closer. We never lost track of the game. There are also times when the drama is such that all you have to be doing is commenting on the action."

In baseball, blowout theater can also become *rain* theater. This is where stories and interviews need to be at the ready, even if you think the forecast is on your side. At times, you might be able to revert to a radio or television station's regularly scheduled programming and wait out the weather that way. If not, get out your hat and cane and be ready to tap dance. Like all good performers, it's up to you to make sure the show goes on no matter the technical problems or, in this case, the weather.

■ The Minors: from play-by-play to pulling tarp

Jon Mozes' first job after graduation from the University of New Haven was announcing for the Abilene (Texas) Prairie Dogs of the North American Baseball League, an independent minor league. This was a Q&A conducted with Jon while he was on the job:

Q: How did you get the job?

A: I networked through a family friend who knew somebody who worked as an intern with another team in that [North American] league, San Angelo. That team president is also the team president in Abilene.

Q: What did you have to do before you landed the job?

A: I networked through seven different guys. A total of about 15 or 20 phone calls. Probably the same amount of emails too.

`Q: What's the typical game day like for you?

A: We're in the office at 9 am. Normally our general manager calls us into the office and takes stock of where we're at. Most of the morning is spent cleaning up any media stuff we have to do with the players, appearances, roster moves—I write the news releases for those—and update our website. I print the roster insert for our eight-page game program, which includes updated stats, bios, and standings. Then, a lot of the day is spent doing sales stuff, cold calling through our chamber of commerce book and the phone book, trying to sell tickets to groups. Then I take 45 minutes for lunch. Afternoons for road games—I don't broadcast those—but I'll

Jon Mozes, courtesy of Mark Fanta

spend a half-hour to 45 minutes preparing for our pre- and post-game shows, then continue with sales stuff or any other stuff that's need around the office. For home games, I'll spend some time preparing for the broadcast and be at the ballpark for batting practice. I also have to be available to help pull the tarp off and on the field.

Q: Tell us a story.

A: When the team president and the radio station negotiated our deal, they did not really think about the details like broadcasting over a phone line for road games. Plus the mixer they gave us did not have a telephone port in it. So my broadcast partner had to lay out more than $250 in wires and a telephone adapter. We also had to purchase the phone to actually place the call. And they didn't have headsets for us so we got a pair from another club team. One of those headsets was duct-taped together and was unusable, so we used a handheld microphone for the second voice.

Q: How much money do you make?

A: I get $400 a month, plus housing—although I pay $100 a month rent for that—the balance was traded out for advertising space. They actually bumped my stipend, though, to cover the hundred bucks. My broadcast partner was there before so he makes $500 a month plus housing.

GAME AND STUDIO ANALYST

Whether you are a former coach, athlete or simply a fan who is a trained broadcaster, the word "color" is inherent to the primary role of the analyst. They need to offer an element of color so that their comments enhance what was heard from the play-by-play announcer. This is true of both radio and television. Too many times the analyst will simply restate what the radio play-by-play man already said or redundantly talk about the replay the television viewer can already see.

The former player or coach has a number of assets that will help him or her to add true "color" to the broadcast.

EXPERIENCE

Coaches and players have been there, done that. They know what it's like to be in the same or similar situations that are being played out in a game. To that end, they need to be able to relate their vast storehouse of knowledge. If a play worked or didn't work, give the fan the all-important *why* it was or wasn't a success and how it might have turned out differently. The same goes for strategy. In fact, the really prescient analyst will try to predict what he or she thinks will happen based on the way a game is going or what strategy is about to be employed.

CREDIBILITY

The previous experience of a player or coach gives them the authority to provide the spice, which is to not only comment but also criticize. While such comments or criticism may be tempered by the nature of their relationship to the team or league, a good honest evaluation of what's going on will add an important dimension to the broadcast. As long as it's not perceived to be malicious nor personal, it's almost incumbent upon the analyst to dispense a dose of honesty.

STORIES

They were experienced in the field, the court, the locker room, or clubhouse. They occurred on the buses, hotels, and airplanes. Stories. If it's clean, if it doesn't harm anyone, and if it's somehow germane (most times?) to something happening in the telecast, a good story is something everyone likes to hear. Of course there has to be time in the broadcast for that story, something that's normally tougher on radio than on television.

But if the play-by-play person and the game situation can provide the opportunity for it, go ahead and tell it. Just know you might have to condense it or truncate it for the purposes of making it fit into the situation.

BE CHEMICAL

Providing the analyst's side of chemistry is Doris Burke, who's been a men's and women's college basketball analyst on both the college and NBA levels.

"Chemistry, in part, is based on repetition," says Burke, who has been working with ESPN/ABC since 1991. "The beauty of being an analyst for a team is you have a certain amount of repetitions with an individual. You have to get comfortable with where a person likes to deliver their information. You have to understand the mechanics of radio and television."

▪ The "Jockocracy"

The late sportscaster Howard Cosell called it the "jockocracy," the influx that began years ago of former athletes and coaches becoming sportscasters in spite of little or no formal media training. Today, to have that ex-player or coach sitting to the right of the play-by-play announcer is typical.

Because of the credibility they have from their involvement in sports, the former player or coach is given more leeway to make mistakes or not be as polished as the professionally trained announcer who shares the booth or set with him. That said, that ex-player/coach can make the transition easier and be a more polished performer simply by putting in the effort and the time.

Former NFL offensive lineman Brian Baldinger did just that. Baldinger has been an analyst for the NFL Network and Fox, but it was an effort to find his way into that sphere.

"I worked really, really hard. I knew that I had to basically rewire my brain so that the words could come quickly as I was speaking. That wasn't easy [in the beginning] while I was looking at a camera or talking into a microphone. It was unnatural. So I did what I had to do [part-time stringing]. I carried a microphone into a 76ers locker room and talked to a dreadful team led by Dana Barros. I drove up to Madison Square Garden and talked to Derek Harper and Patrick Ewing in the Knicks locker room. I just knew I needed to begin talking. Doing Bucknell football on the radio for $50 a game and doing the pre-game and the post-game along with it. Then playing the tapes back and listening to myself and listening to the idiotic questions or repeat sentences. Basically I just listened. I figured once I made a commitment [to broadcasting], there would eventually be people who would give me an opportunity [to learn]. I didn't get rich doing it but I got a ton of experience."

DO YOUR HOMEWORK

If you've never played or coached the game, you can still provide cogent analysis. Having previously watched or been a fan of the game you're broadcasting helps. But, perhaps more importantly, talking to those who are part of the game—the players, coaches, general managers, owners, and others—will help you gain a tremendous amount of insight. Then, unlike the coach or player who can rely on having played the game, you can tailor your comments to what you know based on what you've observed and with whom you have spoken.

The former player or coach should take a similar approach when preparing for a broadcast. That is, don't just rely on what you know from having been in the sport for so many years. While certain precepts of the game might remain the same, players, coaches, tactics, trends, and rules are updated all the time. What's unique to the game you're broadcasting that night in terms of storylines, stats, and strategy is totally different from any other game. Get into the locker room or clubhouse and talk to the participants. Delve into the resource materials and see who's good at what and then be prepared to tell everybody watching or listening what it all means.

Brian Baldinger, who's been an analyst for the NFL Network and Fox, says preparation for a game or a show is ongoing.

"It never ends," says the former NFL offensive lineman. "I think as a good analyst you have to go outside the game and into the global universe of that sport in order to explain things better or give it perspective. I look at the sport of football as a tossed salad. I constantly keep adding fresh ingredients every day. In other words, I'm always listening to something, reading something, watching something, 365 days a year."

ADD SOMETHING

In a studio show, a pre-game show, or in the open of a broadcast, the analyst provides commentary at the request of the play-by-play announcer or host. This includes important storylines or answers to questions, which are often supported by footage or graphics. A good television analyst will avoid literal commentary by adding thoughts that, again, enhance what the viewer can already see.

During the broadcast, the radio analyst generally has to be more succinct in his or her comments. As soon as there's action of consequence, the analyst needs to be finished. Television tends to be a little more forgiving since the viewer at home can see what's going on, but again, the analyst should be able to wrap up a point before any action of consequence. Generally speaking, the analyst needs to give way to the play-by-play person as soon as reasonably possible. If the analysis happens to bleed into important game action, the analyst should not feel the need to pick up the call of the game but rather step aside as soon as possible to allow the play-by-play announcer to take it back.

Analysts commenting on replays, graphics, and other visuals during a telecast should again take care not to be redundant, but instead try to add to what can already be seen. If a basket is made or a touchdown is scored, tell the viewer how and why it was successful. If a player makes a mistake, say what they could have or should have done. Good analysts in more advanced telecasts have the benefit of stop action replay or the use of a telestrator where certain "teaching moments" are available. This is where an analyst can really lean on his or her deep knowledge of the game.

ULTIMATELY, WHAT MAKES A GOOD COLOR ANALYST?

Here's Baldinger's take on that:

> "I think it's somebody who can explain action, whatever that action is, whether it's sports or business or news or politics. Explain action clearly and succinctly. Most people can't get to the point. A good analyst gets to the point quickly."

Burke sums up the question this way:

> "A lot of things. You certainly have to have a feel for the sport you're covering. I think it helps to have played the game. You have to be incredibly prepared. You have to watch game tape, go to practices, talk to coaches, talk to players. Get a feel about what they're thinking. The feel to know when to tell stories or to use numbers . . ."

> "The one thing I try to keep in mind the entire time I'm on the air is "how can I get the fan close to the place I happen to be lucky enough to be sitting?" Fans want to hear from the stars and the coaches. Those are the people closest to the teams. And if we can provide that kind of access, then I think we're doing our job."

PLAY-BY-PLAY EXERCISES—FOR TELEVISION AND (WHERE APPLICABLE) RADIO

1. Spend a "broadcast day" preparing to do play-by-play for an event by doing some or all of the following:

    a.   Design and utilize a sheet to formalize your information for broadcast.

    b.   Gather the information you need to prepare for the broadcast by:

        i.   Attending a practice during the week or the day of the event.

        ii.   Obtaining official game notes, statistics and other information or publications from the teams, schools and/or league.

        iii.   Research other websites and publications deemed authoritative and accurate.

2.   Test yourself on the rules of a sport.

    a.   Design a permanent sheet for some of the more esoteric rules that you can refer to during a broadcast if necessary.

3.   Perform radio play-by-play of an event with a digital record or a more complete equipment set-up:

    a.   Informally, in a press box or stands.

    b.   Formally as part of an actual broadcast.

4.   Perform TV play-by-play as part of an actual student or community-run broadcast including:

    a.   Execution of show format that may include open, intermission, post-game, graphics, special features, etc.

5.   Try doing play-by-play of different sports, on both radio and TV, taking note of the differences in preparation for and performance of each.

6.   Do any/all of the above as a color analyst.

ENDNOTE

ENDNOTE

7

1. http://sportscasterchronicles.blogspot.com/2006/02/ray-scott-word-according-to-ray.html. Accessed 2009. No longer exists.

Chapter 8

WOMEN IN SPORTSCASTING

ONE WOMAN IN A MAN'S WORLD

Eva Zaccaria had only been on the job for a few months as sports director at WICZ-TV in Binghamton, New York. In that relatively short period of time, she'd already gotten an ample dose of what it's like to be working as a woman in a man's world. There had been the sexual innuendos from the athletes she'd had to interview, the "creepy" postings on Facebook and Twitter, the suggestion from her boss that she "lighten her hair," and the overriding theme that tends to be associated with most women sportscasters: the assertion that *you're not going to know as much about sports as a man.*

"It's important not to give up, and don't get frustrated," says Zaccaria, who hopes one day to be a courtside or sideline reporter in a major market. "If somebody looks at you funny or if a player is trying to hinder your ability to do your job because they won't leave you alone, you still have to be professional and be responsible."

This is the mandate for Zaccaria and the other women sportscasters at television and radio stations: dealing with the prejudice, stereotypes, and sexism that frame their segment of the workplace.

There have been advancements in both the hiring and equal treatment of women sportscasters. The advent of Title IX (see below), the proliferation of national and regional sports networks, and the advent of women's professional leagues in sports such as basketball and soccer have all helped.

But many of the stigmas against women working in a predominantly man's world remain. Simply put, the vast majority of sports covered electronically are men's sports and the vast majority who cover and watch those sports are also men.

WOMEN IN SPORTSCASTING: A HISTORY

The documented history of women in sportscasting is less than a century old. It is replete with pioneers who accomplished a substantial number of "firsts."

In the late 1930s and early 1940s, "Mrs. Harry Johnson" (her first name is nowhere to be found) provided color commentary during her husband's broadcasts for Central States Broadcasting in Omaha, Nebraska. She is acknowledged to be one of the first females to be involved in a sports broadcast.[1]

In 1964, baseball's Athletics were still located in Kansas City and owned by the late Charles Finley. Finley wanted a female perspective in the radio booth, so he hired Chicago weather reporter Betty Caywood to provide color commentary.[2]

The first female sports broadcaster on network television was Donna de Verona. In 1960, de Verona was an Olympic swimmer at the age of 13, eventually winning two gold medals in the 1964 Olympics. She retired from competition after that, but was quickly hired by ABC to provide commentary, particularly for coverage of swimming and the Olympics. In 1965, she would appear on the network's *Wide World of Sports* program, but consistent opportunities were far and few between as she was used strictly as a fill-in. De Verona went on to cover the Olympics for ABC from 1972 to1988, eventually working more than five decades for the network. She won an Emmy in 1991 and settled an age discrimination suit against ABC in 1998.[3]

On June 23, 1972, the enactment of Title IX would help lead to more women becoming sportscasters. Title IX said, in part, that "no person in the United States shall, on the basis of sex, be excluded from participation in, be denied the benefits of, or be subjected to discrimination under any education program or activity receiving federal financial assistance."[4]

This law afforded women the opportunity to play sports and earn funding for their education through their athletic ability. And, as the number of women in sports rose, so did their visibility in sports television.

In 1974, Jane Chastain became the first woman to provide commentary on an NFL game when she was brought into the booth after being hired as a general sports commentator for CBS the same year. However, after she revealed she was pregnant, she was taken off of NBA and NFL coverage and her contract was not renewed when it ran out in 1975. She would move onto politics, becoming a political columnist in the 1980s.[5]

In 1975, former Miss America Phyllis George was hired by CBS to work as a sports anchor and reporter for football, eventually staying with the network for more than a decade. Her responsibilities included co-hosting *NFL Today* with Brent Musberger and Irv Cross and reporting on horse racing. George had a good on-screen presence, but was often criticized for her lack of journalistic experience.[6]

In 1978, Jayne Kennedy, a former Miss Ohio, was hired as a reporter for CBS, becoming one of the first African American women in network sports. She replaced Phyllis George on *NFL Today* for two seasons before moving onto acting.[7]

In 1981, Rhonda Glenn became the first fulltime woman sportscaster for a national network when she was hired by ESPN. Previously she had been a golf commentator for ABC after competing in several US Women's Amateur Championships and two US Women's Opens. She is currently a manager of communication for the USGA.[8]

In 1983, ESPN made Gayle Gardner the first female weekly sports anchor for a network when she was hired for SportsCenter. After ESPN and a stint with NBC, Gardner would go on to do play-by-play for the Colorado Rockies in 1993, become the first female television play-by-play announcer for a Major League Baseball team.[9]

Starting in 1987, Lesley Visser would accomplish many firsts for women in sportscasting after being hired full-time by CBS, following a 14-year career as a sports reporter for the *Boston Globe*. In 1990, she became the first woman to cover the World Series for a national network. In 1992, she was the first woman to present the Super Bowl trophy to the winning team after reporting from the sideline during Super Bowl XXVI. Moving on to ABC, she became the first woman ever assigned to *Monday Night Football* in 1995. She would also become the first woman sports broadcaster to carry the Olympic Torch during the relay to Athens in 2004.[10]

Lesley Visser, courtesy of John FILO, CBS

On December 27, 1987, Gayle Sierens became the first woman to provide play-by-play for an NFL game, calling the Seattle Seahawks–Kansas City Chiefs contest. She did such a good job that she was offered several other opportunities to broadcast games for NBC, but the commitment to her family and her employer, a television station in Tampa, prevented her from doing any more football.[11]

On February 14, 1988, Leandra Reilly became the first play-by-play announcer for an NBA game, broadcasting the New Jersey Nets–Philadelphia 76ers contest for the regional sports network SportsChannel New York. She later worked for ESPN for more than two decades.[12]

In the late 1980s and early 90s, Suzyn Waldman, as a New York area sports reporter, established a number of firsts for women in sports broadcasting. In 1987, she was the first voice heard on WFAN radio when it launched its all-sports talk format, delivering a sports news update. Waldman was the first radio beat reporter for the Yankees and Knicks when she covered the teams for WFAN. She did play-by-play for the Yankees' local TV broadcasts on WPIX. She was also the first woman to become a full time announcer for a Major League team when she became part of the Yankees' radio broadcasts for WCBS in 2005 as well as becoming the first woman to broadcast a World Series game in 2009.[13]

Ann Meyers was a highly decorated basketball player, both in college and internationally. After graduating from UCLA, she was offered a contract with the Indiana Pacers, thus becoming the first woman to sign a free agent contract with a NBA team, though she was eventually cut. She would then do color commentary for the Pacers that year, the first woman to do so for an NBA team, before returning to her women's professional basketball career. After retiring from basketball, Meyers would marry former Dodger pitcher Don Drysdale (the first time two married people were members of the Halls of Fame for their respective sports) She was also offered the Chicago Bulls analyst job in 1993, but turned down the opportunity after her husband passed away on July 3 of that year. She is currently an analyst for Phoenix Suns telecasts.[14]

Robin Roberts was a standout basketball player at Southern Louisiana University, with her experience in basketball eventually leading her to sportscasting. After seven years of moving up through various local stations, she was hired as an anchor for ESPN where she would stay for 15 years. She eventually started to work for ABC News and the *Good Morning America* program in 1995, becoming one of the first women to cross over from television sports to news.[15]

In 1985, former professional golfer and two-time LPGA Player of the Year Judy Rankin became the first fulltime female on-course reporter when she worked the Men's US Open. She continues to work in golf and broadcasting as the lead analyst for the Golf Channel.[16]

Between 1982 and 1986, basketball player Cheryl Miller won two national championships, three Naismith Player of the Year awards and a gold medal with the US Women's Olympic team. After a stint with ABC, Miller would be hired by Turner Sports, leading to her calling an NBA game for TBS in 1996, the first female analyst to call a nationally televised game.[17]

In 1994, Nanci Donnellan became the first nationally syndicated female host of a sports call-in show when ESPN picked up her show from KJR in Seattle, *The Fabulous Sports Babe*. It also became the network's first nationally syndicated weekday program.[18]

In 2006, Cassie Campbell, a three-time Olympic medalist in women's hockey for Canada, became the first woman to do color commentary for Canadian Broadcasting Corporation's *Hockey Night* in Canada. Originally hired that year as a rinkside reporter, Campbell filled-in for regular analyst Harry Neale who was snowed in at his home in Buffalo.[19]

■ A brief history of sexism

Sexism in the workplace goes back as long as women have worked. Many of the women who forged the way in sportscasting and sports journalism did so at great peril, experiencing their own, unique form of sexism.

Suzyn Waldman, whose impressive résumé is detailed in the section above, says "people have no idea what it was like for me 25 to 30 years ago. When I started at WFAN, there were death threats, I would get used condoms and the most hideous letters in the mail. When I went through breast cancer in 1996, I had a guy write me every day asking 'are you dead yet?' and 'I'm so glad you're going to die.' It was just awful."

The following is a brief, far from complete history of sexism in sportscasting:

Jeannie Morris was a writer and columnist in Chicago before working at CBS as a field reporter with her husband, former Chicago Bear and sports broadcaster Johnny Morris. During one game in Minnesota between the Bears and Vikings, she was not allowed in the press box and was forced to cover the game seated outside, above the box, during a blizzard.[20]

In 1977 Melissa Ludtke, a reporter for *Sports Illustrated*, was banned from the Yankees' clubhouse due to her gender. She would go on to sue commissioner Bowie Kuhn and Major League Baseball, winning the right for women to enter the clubhouse.[21]

Even after the Melissa Ludtke incident, locker rooms continued to be unwelcoming places for female reporters. In 1990, Lisa Olson from the *Boston Globe* reported to the NFL that a New England Patriots player exposed himself and made a lewd comment to her. The complaint became public and Olson was actually cast as the villain and a reason to keep women out of sports journalism and out of the locker room. The backlash led her to quit her job and take another journalism job in Australia before returning to the United States.[22]

In 2010 while covering a New York Jets practice, Inés Sainz, a reporter for Mexico's TV Azteca, claimed she had footballs thrown in her direction by a Jets' coach and had players later calling out to her in the team's locker room. In 2013, hockey commentator Don Cherry said that women reporters should not be allowed in locker rooms after games. Cherry was responding to post-game comments made by Chicago Blackhawks player Duncan Keith, who had an exchange with a female radio reporter. Ironically, Cherry is acknowledged to be one of the first NHL coaches to allow women into a locker room when he permitted their entry during the 1975 All-Star Game. At the time, he was the Boston Bruins head coach and he made it team policy to allow female reporters in the locker room.[23]

THE SIDELINE STEREOTYPE

One area where women have been able to make inroads is sideline reporting, so much so that it has led to a stereotype: the good-looking (typically blonde) sideline reporter.

Lesley Visser, whose pioneering achievements as a sideline reporter are outlined in the above history section, is one of the most notable sportscasters of all time, man or woman. She has covered the NCAA Basketball Tournament 31 times, the US Open tennis tournament 29 times and the Super Bowl 22 times during her marvelous career. She was originally hired in television for her pedigree as a 14-year sports reporter for the *Boston Globe*.

> "Somebody once said to me, TV is going to take the wrong part of you. It can for a while, but there are many instances where that is not the case. It's not the case with (other notable sideline reporters) Michelle Tafoya, with Andrea Kremer, Suzy Kolber, Pam Oliver. There are some who happen to be blonde and they're great. Alex Flanagan [NBC, NFL network] is beautiful and she's great."

> "If that is true that [attractive blonde sideline reporter has] become a stereotype, then that is discouraging to me."

Doris Burke, who played college basketball at Providence College, has been an analyst and sideline reporter on regional and national networks for both the men's and women's college and professional games. She says you have to acknowledge that television is a visual medium.

"I don't want to be evaluated on my looks," says Burke. "Although I once had a conversation with a producer who I respect greatly. I said, 'I feel like I'm as good as some of the men calling color analyst work and I wish I had more opportunity.' And his response to me was, "I know this goes against every fiber of your being, but you could dress less conservatively, you can let your hair down. You don't have to dress completely business-like. I'm not saying dress unprofessionally, I'm just saying that this is a visual medium and to a certain extent, you are judged by that." So, I made the adjustment [in appearance], and it may be purely coincidental, but more opportunities as an analyst came about. But how [any one person] chooses to attack it is a personal choice and whether or not you are hired based on that, you also have to be able to look yourself in the mirror and say "am I doing the job appropriately? What is behind my hiring?'"

Still, says Burke, she finds patently unfair the issue of women principally being judged more on their looks than men.

> "Women and men are evaluated completely differently. Dick Vitale, Mike Patrick, Jon Gruden . . . no one is asking how handsome *they* are. No one asks that question. They don't ever seem to be evaluated based on their looks. And to me, that reflects more a societal and cultural scenario that we fight in all areas. People who are considered attractive are paid more, get greater opportunities. I don't think this is necessarily limited to television, but it is there because we all see it when we flick on our TVs and notice it."

Alexis McCombs created, produced, and hosted the talk show *Instant She-Play* on AOL Sports/Huffington Post where three women interviewed top NFL athletes about politics, religion, and other hot topics. She's also served as a judge for the Sports Emmy Awards and is a board member for the Association of Women in Sports Media. McCombs says sportscasting is no different than entertainment or, in some cases, society as a whole, when it comes to judging women based on looks.

> "Typically if you look at leading ladies in film and television, usually it's attractive women. If you look at the people who grace the covers of magazines, typically they try to focus on putting attractive women on the cover. So I think that's more of a society thing as opposed to isolating sports itself."

> "That said, it is a double-edged sword for women sportscasters because on the one hand, [producers] are looking for someone who's attractive to be a sideline reporter. But on the flip-side of that, because a woman is attractive, I think she's more heavily scrutinized."

Some women are content to blatantly utilize their looks in order to become sportscasters or to increase their notoriety in the business. Publications and websites have been known to offer photo spreads of suggestively or scantily clad women, celebrating them as "the hottest women sportscasters."

But Allison Kimmich, executive director of the National Women's Studies Association, says sexism is a societal issue that also includes men.

> "[Women selling their looks] is not unlike the beefcake firefighter calendar. We have to remember that those things go both ways. I think I would be careful to not necessarily point the finger at women. We are, instead, talking about systems and structures. These are institutionalized rewards systems. It's a system

Allison Kimmich, courtesy of Marla Cohen

of power. Yes, it's true that individual people may make choices about "how can I be successful within this system" and we might say they're capitalizing on that, but the systems themselves are really responsible. Again, individuals do have choices under these systems, but I would be more concerned about how we need to challenge sexism and stereotypes themselves versus blaming individuals for trying to work within that."

Whether it be individual choice or the societal "systems" that Kimmich alludes to, one obvious solution for women sportscasters is to excel at both beauty and brains. That is, a woman needs to present herself as someone who is knowledgeable in sports (be it as a sideline reporter or any other sportscasting discipline), but also—without being ostentatious or suggestive—she needs to present herself in such a way that brings out the best in her appearance. Build on what you've been born with, while at the same time working to bust the stereotype with an equally knowledgeable portfolio of the sport you're covering.

■ Playing ball with the Yankees

It can be argued there's no more scrutiny than in New York, the nation's top media market. It can also be argued there is no team with a higher profile in the United States than the New York Yankees. One woman who is in the Yankees clubhouse every game is Meredith Marakovits,

Meredith Marakovits, courtesy of Ellen Wallop/ YES Network

who's been the Yankees' clubhouse reporter for the YES Network since 2012. Here are Meredith's views on some of the issues surrounding a woman working in the Bronx Zoo.

Q: What's it like being a woman in a predominantly male clubhouse?

A: It's different. I think when I was younger, walking in there it could be a little bit intimidating in the sense that you never know what people are thinking about you, what people think when they look at you, what people think your motives are. But as you get older and you're there more, you get more comfortable and you start to realize it doesn't necessarily matter what other people are thinking, it's about what you think about what you're doing and how you're approaching things. You're definitely in the minority—there are a handful of women at best in the Yankees' clubhouse. If you can't be comfortable with that, maybe you need to decide [on a different career].

Q: How do you deal with inappropriate behavior or improper advances from players or team personnel?

A: It's difficult because you do deal with these people a lot. Everyone has a different personality. There certainly is right and there is wrong. It's tough because you are in the locker room environment. There are jokes that are sometimes inappropriate. It depends on how it makes *you* feel—I'm of the mindset that you kind of laugh a lot of stuff off. It is what it is. I'm not saying it makes it right, but at the same time, I'm not going to spend my time as a personal crusader trying to make sure everyone acts 100 percent appropriately all the time.

As far as some of the advances, you hear horror stories from some people. I would think if you go in there and you act professionally and show them what you're about right away, you can eliminate some of that stuff. You do your job, you get in and get out. I think it's when you start approaching things differently that you have some problems. [If there is an inappropriate advance] you kind of brush it off, tell them exactly why you're there and say "it's not happening" and then walk away.

Q: As a woman, how do you draw the line between being feminine and attractive but not provocative?

A: I used to think "what is professional attire and how do I need to dress and to look and to act to be a professional in this business?" And I had always been told you have to wear a suit or you have to wear a blazer and that's what makes you professional. Well, I never really felt comfortable in that attire. It never really felt like me. Depending on the environment you're in, what you're reporting on . . . it used to be behind the anchor desk you would have to have a blazer on, now that has changed as well.

You need to look at yourself in the mirror and see what you look good in and feel comfortable in and ask yourself the question, "is this professional, would I wear this to church, would I wear this in front of my parents, is this something that is going to attract attention for the wrong reason?" I don't think you need to put yourself in a paper bag or burlap sack. At the same time, you don't have to go over the line like you're dressing to go out to a club.

Q: What's your advice to aspiring female sports reporters?

A: What I would say to any female getting into this industry is to be very aware of your environment. Know that there are stereotypes associated with women in this business. And if you don't want to be a part of that stereotype, be very aware of the decisions you make, be careful to remain professional, and people will respect that.

NOW AND THE FUTURE

While the authors have discovered no definitive surveys to support this, empirical evidence suggests women sportscasters are making progress. As we've detailed, they are not only filling the role of sideline reporters but those of anchors and reporters at all levels of the business.

"I don't think the sex of a person is really important in whether or not they can cover a story," says Peggy Phillip, news director at KSHB-TV in Kansas City, Missouri. "I certainly can remember when I was the only girl in the newsroom in the 1970s. I'm sure that it's uncomfortable sometimes for athletes to have a woman in the locker room, but as we continue to evolve, those things are going to become less and less important. I don't think you have to be a man to do a good job in covering sports."

In certain areas of sportscasting, women have made substantially less progress. Play-by-play announcers (most notably Pam Ward and Beth Mowins) and sports talk show hosts (Nanci Donnellan) are still a minority.

Jason Benetti is the director of communications and play-by-play announcer for Syracuse Chiefs, an AAA minor league baseball team. He says:

"It's sad to say, but I haven't come across any women aspiring to be baseball play-by-play announcers. I've either filled in or been a lead announcer in four leagues and I have yet to come upon a female play-by-play announcer and, frankly, when we talk about barriers in our society, that's one that needs to

Jason Benetti, courtesy of Lisa Snedeker/
Wake Forest University

get broken sometime soon. I know Beth Mowins and Pam Ward are doing it at a pretty high level [ESPN], but other than them, you don't really hear about female play-by-play announcers. I think at some point that's going to change, but I do think baseball might be one of the last places to do it because in the Minor Leagues of baseball you're travelling with players and you're generally staying in a room with somebody else."

"That said, baseball, our broadcasting schools, and society should find a way to get females more involved."

John Kincade co-hosts a sports talk show on WCNN, 680 The Fan in Atlanta. He says:

"Women in sports talk? Absolutely. I've gotten to work [in sports talk] with a number of talented women who can more than hold their own. Once again, it's all about opinion. It's about what their eyes see. It's about what their point-of-view is. And I think the more points-of-view that get out there, the better. The more people of every race, color, and creed that get involved in our business, the better off our business is. Because honestly, it's been an old white guy industry for way too long. And I enjoy hearing different people's perspectives."

Sandy Padwe is a professor at the Columbia University Graduate School of Journalism. He says the future success of women in sportscasting is predicated upon their own credibility and the subsequent level of esteem in which society holds them.

"The more women, the better," says Padwe. "But let's not 'ghetto-ize' them in a sense. In other words, make them a cliché. They don't all have to be blonde and blue-eyed to get a job as a sideline reporter. They don't have to do that. There's great work being done by women reporters, let them report. Don't make them into cookie-cutters, don't make them sexual objects."

Fortunately, the women who now cover sports can serve as role models for today's aspiring, female sportscasters.

"I didn't have any role models," says Suzyn Waldman. "There weren't any. I'm old. I had another career before this, on Broadway. There were no women in sportscasting. None. I did this because I wanted to do it. I didn't admire anybody in this business. There were *guys* I loved. But there were no role models because there weren't any women."

Says Waldman, "I keep thinking there's a little girl out there who not only loves sports but knows sports. Maybe she's sitting with a little recorder like we used to do, you know, looking at the television and pretend you're doing commentary. There's got to be someone out there. And I hope they're not discouraged. This is a different world now. I was brought up in the 1960s when we believed you could do anything. President Kennedy said we could all change the world and we thought we could."

Visser adds:

> "I think what's great about it now is that women can aspire to anything they want to do. A young woman now can say 'I want to cover the NFL' or 'I want to cover the Olympics, the Final Four, or the NBA Finals.' They can be a radio reporter or host a radio show. There are plenty of places to do it. And she can aspire to anything."

> "I wanted to cover sports when I was ten years old in 1963. I said this to my mom. Well in 1963, this was like saying 'I want to go to Mars.' Those jobs simply did not exist for women. But there is something that an adult can say to a kid that can change their life. And my mom looked at me and instead of saying, 'what, are you kidding me, girls can't do that,' she said to me 'sometimes you have to cross where it says don't walk.'"

POINTS FOR DISCUSSION

POINTS FOR DISCUSSION

8

1. Discuss what it must have been like for women to overcome certain obstacles during their early forays into sportscasting.
2. Women, discuss how you would handle an athlete, coach, or other team member making inappropriate comments to you.
3. Women, would you lighten your hair or make some other serious, cosmetic change at the request of your boss? Why or why not?
4. Women, is there such a thing as the "sideline stereotype?" If so, what can you personally do to avoid it?
5. Should men be allowed to cover women's sports or should it be exclusively the domain of female sportscasters?
6. Discuss why there aren't more women play-by-play announcers and sports talk hosts.
7. Women, who are your female sportscasting role models and why?
8. Men, discuss what you feel women should do, if anything, to put themselves on equal footing as sportscasters.
9. Will we ever get to the point where women sportscasters are not thought of as anything else but just other sportscasters? Why or why not?

ENDNOTES

ENDNOTES
8

1. Amanda Gunther, Daniel Kautz, and Allison Roth, "The Credibility of Female Sports Broadcasters: The Perception of Gender in a Male-Dominated Profession," *Human Communication* 14(2) (2011), 73.

2. Whet Moser, "Betty Caywood and Mary Shane: Baseball's First Female Announcers," *Chicago Magazine,* September 26, 2012. www.chicagomag.com/Chicago-Magazine/The-312/September-2012/Betty-Caywood-and-Mary-Shane-Baseballs-First-Female-Broadcasters, accessed April 15, 2013.

3. "Hispanic Heritage: Donna de Verona," *Gale.* www.gale.cengage.com/free_resources/chh/bio/devarona_d.htm, accessed May 3, 2013.

4. "Achieving Success under Title IX," US Department of Education, July 10, 1997. www2.ed.gov/pubs/TitleIX/part5.html, accessed May 5, 2013.

5. Lee Walburn, "Locker-Room Blues," *Atlanta Magazine*, June 2007.

6. Brad Schultz, *Sports Broadcasting* (Boston: Focal Press, 2002), 248–249.

7. Sue Reilly, "Jayne Kennedy of Broadcast Fame May Carry the Ball, but Husband Leon Calls the Signals," *People*, January 8, 1979. www.people.com/people/archive/article/0,,20072683,00.html, accessed April 8, 2013.

8. Josh Krulewitz, "Learn More about SportsCenter History with Timeline, Trivia," *ESPN Front Row*, September 4, 2012. http://frontrow.espn.go.com/2012/09/learn-more-about-sportscenter-history-with-timeline-trivia, accessed April 2, 2013.

9. Sally Jenkins, "Who Let Them In?" *Sports Illustrated*, June 17, 1991. http://sportsillustrated.cnn.com/vault/article/magazine/MAG1139880/index.htm, accessed May 1, 2013.

10. "Leslie Visser Biography," LeslieVisser.com. http://lesleyvisser.com/bio.html, accessed May 10, 2013.

11. Richard Sadomir, "First Woman to Call NFL Play-by-Play, and the Last," *The New York Times*, January 28, 2009. www.nytimes.com/2009/01/29/sports/football/29women.html?pagewanted=all_r=0, accessed May 1, 2013.

12. "Sports Broadcasting Pioneer Leandra Reilly Visits Mount Saint Mary Academy in Watchung," *Independent Press,* March 1, 2012. www.nj.com/independentpress/index.ssf/2012/03/sports_broadcasting_pioneer_le.html, accessed April 20, 2013.

13. "Broadcasters," Yankees.com. http://newyork.yankees.mlb.com/team/broadcasters.jsp?c_id=nyy, accessed April 27, 2013.

14. "Biography." *AnnMeyersDrysdale.com,* accessed April 21, 2013, http://annmeyersdrysdale.com/ann/Ann_Meyers/biography.html

15. "Robin Roberts Biography," *Good Morning America*, October 2, 2004. http://abcnews.go.com/GMA/robin-roberts-biography/story?id=128237&page=2#.UOmsLYnjkdI, accessed May 3, 2013.

16. "Judy Rankin Bio," LPGA.com. www.lpga.com/golf/players/r/judy-rankin/bio.aspx, accessed April 23, 2013.

17. "Hall of Famers," Basketball Hall of Fame. www.hoophall.com/hall-of-famers/tag/cheryl-miller, accessed April 23, 2013.

18. Michael Kruse, "The Ballad of the Fabulous Sports Babe," *Grantland*, September 11, 2012. www.grantland.com/story/_/id/8337825/catching-sports-talk-radio-host-nanci-donnellan-fabulous-sports-babe, accessed June 21, 2013.

19. "Biography—Cassie Campbell," Cassie77.com. www.cassie77.com/webpage/1002348/1000 608, accessed June 3, 2013.

20. Lou Schwartz, "Women in Sportscasting: A Brief History," *American Sportscasters Online*. www.americansportscastersonline.com/womeninsportscasting.html, accessed April 14, 2013. Linda Witt, "On TV and Off, Johnny and Jeannie Morris Star in the Sporting Life," *People*, November 3, 1975. www.people.com/people/archive/article/0,,20065812,00.html, accessed May 3, 2013.

21. "Women Journalists in the 21st Century: Melissa Ludtke," *JAWS*. www.jaws.org/2012/01/27/ women-journalists-in-the-21st-century-melissa-ludtke, accessed June 20, 2013. Schultz, *Sports Broadcasting*, 202.

22. Schultz, *Sports Broadcasting*, 204.

23. Brian Baker, "Don Cherry First NHL Coach to Allow Women in Lockerroom," *Toronto Sun*, April 30, 2013. www.torontosun.com/2013/04/30/cherry-first-coach-to-allow-women-in-locker-room, accessed May 13, 2013.

Chapter 9

SOCIAL MEDIA AND THE WEB

HOW FAST CAN WE SEND 140 CHARACTERS?

January 8, 2012. NFL playoffs. The Broncos and Steelers are tied 23–23 at the end of the fourth quarter. On the first play of overtime, Tim Tebow throws an 80-yard touchdown pass to Demaryius Thomas. The play takes 11 seconds and sets a record for the quickest ending to an NFL overtime. In the moments after Thomas crosses the goal line to win the game, Twitter explodes with activity at the rate of 9,420 Tebow and Denver Bronco-related tweets per second. The frequency of tweets sent sets a record for a sporting event: 9,420 bursts of user-created content every second.

While Tebow's tweetfest set the bar for a sporting event, a few months later in July 2012, Twitter reported fans of the Euro 2012 Soccer final tweeted at a rate of 15,358 tweets per second as Spain tallied the winning goal against Italy. Overall, the match generated more than 16.5 million tweets worldwide.

At the London Olympics in August 2012, RadiumOne, a social media consulting company, estimated the number of items shared on the open Web during the 17 days of the games at 306 billion pieces of content. That is an average of 208,333 items every second for 17 days. Facebook had 102 billion items shared and Twitter reported five billion tweets.[1]

A few months later, in February 2013, Twitter announced a new record of 24.1 million tweets sent the night of Super Bowl XLVII, an average of 231,000 tweets every minute of the game.

Clearly, the audience is actively contributing to and participating in the sportscasting experience like never before.

Social media is the most rapidly evolving topic in this textbook. Many of the most popular applications were founded and launched into prominence in a very short amount of time. Facebook (founded in 2004), Twitter (founded in 2006), Instagram (founded in 2010, acquired by Facebook in April 2012) and Vine (founded June 2012, acquired by Twitter in October 2012) are all examples of social media applications that were adopted early and often by a wide range of people. From high-schoolers all the way up to giant corporations, social media enables an immediate and two-way conversation. The website Mashable estimated that 80 percent of people watching a sporting event on TV and 60 percent of people attending live events are checking in on social media during the game.[2]

These tools are a normal part of the sportscast, and learning to use them to your advantage can make a major difference in building your brand and connecting with your audience. Many reporters, announcers, and sportscasters now incorporate social media into the delivery of information before, during, and after an event. A Sporting News Media survey in 2013 found that a solid quarter of sports fans use some form of social media to keep up with their leagues, teams, and players. Major League baseball, the NBA, NHL, and NFL are all available online and this same survey found that close to a third of all fans are watching sports online via a personal computer.

Leagues, teams, and players are aware and taking advantage of social media in a variety of ways. The NFL has a blog for the entire league and, prior to the 2013 season, they hired a blogger to cover each individual team. A popular NBA team such as the Los Angeles Lakers has millions of followers on Facebook, Twitter, and Instagram. These are followers who can get information from their team in a matter of seconds. The NBA is experimenting with Twitter as a delivery method for playoff game highlights.[3]

Major League Baseball keeps a tight reign over what video can be released of their games; however, the league tends to be very open about the use of social media. Baseball, an innovator in the use of the Internet to provide content for their fans, established a "Social Media Clubhouse" for all teams to produce content. In March 2012, MLB released a social media policy that encouraged players to use social media to "connect with fans in a positive way." Along with this encouragement came some things for players to remember. These included reminding players that what they post in social media is public content, to keep the content as safe as if they were speaking at a press conference and to refrain from sending anything in the "heat of the moment."[4]

The new wrinkle in this delivery of information is that the audience can talk back! Erik Brady and Jorge Ortiz wrote in *USA Today* about a baseball player deleting his Twitter account for several reasons. The player was apparently tired of dealing with "haters" and was also upset that he "gave way too much of himself." However, even though the player removed himself from the conversation, that didn't stop the audience from continuing to tweet and comment about him. While social media managers would advise people to avoid being drawn into arguments with folks on social networks, for many people, ignoring negative comments is "easier said than done" according to Josh Thole, a Major League Baseball player, who stopped tweeting because of all the negative comments he was receiving. Brady and Ortiz also talked to Nicco Mele from Harvard University who points out that tweets or comments on social media from the team, players, or even the media are "an unfiltered relation, direct access" from the person in the spotlight or covering the game to the fans.[5]

Urooj Kazi of Social Media Today reminds her readers that the key word in social media is the word "social." If we are aware of others and how we present ourselves in person in social settings, why not have the same awareness when we interact with people through social media? In addition, Kazi recommends giving folks some background information about yourself, engaging in conversations, and staying positive with your comments.[6]

■ **Kelley O'Brien, Director of Social Media for Krispy Kreme Doughnut Corporation**

Kelley O'Brien is a power user of many different social media platforms and networks. She offers advice on developing your personal brand, effective use of social media, and staying current with the latest trends.

Branding, in the literal sense, comes from the tradition of burning a mark onto a piece of property or livestock so anyone who looks at those items will know who they belong. While being able to see the burn mark on a cow's hind-quarters so no one steals dear old Bessy had very practical origins, the modern definition of branding goes a bit further. Branding now means that instead of simply searing into the flesh of livestock, companies now want to imprint their company onto your brain so that when you see the golden arches, you think McDonald's. When you see the sphere with blue lines, you think AT&T. When you see the letters E-S-P-N with a line through the top third of the letters, you know to think of the self-proclaimed worldwide leader in sports. In addition to knowing the company, branding also has the added impact of transferring implicit information about a particular product. Branding allows our previous experience or the experience reported by others to give us information about that company, person, or—in the case of sports—members of the media, athletes, coaches, leagues, and other ancillary people associated with sports such as officials, bloggers, or commissioners. We will likely trust that ESPN will produce a high-quality show when we watch an event regardless of the sport just like we know that McDonald's hamburger will taste the same whether we purchase one in Philadelphia, Fresno, or Phoenix. Branding allows previous work to carry forward and build the brand over time.

You can develop your personal brand that will allow potential employers, followers or co-workers to know you through the effective use of social media and the internet. As you grow your brand, especially through social media, you will develop a footprint based on the publishing of your work and from the benefit of followers who can spread your brand for you. Several key steps should be taken to effectively use social media to build your personal brand and to stay current with the latest trends.

The first step to create your personal brand is to reserve your name under all relevant social media platforms under their same consistent handle. If you stay consistent, you can reap the benefits of that cross-platform consistency. For example, if you're writing blog posts, or tweeting, or posting on Facebook, you can link across all those platforms. This doesn't mean you should post the same content on every platform, rather create different experiences in different areas. In addition, on many of these sites, it is a good idea to have two different accounts. One is for your professional persona and one for your personal life. This doesn't mean you can't have any personality with your professional accounts, but understand the fine line between showing everyone how much fun you had in your Halloween costume versus sharing all your personal information with your audience.

We all have a social media past in our very near future. That means that everything we post is very public, so you want to post with a careful conscience about what you are entering into the social media public record. People will expect and appreciate seeing you as a real person, but again, with different social media platforms, you have different opportunities to show different facets of yourself. For example, Twitter is a short burst of info, while you can take more space to post something on Facebook.

Also, you might want to avoid discussing too much about the parts of your job that can make you seem unappreciative of your position. For example, "they ran out of red wine in first class on my way back from the game" might not endear you to too many fans.

If you establish yourself as an expert on a particular entity, whether a team or teams, you need to be very careful about the veracity of your information. Your status as a source is built upon your credibility and accuracy. By citing sources, promoting across platforms, and creating a social media footprint, you can grow your reach to different folks.

In terms of the number of posts per day, for Facebook, you should be posting 1–4 times a day, although you might post one or two extra times on days when the news warrants. For Twitter, in general, the sky's the limit! Usually, if you are tweeting a bunch of times or engaging in a Twitter chat or something that is going to explode in your followers' inboxes, as a courtesy, you might want to send a warning that they are about to receive a barrage of tweets.

O'Brien notes that an application like Twitter is a perfect platform for a live event. Short, frequent descriptions of an event taking place in real time can allow you to have that quick conversation with your followers.

To build your audience, here are a few strategies. You want to use popular hashtags that are relevant to get your message in front of interested people. In addition, you can follow like-minded people and hope they follow you back to not only connect with them professionally, but also to tap into their followers. You should answer directly folks who have sent you messages. In addition, hashtags can give you a connection to several folks with similar interests who would potentially share your material with their friends, and thus grow your audience. The key with hashtags is to know the relevant topics that are trending and accurate. If you try to make up original hashtags, you want to make it something that people will find interesting and clever, and never mess with established hashtags if you expect people to find, follow, and share what you post.

To keep up to date on technology, O'Brien suggests reading websites such as Mashable and magazines such as *Fast Company*, and gain an understanding of Search Engine Optimization (SEO). To measure your effectiveness in the realm of social media, you will need to know about analytics. These stats will give you a sense of how many people are reading, sharing, linking, liking and/or retweeting your material.

USE OF SOCIAL MEDIA BY THE MEDIA AND ATHLETES

Associated Press (AP) is a valuable source for all journalists. It provides guidelines on standards and practices for working media based on decades of thoughtful introspection on the practice of news coverage on a variety of mediums. AP gives clear guidelines on a wide variety of topics for journalists. For example, it makes clear definitions of terms such as "on the record" and "off the record" for reporters of all media to understand what information can and cannot be used. With the rapid application and adoption of social media, AP published a guide for how members of the media should approach social media. Some highlights of the AP Social Media Guidelines that are relevant to people working in the sportscasting industry include:[7]

- Have one account per social network for both personal and professional use
- Be aware that personal opinions can adversely affect the reputation of your employer. This includes the avoidance of "trash-talking" about people or teams
- Assume the target of your post will read your post. This might impact not only your relationship with that person, but current and future interactions with other people at your media outlet
- If you are covering a certain subject or story, you should link back to your media outlet and try to be "even-handed" in your comments or tweets. If your comments

on social media are being used to collect audience reaction or opinions, you should look for a well-balanced collection of thoughts

■ Use privacy settings to your advantage while keeping in mind that nothing is "truly private." If it is out there for one person to see, you can assume it can be out there for *everyone* to see

■ A fine line exists between making connections with "sources, politicians and news-makers if necessary for reporting purposes" versus associating with those same sources as a personal preference. In other words, as a reporter you need to make a clear distinction between personal preference or advocacy of a politician or athlete versus reporting their activity as a news story. As a reporter, you should be very clear whether you are writing as a member of the fan base or as a reporter. Granted this is often a blurred line, but being clear will allow you to steer clear of any potential conflicts of interest in your reporting. The AP recommends that you avoid personal interaction and "liking" or following "figures on both sides of the controversial issue"

■ The AP talks about who you should serve first when covering breaking news. On the one hand, you need to make sure your news outlet is getting the relevant information, while at the same time your immediate publishing of information through social networks can also be a great way to break news. The challenge for you will be how to walk the line between being a reporter for the station and building your own personal brand by being in front of the news. This issue would be something that you would definitely discuss with your news director or supervisor before you dive into this type of situation

■ A critical carryover from traditional news reporting on social networks is verifying sources. You should not take a tweet, post, or picture from a social network and assume the material is from the official source without establishing a connection to that source. You should treat the information found on a social network similar to how you would treat a phone call. Fake accounts are very easy to establish on social networks and if you have any doubts, you are better to leave it out of your reporting

■ When interacting with the consumers of your content, the AP recommends a civil and respectful tone. As common sense would dictate, avoid drawn out rants and arguments with your audience on social media sites. These "discussions" tend to "become less constructive with each new round"

■ If you make a factual error with something you post on social media, it should "be corrected as quickly and as transparently" as possible. You should admit to the error and provide the correct information

Athletes, teams, and leagues are also taking to the social media universe to send out information and to connect with fans. Christopher Craft wrote about the explosion of social media and the impact on sportscasting. Craft discussed the 2012 Olympics in London being dubbed the "Socialympics" because of the prevalence of social media being used to convey information about the games. As mentioned earlier in the chapter, the fruits of social media were evident by the 306 billion pieces of social media shares over the course of the Olympic Games. In addition, Craft says that, more than ever, news items are coming from athletes and teams themselves rather than traditional new media outlets. In some cases this allows athletes to communicate directly with fans. In other cases, this direct, unfiltered connection can cause some issues.

For example, in 2011, Arian Foster, then a player for the Houston Texans, tweeted an MRI image of his hamstring in the preseason. He wrote "the white stuff surrounding the muscle is known in the medical world as anti-awesomeness." ESPN had their medical expert look at the image and offer a diagnosis that the injury was "significant." Some folks thought this was an indication of a serious injury and others questioned if he was sharing private team information. While the tweet didn't violate the NFL's social media policy, the Texans released a statement that "disclosing medical information" was a violation of team policy. Foster later stated the tweet was meant to "make fun of the whole situation." Clearly, this type of direct access from athlete to a social media public is breaking new ground for the entire sportscasting establishment.

■ Fans as Producers of Content (or how a YouTube Video of a NASCAR Wreck Became a Public Relations Riddle)

In February 2013, on the final lap of a race at Daytona, Kyle Larson's car crashes and sends debris into the stands. Several spectators are injured and require medical attention at a local hospital. In the stands near the accident, Tyler Andersen is recording a video of the wreck on his cell phone. When he goes home after the race, Andersen uploads his video to YouTube. NASCAR, citing its ownership of everything related to the race, contacts YouTube to remove the video. Steve Phelps, NASCAR's chief marketing officer says the video was removed "out of respect for those injured in today's accident" and "to err on the side of caution" because NASCAR wasn't sure about the health of the injured fans. When news of Andersen's video removal hits social media, a conversation starts on social media about the removal of the video. The discussions are mostly negative and range from copyrights laws to censorship of fans by NASCAR. How does NASCAR respond? It allows the video to be reinstated and issues a response that says: "Our partners and users do not have the right to take down videos from YouTube unless they contain content which is copyright infringing, which is why we have reinstated the videos."

Jess Smith on her blog *Social 'n Sport* analyzed this incident and wrote about the lessons NASCAR and other sports entities might learn from this incident. Essentially, companies should understand that the messages sent by fans through social media are instantaneous and spread quickly. If you are a company trying to keep up with this trend, the goals should be consistency of your social media strategy and plans, clear communication in a timely fashion, the encouraging of fans to be partners in the coverage of your sport, and an awareness of how your actions will be perceived. NASCAR was slow to even acknowledge the crash itself. It waited until the next evening to make an official statement about the crash, which, as Smith points out, is "way too late by social media standards."[8]

WEBSITES AND BLOGGING

In addition to social media, web sites are still a key piece to your personal branding plan. While your Facebook and Twitter pages provide great information, having your own webpage is meaningful for a few reasons. Dan Schawbel of Mashable wrote about creating your own personal brand. In his plan, he wrote about the "need to own yourname. com or a website that aligns with your name in some fashion."[9]

One option is building your own website from scratch. While this is still an option for you, the expertise and cost of designing, building, and keeping a website built from scratch is difficult task. If you can afford this luxury, because you have the knowledge, time, money, or some combination of those, then you are in a great position. Knowing HTML, CSS, and the details of Web development and publishing are viable and valuable skills. For other folks, many options are available to still have a Web presence in the form of pre-built websites.

Another option for promoting a website presence is to create and maintain a blog. A blog, a term shortened from the term "Web log," is a website that allows a user to publish posts. Some blogs will also allow more customization of the look of the page as well as providing the ability to have several pages within the blog. Companies such as Tumblr, WordPress, and Blogger allow you to create a blog for free. They vary in complexity and layout, but they all basically have simple interfaces that allow users to post content without knowing what is happening under the hood of the website. You can post text, pictures, and video as well as link your social media to appear on your blog page as well.

Websites allow you to have a living portfolio to showcase your work and talents. While social media sites can and do change their rules of access or layout of their domains, an advantage of having your own website or blog is that you control the content, layout, and presentation of your work. Your personal website or blog can be a landing page for all your social media. While the applications might change or develop over time, your personal Web presence will be populated and maintained by you. Therefore, you can adjust, add, or subtract any pertinent information. While it is important to have your website or blog and social media well established, you also would like to know who is actually seeing your content and knows about your personal brand.

ANALYTICS: MEASURING YOUR BRAND

"Analytics" is a widely applied term that refers to a range of ways of looking at data to find meaningful patterns. In terms of your social media and online presence, "analytics" refers to measuring your effectiveness at reaching your audience. For your personal branding, different tools can provide a wide variety of information about how effectively your brand has been received by various audiences. These measurements can provide information about where you are succeeding and where you might want to focus some attention.

Mike Daniels, Richard Bagnall, and Don Bartholomew have developed one model to break down social media measurements. This model uses exposure, engagement, influence, impact, and advocacy as various "stages" to measure the effectiveness of social media.

Exposure is your audience seeing your content. For example, you might post a link to the latest package you produced for your local news station, or your post-game interview with the winning coach. *Engagement* is the "interaction that occurs" by people responding to your content. Commonly, this might be views of your post, following you as a content provider, or "liking" your channel or post. *Influence* is the stage where you have the "ability to cause or contribute to a change in opinion and behavior." This could mean that after seeing your content, someone is more likely to promote you as a content provider to someone else. *Impact* is a measurement of how effective a "social media campaign, program or effort [is] on the target audience." Did you succeed in convincing someone that you are an effective reporter, video editor, or whatever you were trying to show with your social media content? Finally, *advocacy* is the stage where you have a "call to action." For a company, this might be buying their product, subscribing to their service, or simply changing the opinion of the target audience member. For you, this might be convincing someone to hire you or to believe that you are an expert on the team or sport you are covering and discussing.[10]

Once you have some goals set up for what you want to expose, engage, influence, impact, and advocate, you now need to find ways to measure your success in each of these stages. To do this, you can use a company that has developed strategies to measure a wide range of data. They can also take that data and using various methods of analysis, provide you with their measure of effectiveness.

For example, Klout is a company that will take data from various social networks and produce what they call a "Klout score." According to their website, Klout measures more than 400 different "signals" from social media networks. These signals include views, retweets, likes, and follows. What Klout provides is their analysis of your data about how effective you are at creating some kind of action from your audience. Many other companies, such as Hub Spot, provide similar information. As with many other areas of social media, this field is rapidly expanding and evolving and keeping track of trends and developments should be part of your social media strategy.

For your personal website or blog, Web analytics provide data on the traffic visiting your website. For example, Google Analytics will give information about what search engines or social media networks refer users to your site, as well as how many direct visitors clicked to your site. In addition, Google Analytics can provide information about advertising on your site, email marketing, and what links users clicked within your site. These insights can help you understand how effectively your site is performing, and guide you to places where you might improve the layout of your site to increase traffic.

A FINAL THOUGHT

With the Internet and various social media applications, the world is closer and more accessible than ever before. Of course, this also means that we as individuals are just as accessible and available to the rest of the world. As we share more of our lives online and work to have our presence known, the concepts of privacy and anonymity are changing and evolving. The data and information we share leaves a trail for many people to see and glean information.

The challenge for you, the budding sportscasting talent, or anyone involved in covering or broadcasting events is to become an active and effective user of social media. This means both as a producer and as a consumer. By using the guidelines and strategies outlined in this chapter, which by the very nature of this topic are likely outdated as soon as they are typed, as well as following current industry trends, social media and the Web can be effective tools. Your challenge will be to evolve with the times and use the tools to your advantage.

POINTS FOR DISCUSSION

POINTS FOR DISCUSSION 9

1. Find five sportscasters on social media. Analyze their balance between reporting hard news and opinion. What is their frequency of posting on social media? Weekly? Daily? Hourly?
2. What do you think is an effective use of social media for the following positions on the crew:
   a. On-air talent.
   b. Reporter.
   c. Producer.
   d. Director.
   e. Can you name any other positions that might have a use for social media?

3. What are some of the immediate benefits and potential pitfalls of using social media?

4. Research ways organizations use to analyze the effectiveness of social media? What are media analytics?

5. How would you use social media to promote yourself? How would you create a personal brand?

6. What do you think are the most effective social media platforms? Why?

7. What are the pros and cons of having a personal relationship with an athlete you are covering as a member of the media? How could you make sure this relationship doesn't undermine your credibility?

8. Find an example where social media was the primary source of information for a sporting event.

9. What does the term "trending" mean? Find the most popular topics for the past month on social media.

10. Find good examples of power users of social media users. Why is their use of social media so effective?

11. What do you think the future of social media and sportscasting looks like? How might social media augment sports coverage for the media, fans, athletes, coaches, teams and leagues?

SUGGESTED
ACTIVITIES
9

SUGGESTED ACTIVITIES

1. Create a website or blog to create content for your personal brand. Perhaps you want to write about sports in general, or a specific sport or team.

2. Create and develop your social media presence. Research if there are newer social media platforms beyond Facebook and Twitter that may have been adopted.

3. Use one or more media analytic tools to measure your effectiveness. Try to develop some strategies to increase your reach.

4. Develop an original hashtag with a group and see if you can get others to use that hashtag in a post.

ENDNOTES
9

ENDNOTES

1. "The 2012 Sharing Olympics." www.jeffbullas.com/wp-content/uploads/2012/08/Radium One-Olympic-Sharing-US-081312-FINAL.jpg, accessed March 17, 2014.

2. Sam Laird, "How Social Media is Changing Sports," Mashable, April 27, 2012. http://mashable.com/2012/04/27/sports-social-media-2, accessed September 1, 2013.

3. Roger Groves, "How Twitter Amplify May Change Sports and Social Media as we Know it," *Forbes.* www.forbes.com/sites/rogergroves/2013/08/21/how-twitter-may-change-sports-and-social-media-as-we-know-it, accessed September 1, 2013.

4. MLB Social Media Policy, March 12, 2012.
5. Erik Brady and Jorge L. Ortiz, "For Athletes, Social Media Not All Fun and Games," *USA Today*, July 31, 2013.
6. Urooj Kazi, "Twitter Etiquette for Aspiring Power Users," *Social Media Today*, September 23, 2013. http://socialmediatoday.com/urooj-kazi/1762456/twitter-etiquette-aspiring-power-users, accessed March 17, 2014.
7. Adapted from the AP Social Media Guidelines published July 24, 2012.
8. Jessica Smith, "NASCAR's Decision to Remove a Fan YouTube Video: Five Lessons Learned," *Social 'n Sport*, February 24, 2013. http://socialnsport.wordpress.com/2013/02/24/nascars-decision-to-remove-a-fan-generated-video-five-lessons-learned, accessed October 20, 2013.
9. Dan Schawbel, "Personal Branding 101: How to Discover and Create Your Brand," *Mashable*, February 5, 2009. http://mashable.com/2009/02/05/personal-branding-101, accessed December 4, 2013.
10. Don Bartholomew, "A New Framework for Social Media Metrics and Measurement," *MetricsMan*, June 12, 2013. http://metricsman.wordpress.com/2013/06/12/a-new-framework-for-social-media-metrics-and-measurement, accessed December 4, 2013.

Chapter 10

PRODUCING

INTRODUCTION

A producer is someone who takes raw elements and makes them into something. In television, a producer can have many forms. In sportscasting, the producer plays an important role in bringing together these raw elements and, along with the rest of the crew, shapes them into a product that tells a story or many stories. The producer begins their job long before the show fades up from black by researching, writing, and organizing the mission of the show. Once the show begins, the producer has an ever-changing list of questions that need decisions.

CAPTAIN OF THE SHIP

Imagine an old sailing ship getting ready for a long voyage. What would need to happen before, during, and after leaving port? Certain events you know will happen and you can plan accordingly. For example, you will hopefully be able to predict how long the voyage is going to take and how much supplies you will need to bring. Other events might not be as easily predictable. For example, a piece of the ship might break and you will need to either fix the part out at sea or hopefully have other means of making it to port. Regardless of what happens, the captain is responsible for everything that happens on that ship. The good, the bad, and the ugly will all rest at the captain's feet and the success of the overall voyage will be in direct relation to how well the captain prepared in terms of crew, supplies, maps, and the ability to navigate through unforeseen circumstances.

PRODUCER AS CAPTAIN

A phrase that would serve a sea captain and a sports producer very well is "plan for what you can, prepare for what you can't."

In a sports production, the producer is the captain. Sometimes they will know pretty much exactly what is going to happen. For example, a scripted studio show, with finished packages that are produced in a similar fashion week-in and week-out has a certain level of predictability that can allow a producer to follow some kind of formula to make sure the show goes off without a hitch. During a live event, most of the show is about following the action as it unfolds and trying to deliver the story of the event as it happens. In many cases, the predictability of the show is a mixture of scripted and unscripted events. This leads to using the above axiom to handle most productions. A producer will come into a show with a plan for everything that can be relatively predicted to happen—for example, the open of a show. In addition, the producer will prepare for a myriad of situations that might occur throughout the show. For example, if the event is a football game, a producer will come up with standard operating procedures for what happens when a team scores a touchdown, makes an interception, or calls a timeout. While producers might not be able to predict exactly what will happen, they can put the announcers and crew in position to make decisions in the flow of the show.

This brings us to a very important role of the producer. Depending on the size of the show, the crew working with a producer can range from a small group of people to a cast of more than 100. A producer needs to know and understand everyone's role during a show. However, this doesn't mean a producer attempts to *do* everyone's job, but knowing what folks are responsible for and knowledgeable about can help a producer make decisions and ask questions that can put people in positions to succeed. For example, if a basketball coach is scheduled to do an interview on her way to the locker room heading into half-time, a lot of preparation and distribution of information would need to happen. A producer would need to tell this to the crew, including director, announcers, camera operators, and audio mixers, and understand how each of those folks integrate into the show. This understanding will guide the producer to make decisions and ask the crew to perform functions within reasonable expectations. For example, the producers needs to know how fast can a camera operator can get into position with proper audio, and smoothly integrate this into the flow of the show without taking too much time, which could upset the coach because they are losing valuable locker room time with their team. Knowing and understanding the job roles of the crew can help a producer plan and anticipate.

Returning to our ship analogy, a captain needs to prepare equipment and supplies needed for a sea journey. Similarly, a producer needs to prepare and plan for the journey of the show. Along with the director, and perhaps with input from venues, teams, and broadcast outlets, a producer needs to make sure the equipment and supplies are available for the crew, as well as devise a plan for how those resources will be utilized.

HUMAN RESOURCES

Wearing Many Hats

A producer wears many hats, as we have discussed. One important role of a producer is similar to a human resources manager. A producer is in charge of a large group of people, and these people will look to a producer to answer a lot of questions. For example, when's lunch? Where do we park? Who do I invoice for my work? How long will we be here? The list of information a producer must keep track of is long and detailed. And he or she will have to know the answer or know who to ask at a moment's notice. This also means that the stress and challenge of producing a show is compounded by dealing with many issues above and beyond the scope of the technical and creative aspects of a show. And guess what happens when someone is pulled in many different directions simultaneously without a lot of time to get everything done? Tempers can be strained and tested, that's for sure. So keeping one's cool is a skill for a seasoned and successful producer. The environment can be highly stressful normally, so being able to navigate the issues either with a smile or at least a decent sense of humanity can go a long way toward getting the crew to come along for the potentially bumpy ride.

This doesn't necessarily mean that a producer can or needs to be everyone's friend. Sometimes, someone needs to do a dirty or less than pleasant job (empty the trash, get the coffee, wait for the tape melt) and the show needs a decision to be made who gets the short end of the stick. The full meal break for a crew is in jeopardy because some pre-production is running long. The producer will need to make the call if his crew will be a little rushed or if the tease is "good enough." You can imagine a crew that is working a 12-hour or longer day might be sensitive about being asked to skip part or all of a meal break, which might be their only break of the day. And if a producer is the person making that call, well, friendship might need to take a back seat to getting the job done. Ideally, this will never happen, but conditions are not always ideal.

Setting the Tone

In a similar vein, a producer will often set the tone for an entire production in how they deal with people in a myriad of situations. This harkens back to understanding the jobs of people around the crew. If a producer has a positive attitude, says "please" and "thank you," and generally has consideration for members of the crew, even when making decisions that are not the most pleasant, you can guess how that can have a positive impact on the production. Conversely, a surly, profanity-laced and rude producer will likely have a less than enthusiastic crew when he needs an extra few minutes to edit or requires a challenging camera position set up at the last minute. I'm not suggesting that most crews will be any less professional based on a producer's attitude, but I am suggesting that many producers will not get second and third chances with an A-list crew if they are impolite or inconsiderate. As a producer, you might have all the great ideas and plans worked out, but if you alienate your crew, you will have less success in the long run. Be positive, and you will gain the benefit of having folks ready to work with you even in the most trying and difficult situations. And you can bank on several situations in your career that will be unforeseen and unpredictable when various members of the crew will save a producer's bacon by speaking up or working above and beyond the call of duty to make something happen.

While many technical positions are freelance, and thus they tend to be hired on a show-by-show basis, often a producer and director will have some direct input in who is hired for a show. For some sportscasts, such as those for the NFL, a producer and director will be paired for an entire season of shows. So, they might have 17 weeks of Sunday football games, and of course the preference is to have a crew that is as consistent as possible. This allows for familiarity between the technical crew and the producer and director that leads to easier set-ups and less confusion about what is expected week-to-week. Many crews remain together for several years. This is a function of a producer and director hand-picking members of the crew and passing that information on to the folks who do the hiring of freelancers.

As you can imagine, this is another function of the rapport developed by the producer and director with the crew. And depending on considerations such as the budget for travelling to different cities, a producer may only be able to travel in and hire a select few to be on her crew. The development and practice of people skills is the subject of several books beyond the scope of this text but suffice it to say, paying attention to the humans behind the cameras, microphones, tape machines, and various other pieces of equipment can go a long way in preparing for the unforeseen events of a production. The history built up between the producer, director, and members of the crew can be similar to the chemistry of a winning sports franchise. They will be able to anticipate not just the potential problems, but also get shots before a director calls for them, cue up packages before a producer asks, play a song going to break without a cue, and maybe even have the right amount of cream in their coffee on the way to the venue! All this hopefully adds up to a much more pleasant work environment in a world of often-chaotic productions.

Budget

In addition to the hiring of the crew, the producer is often tasked with dealing with the budget of the crew. While we will go much deeper into this topic in Chapter 18, we should mention that the costs involved with a production are never unlimited and are often shrinking. A producer will need to maximize the dollars available and make decisions about crew, equipment, and any special tricks or treats a production might need; for example, a special camera mounted outside the venue to show the crowd outside, microphones on a player, or some new special effect the home office wants to try out. Most of these will incur some added expense and will definitely need to be incorporated into the plan of the production. If you pay for something, people writing the checks expect to see that new gizmo on the air at some point. We go much more in depth about the money trail in Chapter 18, and a producer is often right in the mix of those plans, making decisions and shuffling resources.

Relationship with the Director

One important relationship for a producer is with the director. In some cases, a producer will work with the same director over many shows, and they can form a symbiotic relationship that allows a crisp flow of information based on knowing the style of a show and several discussions before and after production. A director needs to understand the goal of a production and work closely with the producer to make this happen.

Dave Harmon of HBO has worked with many directors over the years and recognizes the huge task that a director is handling. A director has so many decisions and facets to pay attention to that a producer can help guide items such as replays or stories being told. Harmon says having a good relationship with a director can help a producer in a couple of ways. First, having the same vision as your director can help foster a healthy atmosphere around the production. Harmon wants people to feel confident to make suggestions, take risks, and offer new ideas. If a producer and director are on the same page, then all the different sets of eyeballs and creative minds around the production will be able to augment the production: 50 or 100 sets of eyes will always catch more than just the two sets of the producer and director.

Another benefit is from a content and storytelling standpoint. If the producer and director each understand the other's philosophy and direction for the show, both in terms of big-picture items and for an individual show, then they can help each other achieve certain goals. This can go beyond telling certain stories and can delve into more subtle issues related to a production. For example, if an announcer has been criticized for certain aspects of their performance or commentary, then a goal for a show or series of shows might be to improve that announcer's confidence or likability. No one, other than the director, can assist a producer with those types of goals in the subtext of a production.

Relationship with On-Air Talent

On-air talent are an incredibly important part of producing sporting events. They provide commentary and analysis for most of what we see and hear. The relationship with talent is an important part of the producer's role to have a successful production. Various producers have a variety of ways they handle talent and different styles will work for different people.

Chris Dachille, the Executive Sports Producer at WBAL-TV in Baltimore, is good friends with his talent because this allows for open communication. Especially in situations where time is an issue, free-flowing discussions, even if they may involve passionate arguments, give the producer and talent a chance to communicate effectively. For example, if a package is not included in a show and a reporter really believes his work should be included, then the ability to be heard and considered by the producer is very important for their relationship.

For Dave Harmon, relating to talent also involves the building of respect for talent. Liking each other is important, but respect and trust need to come first. Why? Talent rely on producers for a tremendous amount of information. This information can be stats, content of a replay, counting to break, or a myriad of other situations that an announcer needs timely guidance for in order to have a smooth performance on air. If an announcer gets bad information from a producer, then a producer can become invisible to the announcers. No one benefits from that perception and fixing a relationship that has trust issues can be very difficult. Harmon says an announcer needs to know that the producer is giving information to make the announcer look better *and* to improve the show. If the producer and announcer have that trust, then the show can go to a lot of great places. An announcer with a trusted producer in their ear can help guide and improve the event and will allow the producer the flexibility to change items or plans in an instant and the announcer will not hesitate or question these quick decisions because they know the producer has their best interests at heart within the context of the production.

DECISION-MAKER

Where are we going? What's next? What's after that? Should we show that shot of the manager with his head in his hands? The replay of the horrific injury? The streaker on the field? When are we off the air? Do we need to fill time? Who should we interview post-game? Do we need more satellite time for a feed?

The questions to a producer during an event are wide-ranging and often seem never-ending. Sometimes they are ahead of these questions, but most of the time the decisions are coming fast and furious. A producer needs to keep track of every decision, but not necessarily make every one of them. Read that again, and make sure it sinks in. If a producer made every decision of a show, little would move forward.

People are in place to do their job, and if a producer attempts to micromanage every decision, then nothing could be effectively done. So, a director calls appropriate shots, maybe based on a conversation with the producer that says they cannot show anyone running on the field as per league media rules. So when a fan runs on the field, a director already knows to show anything else besides the fan. Another example: if a tape operator is editing a highlight package, and seven camera angles exist, the operator will make a decision about which angles to use, again, most likely based on a conversation or understanding that a producer would like a mixture of angles if possible. For both of these situations, a producer might not verbally tell each of these people their decision, but the producer is aware of them because they will see them on air.

The tone and style of coverage are all nuances that a producer will convey to key members of the crew. For coverage, is the production looking for balance or more slanted towards one team or player? Is the production more about marketing the sport or team than actually covering the action? Is the production there to sell tickets or get the sponsored elements into the broadcast? Is this event part of a national network trying to be objective or is this a local high school network trying to promote specific teams or players? These are all decisions a producer will make—sometimes alone, but often with input from management and the folks who are paying for the production.

The style and magnitude of the event will relate to the resources available for the event. Obviously, a professional football playoff game will have a lot more resources than a local cable channel's production of a regular season baseball game. That does not mean, however, that the decisions of style, tone, and coverage will be different. The production ultimately has to tell the story of the event, whether it be with four or 40 cameras.

These decisions should be communicated before a production begins. The planning for an event starts long before the truck pulls in or the studio engineer fires up the lights.

PRE-PRODUCTION

Chris Dachille's role is to produce the sports segment for the news shows on WBAL-TV in Baltimore. He says a producer needs to know a little about everything to be a producer. Dachille says this knowledge needs to go beyond the rosters, game results, and content you are dealing with, but also the community where you are working. You need to know what the viewer wants to see. Dachille gains this information from a variety of sources. He talks to people as well as researching previous coverage of events in the newspaper and, if available, what the station has covered before. This research will yield a pattern. You can then make decisions about repeating this pattern and what new ideas might fit in with the market.

For example, in Baltimore, the ebb and flow of sports seasons has been established for many years. Dachille also pays attention to the power of his local angle. He is looking for stories that you will only see locally and generally would not see on SportsCenter.

Dave Harmon, a producer at HBO, says the process of finding stories is one that begins long before a show. In general, this is a group effort. The producers, associate producers, and production assistants will meet and discuss what ideas they have internally as well as what is being talked about and written by other folks.

For example, if two boxers are fighting a rematch after a controversial decision, obvious topics would be talking about the first fight, the fighters' preparation, and implications for each fighter if they win or lose.

Ultimately, the producer and executive producer will come up with a list of potential storylines. Then, before the event, the talent, director, and producer will meet with the participants of the sporting event, and more ideas are generated. Harmon will keep all those potential threads in mind when an event starts. He will be constantly checking to see which of those ideas are alive, which ones have changed, and consider if any new stories have emerged since the event started.

A producer's preparation will depend on the resources and time available, as well as the magnitude of the show. In any case, a producer will need to spend time understanding the event, the participants, the potential stories and angles to be covered, and what is necessary to set folks up to succeed.

Research

A producer cannot do their job effectively without preparing for the event by doing research into several areas, and engaging in discussion with members of the crew and other support personnel.

One place to start is the history of the event being produced. This means players, teams, league history, and anything related to the background of the event taking place. Is this a rivalry spanning several generations or is this the first meeting between the teams? Perhaps this is a once-off meeting between two tennis players that is showing off a new facility. Knowing the participants and significance of the event can guide many of the decisions mentioned above.

A producer will also need to meet and discuss the event with the announcers. They might have specific knowledge or expertise that can help a producer tell the story of the event or game better. They also might have access to guests or potential interviews that could be incorporated into the show.

Another area to pay attention to is the potential audience for a show. Is there a target demographic or several that need to be accommodated for a particular show? This would guide style and other decisions such as music selection, the pace of cutting, or the high-lighting of packages.

Pre-Built Graphics and Packages

Heading into a show, a producer will hopefully know certain elements, such as how they are getting on and off the air, the graphic package available, and whether they can bring pre-produced elements with them to the production. Depending on the resources of the production company or network and the facility used to produce the show, some or all of the pre-production will have to be done on-site during a set day or production day in the truck or studio.

However, in some cases, a producer will have the ability to pre-build graphics, video elements, and packages. This would help a producer save time on the day of production, or set days leading up to the production day. In addition, graphics are often created on machines that are already set up with graphics programs or video-editing software ready to go, and do not require as much preparation as might be the case in a truck.

So, a producer might build some lower third graphics with statistics that won't change before the show, or edit a package highlighting a player or coach that can be used some-time during the show. Often, these can take a little more time to produce and can benefit from being produced outside the hustle and time-constrained environment of a show day.

Production Meetings

Before a show begins, a producer will ideally have a production meeting with several people, including announcers, production personnel, tape operators, graphics designers, and the director. Sometimes, due to logistical constraints, these meetings might be com-bined into one large meeting. Nonetheless they provide important face-to-face commu-nication about expectations and plans for the show. The point is to let folks know what the producer expects and to go over the rundown and pre-production schedule.

HELPING THE PRODUCER

A producer often has a few folks assigned to help keep track of all the material and resources at a producer's disposal. The volume of graphics and tape elements, both pre-produced and produced on-site, can be voluminous and unwieldy. An associate pro-ducer or production assistant will be on-hand to help keep track of and organize these elements and other areas of the show.

In general, an associate producer (AP) is the right-hand of the producer. They are there to make sure equipment and material arrives on time, to talk with the graphics or tape or audio operators about building packages or elements, and, during the show, to know where these elements are stored to be offered as elements of the show. APs are often attached to a certain producer or show and become very familiar with the flow of production. They can fill-in for a producer if the producer is called away on other business and, in terms of career paths, this is a likely stepping-stone on the path to the producer's chair.

More of an entry-level position, production assistants (PAs), are often tasked with jobs commensurate with their level of experience. They might operate a prompter, run scripts, log footage, or other jobs that are critical to a production. Many PAs start with little or no experience, but hopefully ask questions and quickly gain knowledge necessary to become an integral part of the show. Not to sugarcoat this job, they are also sometimes the folks who run for coffee, give rides to and from the airport, help transport tapes, hard drives, or other equipment to and from a hotel, and other critical, but not so glamorous jobs associated with a production.

Dave Harmon has seen many production assistants over the years and observes the value and potential of folks in these positions. Even when they are in this entry-level position, Harmon is not just observing if they will be successful as a PA, but he is evaluating if they could be successful as a producer. You might be wondering how you can effectively show your ability to lead an entire show while you are in such a beginning position. Harmon says that rising to the level of producer does not require that you know how to do every job, but you will need to understand the purpose of every job and know how they can help a show. A PA or AP who shows fundamental interest in not only doing their job but also understanding the big picture of all the pieces in the machine that produce an event or show demonstrates their promise for the future.

This machine starts weeks before with people assigned roles or freelancers hired. All those people have specific responsibilities for that particular event. A PA might be given the task of researching video clips or compiling a list of relevant graphics from previous shows or an AP might be asked to build the opening video for the show, also known as a tease, or they might be asked to produce a video package that can be rolled into the show.

Again, these people who will support the producer can gain valuable understanding of the entire show by paying attention to who is doing their job well. In the heat of production, you might not be able to ask in-depth questions of the people all over the production. Over time, by working on several productions, a PA or AP can become aware of people and the various roles they play in the production machine. Harmon says the implications of understanding the gears of the machine have far-reaching effects. If something is going wrong, or if a gear isn't doing its job, and the producer either doesn't understand that person's job or can't help them either correct the issue or help them be able to do their job, then all the gears can be affected and, in the case of a live event, the machine might grind to a halt. When the producer is in tune with the various gears, they can help keep things moving, troubleshoot before situations get too out of control, and keep the production/machine moving forward.

PAPERWORK

A producer will also have to provide the physical roadmap for a production. This will be in the form of a rundown for the show, scripts for talent, timing sheets for commercial breaks, and perhaps a schedule for the day.

A rundown breaks down each element of a show item by item. A rundown will have room for important information for several members of the crew. Each item will likely have a certain letter or number to make it unique to the show. When a producer says, "We are looking for item 114," anyone on the crew can look at their rundown and know what they are talking about. The rundown will include a slug, source, and some timing information about that element. The slug is a brief description of the element, for example, "Smith SOT" or "Eastern Conference Standings." The source listed on the rundown could mean a camera shot, graphics element, tape segment, or some other source in the production. Identifying the source on the rundown will help the crew know if the sound is on the element itself or if an announcer will be providing a voiceover. Including timing on the rundown helps the crew know how long an element runs, if applicable. Often the timing of an element is in reference to the overall length of a segment.

The value of a rundown is that each item can speak to several different people. For example, if item 110 is an interview with the head coach, then many pieces of information can be gleaned. For example, the director knows this is coming from a tape machine, the technical director (TD) knows to be ready to take that tape machine, the audio person will know they will have to track that tape machine, and the producer will have communicated to the announcers that they will have to lead to the tape machine. All that information from one tiny line on a rundown!

Developing a useful rundown is a valuable piece of a producer's toolkit to convey information in a meaningful and concise way to several people on the crew.

PRODUCTION

All the planning has taken place, or as much as time will allow. Often, there will be items that will happen live, and you can only prepare for them. But the puck is dropping, and you have to press forward with your plans and preparations.

While this chapter has talked a lot about the elements of the production and the steps leading up to fade up from black at the beginning of a show, the key to the entire process is to convey a story. This is guided by the goal of the show, the flow of the event, historical events, and anything that helps people who are not there get a visual and aural representation of what is happening.

A key to this process is how a producer works with a director. We mentioned earlier that the producer is the captain of the ship and spends a lot of time working out the path of travel, gathering resources, and hiring a crew for the massive journey across an ocean. In this metaphor, the producer essentially shares the steering wheel with the director once the show launches out to sea. The director is calling camera shots, inserting graphics, rolling tapes, adding music, and putting the producer's plan into action. The director is often asking the producer where they are going next, to make sure items are getting in. If the show is scripted, these questions are generally asked less. During a live sporting event, often the elements are shifting depending on the action, or on whether something is sold with advertising, or simply the changing flow of the game. The dynamic of a producer and director is another critical piece of the flow of the show. If they are in sync, the show can have a nice rhythm. If not, look out! Communication breakdowns are killers in terms of getting ideas out on the air. Hopefully, this relationship is worked out before the show starts, and even better is if these two have worked together several times before so they can help each other get the most out of a production.

As mentioned earlier, the stress and time-crunch of a live event calls for as much patience and clear communication as possible. When a producer can keep their wits about them and remain relatively calm, they set the tone for the entire show. A producer will likely have a list of items to incorporate into the show to help tell the story. These items might be pre-produced, created on the fly by the graphics or tape operators, and could be influenced by the story of the game, a milestone achievement during the event, or a sponsored element that needs to be incorporated into the game.

This is also where the rapport of the producer and crew becomes critical. A producer is likely sitting in a truck or in a studio far away from the action and is focused on several different tasks at the same time. So, a crew member who notices someone limping off the field, or who knows an interest statistic to sell to the producer can make a show much more interesting than if they were not paying attention and looking to help tell the story.

The details of the show range from going to breaks on time, to accommodating an announcer's request for a shot of a player to tell a story, to dealing with malfunctioning equipment. Again, this is where the people skills we mentioned earlier come into play. On a smaller production, a producer will likely wear many hats and need to keep track of many of these details themselves. As productions get bigger, a producer will potentially have less specific tasks to do, but will be checking in with a larger number of people.

After the show, a producer will need to make decisions about how and when to sign off, tape melts, post-game feeds, and any other responsibilities of the crew.

POST-PRODUCTION

After the show, a producer's job might not be done. The show might need to be edited for air or re-air. If the show is too long, it might need to be condensed for a shorter window for broadcast. In addition, a producer might be involved with packaging the show for some other form of distribution such as on-demand or DVD.

POINTS FOR DISCUSSION/ACTIVITIES

POINTS FOR DISCUSSION/ACTIVITIES

10

1. What other jobs are similar to a producer?
2. What are the different "hats" a producer might wear before, during, and after a production?
3. How can a producer set the tone for a production? What might be your strategy for setting a positive tone if you are the producer for an event?
4. Imagine you are hired to produce a college basketball game. What are some basic people and items you would need to include in your budget? How might this budget change if you were doing a game at a small college on a local cable network versus two top ten ranked teams on a national network?
5. Why is it important for a producer to have a good relationship with a director?
6. How can a good relationship between talent and producer help a show? What are the potential problems and benefits to the content of the show?
7. Describe the role of APs and PAs on a show. How can these support roles potentially indicate future success as a producer?
8. Create a rundown for a five-minute pre-game show for a sporting event. How might this change for different sports? What different types of elements could you use (for example, graphics or sound bites, or video packages, or announcers talking on camera)?
9. Describe a rundown. Why is this a useful part of a producer's plan for a show? What items are typically listed on a rundown?
10. Get in touch with a sports producer and interview them about their relationship with directors, talent, crew, and their bosses.

11. How might your coverage of an event be impacted by who is paying for the production you are producing? For example, if a team is paying for the show versus a regional sports network. What do you anticipate would be some issues with coverage that you might have to avoid versus what types of storylines would you be encouraged to cover?

Chapter 11

CAMERAS AND VISUAL COMMUNICATION

THE EYES OF THE SHOW

The history of sportscasting features a long lineage of images that capture not only the moments of a particular game, but encapsulate life-altering moments for generations of fans. Consider Michael Jordan. His legacy can be firmly explained by opening an NBA stat book and pointing to his massive volume of work in terms of points per game and NBA championships. However, his legend is undoubtedly cemented by the myriad of images available that showcase the highlights of his career. An Internet search can easily turn up his best games and key moments and even fan-produced videos that show their picks for his top ten achievements. For each moment, a camera was close by to capture the action and bring his exploits to the eyes of millions of fans. Cameras at sporting events are the eyes of the show. They provide a visual basis for viewers to see the action, up close and personal, in order to get a better sense of the action from the perspective of the players, coaches, and fans.

ANYONE CAN BE A CAMERAMAN

That is not the most auspicious headline for people who make operating a camera their living, but it is the truth. Cameras are, for the most part, user-friendly in capturing an image. And most consumer models have an "auto" feature that relies on the engineers who designed the camera to help you make a nice picture. However, there is a major difference between the home movie of Abbey learning to ride a bike versus the latest Hollywood blockbuster with the dashing face of Leo or Jack. Some of that is the quality of the equipment and some of that is the skill and artistry of the people behind the lens.

Part of the challenge in describing the role of a cameraperson is that most people think operating a camera is relatively easy. We have all picked up a camera at some point and clicked a picture or recorded a video of Aunt Alice carving the Thanksgiving turkey. Knowing how to put a camera into record mode does not make one an expert. The skills of a cameraperson are a detailed combination of the technical skills needed to set the camera up and record a technically proficient image as well as the craft of being a visual storyteller who understands aesthetics and the basics of visual language. On top of those traits, a cameraperson needs thousands of repetitions to know how to get a certain shot or, at the very least, have the ability to figure out and troubleshoot visual riddles on the fly.

To put it another way, consider a ballpoint pen. If you hand this to anyone, they can figure out how to make marks on a piece of paper with the ink in the pen. No big deal. However, ask someone to draw an apple or to write a poem with that pen and the game instantly changes. Similarly, a cameraperson needs to be able to draw with their lens and write with the pictures they capture with their camera. The fine art and poetry created by a cameraperson provide the currency that helps make sportscasts successful.

In this chapter, we will discuss the technical and theoretical side of the camera in and around sporting events. While we will cover most of the basics, keep in mind that they are just that, the basics. To truly understand and become proficient at running a camera, nothing can replace hands-on training, thoughtful critique from a professional with experience as well as deeper study of the equipment and theory through trade publications, books, and articles.

In addition to those nuts and bolts, the successful camera operator brings a certain degree of artistry to the production. Throughout this chapter we will be hearing from Greg Farnese and Todd Palladino. They are two very accomplished camera operators who have worked on hundreds of sporting events all around the world. In addition to a thorough understanding of the camera, lenses, and technique of camera operation, they also bring a strong sense of the philosophy of camera operation. This includes preparing for shoots, working with fellow camera folks and relating to the director, among other intangibles.

Farnese values the ability to have an eye for a shot. When you can understand the storyline outside the field of play and know what is happening around the game, that information can inform your shots. Anticipating your next shot can help educate the audience with a visual. In essence, you are thinking like a director. This means paying attention to the previous shot knowing what will complement that shot. If a player just made a key play, perhaps there is the shot of a coach or a teammate that can augment that shot. If you pay attention, do your homework, listen to the director and the announcers, you can help make the show better.

Todd Palladino is also a freelance camera operator with many professional events under his belt. For Palladino, knowing the basics is very important. Modern cameras will do a lot of the "thinking" for you, but understanding how to take control of the camera will allow you to own the finer points of composing a shot. Palladino talks about having the ability to stay relaxed, but also very focused and able to block out the crazy situation around you, whether that is the crowd, the exciting play, or the weather. The basics of camera operation are easy, Palladino says, but having an instinct about the type of shot needed at a moment's notice will make a huge difference in your development as a camera operator.

RELATING TO THE DIRECTOR

During a live event, a camera operator will have a specific set of shots they will be responsible for getting. The director most often conveys the camera operator's responsibility during various parts of the event. Depending on the sport and the number of cameras, these roles can be anything from very specific and situational to very vague and up to the creativity of the person running the camera.

For example, the game camera at a basketball game will have the important responsibility of covering the action from baseline to baseline. This will be a wide shot that might zoom in slightly as the team sets up in the half-court. In some situations, this camera might go in tighter for an iso shot of a coach or player, but during game action, this is the safety camera that always shows the game. In comparison, there might be another camera with the task of recording only color shots of players, coaches, and fans. They might be specifically directed to *not* worry about game action and instead find a group of players and wait for the reaction to the big shot. Or this camera might be tasked with finding a player's family and wait for a reaction to that player's triumphant return from an injury.

In all cases, a director will have told the operators of those cameras what is expected from them.

■ **View from Behind the Len**

Greg Farnese has interacted with many different directors as a freelance cameraman. Any production he encounters is about relationships between members of the crew. A very important relationship is camera operator to director. The more you work with a director, then the more you can know what they are expecting. How does he approach directors he hasn't worked with before? Farnese relies on the pre-show camera meeting to begin communication and he will ask questions to help him clarify expectations. With a director he has worked with many times, the camera meeting might not be too extensive because the camera crew will have a working knowledge of their assignments. Farnese will take the camera meeting as a chance to refresh the role he needs to fill for his director.

In the end, the key to having a good relationship with a director for Farnese is having a rapport that reflects clear communication of expectations as well as the trust that will allow Farnese to try new things and offer interesting shots in the heat of a live moment that will enhance the overall show.

For Todd Palladino, on every shoot, he gets a feel for a director very quickly. Palladino tries to understand if this is a seasoned director or someone early in their career. The relationship of director to camera operators is very important to Palladino. If there is a respect from the director to his camera crew, they can work as a team. The camera operators will fight for shots and do as much as possible to make a show better. The bond of a crew can be very strong and, Palladino's experience, allows for folks to anticipate the needs of a director and follow their lead almost without words. This also creates a positive environment for people to offer new ideas and take chances that can greatly improve a show. A good director will know and understand the potential of the crew as well as logistical limitations of their crew.

CONTROLLING LIGHT—THE ESSENTIALS OF CAMERA

Expert camera operation can be discussed in terms of the amount of light getting through the lens of the camera. If you learn to control light getting into a camera, you can create beautiful images. We generally control light in three major ways on video cameras: gain, shutter speed, and the aperture.

Gain

If you have ever used a still camera, you might be familiar with ISO (or ASA if you go back to putting actual film in a camera, in which case you might also remember dials on the television and a world without cell phones . . . but we digress). In a digital still camera, ISO will determine the sensitivity of a camera to light. The higher the ISO, the more sensitive the camera will be to light. On a video camera, this is a control called *gain*. If you are in a dark lighting environment, by turning up the gain on a video camera, you can capture an image without much light. Sounds good, right? However, when you juice up the gain, you tend to give back some of the quality of the image in the form of digital noise. So, while high gain isn't perfect, sometimes you might not have any choice. But remember that using gain often brings grain to your images.

Shutter Speed

Another parameter that controls light is *shutter speed*. This measures how long it takes for the shutter to be open for each frame of video that is captured. This is usually measured in parts of a second—1/60th, 1/30th, 1/24th—all the way up to really fast shutter speeds on some cameras to 1/10,000th of a second for some high speed shots. The quicker the shutter speed, in other words the shorter amount of time you have the shutter open to capture each frame of video, the less light can get through the lens. In sports, oftentimes the action is very quick, so you want to be able to see every move, dive, and score very clearly. Therefore, sports video often uses a higher shutter speed. So what do you think is the impact on light? You need more light to compensate for the faster shutter speed.

Aperture

Technically speaking, the aperture is the opening that allows light into the lens. This opening is controlled by the iris, which is a moveable ring of metal pieces that open and close. OK, so that is a very technical way of explaining the simple fact that something in the lens opens and closes and allows light into the lens. Whether you want to think of this in a complicated or easy way, the fact remains that this is the third way to control light getting into the lens. We measure the amount of light getting through the iris in terms of f-stops. In photography, f-stops are marked on the lens to let you know how much light is getting through. On most video cameras, a knob or wheel labeled "iris" will give you some measurement of an f-stop that is displayed on your viewfinder or screen. The higher the f-stop number, the smaller the aperture, thus the less light gets through the lens. In contrast, the lower the number, the larger the aperture, the more light will get through the lens.

The Relation of Gain, Shutter Speed, and Aperture

OK, you might be saying, so what? Gain, shutter speed, and aperture control light. This is true. But the key part of understanding their relationship is how they can help each other in getting you the image you want.

Let's use an example to illustrate this. Let's say you are recording a football game on a bright sunny afternoon. People are running all over, and you want to use a fast shutter speed to capture the distinct movements of the players, the ball, and everything that is flying all over. So, you go into the settings of the camera and set your shutter speed to 1/1000th of a second. And bang . . . your image gets kind of dark. Because you understand shutter speed, you know that the fast shutter speed you chose is going to let in less light. But, you also know that there are two friends of shutter speed—aperture and gain—that are going to allow you to let more light in. Your choices would be to bring up the gain, to make the camera more sensitive to light. But, by doing this, we might risk adding some digital noise to our image. Since we are recording on a bright day, our better option will likely be to open the aperture to a lower f-stop number and thus allowing more light into the camera.

The key parts of a video camera are the lens and the charged coupled device (CCD). Without getting too technical here, the lens controls the amount of light getting through the lens (as well as focus and in most cases allows for zooming in and out) and the CCD is the fancy plate inside a camera that takes the image getting through the lens and turns it into an electronic signal to be saved on your record material. You might be recording on a memory card (such as SD or Compact Flash) or something old school like a videotape.

■ Fwigs

No matter what camera you pick up, you will need to learn the basics of operation for that camera. While each camera will have its own particular sets of parameters, menus, and functions, all cameras essentially perform the same tasks. Therefore, no matter what make or model you pick up, there are some basic things you need to know. One common mistake a student or novice operator will make is to become very familiar with camera model XYZ-50. They know the buttons and zoom controls and menu inside and out. And that is wonderful as long as you only ever need to use camera model XYZ-50. However, invariably, you will grow up and move out of the house you grew up in and someone will hand you a camera with model number ABC-100. Now what? You know how to hit the little button on the front to make the picture the right color, but on the ABC-100, you can't figure out anything! Where do you start? What do you need to know? What are the questions you should be asking to know the basics of any camera someone hands you? Never fear . . . FWIGS is here!

To help you remember the basic questions of operating any camera, we offer a simple acronym, FWIGS. For each of these items, sometimes you will have the ability to go between manual and automatic, and you will need to know when each of these items is useful to create a compelling and technically proficient image. (And we even cheat a little by having the last "S" count for two things, but hey, it's our acronym, we can do what we want.)

FWIGS stands for:

Focus: Understanding how to work the controls to focus the lens is very basic, but critical for you to understand. Controlling focus allows you to guide a viewer towards different parts of the screen by having parts in focus and parts less in focus.

White balance: Knowing how to make a camera sensitive to different lighting environments is important. Setting the white balance tells the circuits of a camera what type of light is hitting the lens. For example, sunlight is more blue and indoor lighting tends to be more orange. By setting the white balance, an image recorded by the camera will have the correct color.

Iris: The iris controls the amount of light getting into the camera. This is often measured in f-stops. The higher the f-stop, the less light enters the camera.

Gain: Sometimes you are recording in an environment that is a little too dark. Gain allows a camera to be more sensitive to light in those darker lighting situations. One word of caution, by adding more gain into an image, you tend to add digital noise or grain to your recording.

Sometimes, you need to sacrifice the quality of the video in order to get a particular piece of video.

Shutter speed: How fast a shutter opens and closes will impact the type of action you can see. For very fast movements, you will tend towards a faster shutter speed. This will allow you to see distinct movements with more clarity, but will also require you to have more light in a particular environment. Conversely, a slower shutter speed will allow more light into the camera, but will be subject to motion blur if a person or object moves too fast.

And then we also reference 'S' in a second sense, **sound**. I know this means we should be calling it FWIGS-S, but that is not as elegant! Also, generally, the first parameter you will set is white balance, but then we would be calling this mnemonic Wh-FIGS-S, which is really messy!

In the end, you should try to get your hands on a camera before you need to use it for an official recording. Using FWIGS can guide you towards the basics of any camera you might have to use. By asking how to do those five things, plus audio, will point you towards answers that will allow you to properly operate a camera.

KNOW MORE THAN THE BASICS

The first step in learning how to use a camera is to understand its basic operations. Utilizing a strategy as laid out with FWIGS in order to learn focus, white balance, iris, gain, shutter speed and sound is a great way to get familiar with any camera. Beyond those concepts, to take advantage of the powerful impact of images, you need to get beyond those basics to more advanced concepts. The following is an introduction to more advanced camera techniques and theory that an expert camera operator will understand and be able to control whenever they pick up a camera.

Composition and Aesthetics

Learning the jargon associated with camera shots is important because you can speak the common language among professionals. This allows folks to be on the same page to communicate expectations as well as label shots for editing. The three main compositions for a camera are long shot (LS), medium shot (MS), and close-up (CU). Different directors and camera operators might have slightly different framings for each of these terms, but generally they are full shots of the entire body (LS), half of the body (MS), and the top part of the body from the shoulders to the top of the head (CU). We can further refine close-ups by adding medium close-ups (MCU), which is the chest to the top of the head, and extreme close-up (XCU), which is an extremely tight shot, for example, of an eye. In addition, we can add additional identifiers such as two-shot, to show two people in the same shot, or extreme long shot (XLS), which is a wide master shot of an entire scene. Using these terms as guides allows crew members, producers, and talent to speak a common language.

Depth of Field

When we describe the area of an image in clear focus, we call this the depth of field. A deep depth of field indicates most of the image is in clear focus, while a shallow depth of field has only part of the image in clear focus. Depth of field is a powerful compositional tool because it helps to guide a viewer towards parts of the screen where you want to point their attention. Controlling depth of field is a function of three main criteria: amount of light, focal length, and distance to the subject. Each of these can impact the amount of an image in clear focus. These are not the only factors but, in general, these are the main factors at your disposal.

By decreasing the amount of light getting through the lens, you will lessen the amount of an image that will be in clear focus, in other words, a more shallow depth of field. Increasing the amount of light will allow more of the image to be in clear focus and thus a deeper depth of field. To think of this in a concrete example, imagine you are in a packed classroom and trying to capture a single student in the front row. If you have all the lights on in the classroom, and thus have a lot of light, you will see most of the students in class. By turning off the main light, and either using ambient light or adding a small artificial light, thus greatly reducing the amount of light, you will control the amount of the image you will be able to see in clear focus.

Technically speaking, focal length is a measure from the focal or optical center of a lens to the focus point. That is a very fancy explanation, right? In terms of depth of field, we can understand focal length by relating that measurement to zooming a lens in or out. When we zoom out, or get wider, the focal length will decrease and we will allow more light into the lens. As we zoom in, or get a tighter shot, the focal length will increase and we will let less light into the lens. Guess which way will help make a more shallow depth of field? If you guessed a longer focal length, go to the head of the class. A longer focal length, in other words zooming in, can help you make the depth of field shallower.

The last parameter, distance to the subject, is simply how far or close you place the camera from the subject. By getting closer to the subject, you will be able to have a shallower depth of field. Moving away from the subject means you will be able to see more of the background, allow more light into the lens, and generally have a deeper depth of field.

Thus by combining all of these elements, you can control what is in clear focus in a scene. Less light, zooming in, and getting closer to the subject will give you a shallower depth of field than more light, zooming out, and getting farther away. Understanding and practicing these techniques will give you a powerful compositional tool to use.

Pans, Tilts, Zooms, Pedestal, Dolly, and Truck

To become a proficient camera operator, you will also need to know about movements associated with the camera. Some moves involve moving the entire camera, some only pivot the camera on its mount, and others take place within the lens.

To *dolly* or *truck* a camera means you are moving the entire camera along with the tripod or pedestal the camera sits on. If you move the camera up or down in space, this is called a *pedestal move*. If you move directly towards or away from your subject, you are *dollying in* (getting closer) or *dollying out* (getting further away). When you *truck* with your camera, you are moving the entire camera and mount left or right parallel to the subject.

Panning and *tilting* involve moving the camera on the tripod or mount, but not the mount itself. To pan means to move the camera left or right. Tilting involves pivoting the camera up and down on the mount.

Zooming is a function of the lens and involves moving the glass parts inside the lens. When you zoom out, you are decreasing the focal length of the lens and show a wider angle of view. To zoom in, you increase the focal length and move in towards a particular part of a scene.

LIVE EVENT PHOTOGRAPHY

During a live event, a camera operator is a crucial element in the production. However, their creativity and vision must fit into the overall plan for the production. This vision and plan is most often set by a director, but can be heavily influenced by the producer and on-air talent, as well as the event itself.

Utility: Probably Your First Job

If you are interested in becoming a camera operator, or basically any technical position on a crew, the place you are likely to start is as a utility. Utility is a position on the crew that is hired to help out various member of the crew. During an event, they might be there to make sure a camera operator's cable doesn't get tangled as they walk around, or hold a parabolic microphone for the audio department, or maybe run different items such as stat sheets, bottles of water, or coffee around to people on the crew. This is not a glamorous position by any means; however, it often affords you the opportunity to meet folks on the crew and ask technical questions and, after developing a relationship over several shows, perhaps get some hands-on time with professional grade equipment.

If you are interested in learning about the cameras used during live sporting events, the only way you will have a chance is during the setup of a show.

We will talk more about the utility position and how to approach your career through this position in Chapter 17.

Before the Show: Setup and Camera Meeting

Obviously, the first job task for camera operators is to set up their cameras. Often, the camera department, along with the utilities for a show, will work as a team to set up the cameras. Once they are set up, operators will be responsible to "fax" out their camera. Fax is a chance for an operator to make sure they can hear the people they are supposed to hear (for example, the director and perhaps program audio) and check that all their equipment is functioning properly.

Most live events have a camera meeting as part of their preparation. This is a meeting where a director will lay out the visual coverage plan for an event. The director will go over each camera and the coverage plan for that specific camera. For example, one camera might be responsible for nothing but the main action of the game or event. Even when the production is in a commercial break, this camera has to be focused on the overall field of play. While this might be the most creative position, the game camera is a critical piece of the puzzle because that is the camera that is most often viewed by the folks at home trying to watch the action. Another camera might be a handheld camera with the sole assignment of getting shots of the crowd, coaches, and players. Another camera might be assigned as a wide shot used for use by a color analyst or for video review by an official. This camera meeting is very important to get all the camera operators and the director in sync. This is also where a camera operator can ask any questions they might have about the production.

During the Show

Once the show begins, a camera operator should have an idea of the coverage expected from their position. He or she could be isolated on a particular player or coach, or an area of the field, or maybe hunting through the crowd for different shots. For example, in a football game, a camera operator might be assigned to follow a particular wide receiver when the home team is on offense, and on a running back for the other team. They will follow that player no matter what.

On occasion, a camera operator might come up with a shot or go find a shot that a director might call for on the spur of the moment. For example, the announcer might be telling an off-the-cuff tale about a retired player, and the camera operator might remember a retired jersey up in the rafters, go frame it up and sell that shot to the director. Listening to the telecast and carefully following the flow of the game can help a good camera operator become an integral part of the show by adding and selling visuals to the director.

■ After the event, but sometimes before signing off the air, a camera operator might have post-game responsibilities such as recording interviews, post-game press conferences, or other production elements that need to be recorded. For example, an announcing team might need to record a post-game "hit." By "hit" we mean a recorded segment featuring the talent for the game that is shown later in a sports news show on the network the game aired or on the Internet or as part of a different production

After the Show

When the show ends, the camera operators will be responsible for striking and putting away their camera. The term "strike" means to break down all the equipment and put it back in a storage location. If you are working on location, this would mean packing the mobile production unit. Sometimes, a show will be set up for several days, for example at a golf tournament, but in many instances, a show will setup, shoot the event, and strike in the same day. If you are working in a studio or at another venue where the equipment might be installed on a more permanent basis, then the strike might be just putting equipment into a standby position.

ENG CAMERA

ENG stands for "electronic news gathering." This style of camera usually means you are recording all the video and sound by yourself. You will not have a studio or truck with you. You might have a camera assistant or an audio person with you but oftentimes it is just you. You might be assigned to go out to a high school football game or a college basketball game to get enough footage to cut a highlight. Or you might go out and setup an interview with a coach or player, with lights and a nice background setup in a locker room.

No matter the situation, you will need to prepare. In the case of a live sporting event, the type of sport will dictate decisions such as your location at the venue and the equipment you might need. Most often you will bring along a tripod for the camera and headphones to monitor your audio. In terms of location, think about the goal of the shoot. Are you there to focus on the star quarterback? Then you might think about being a little ahead of the offensive line of scrimmage to allow him to throw towards you and see his face or at least the front of his helmet. If you need to capture the state's leading softball pitcher, do you set up behind home plate or up in the stands to get the best shots? Perhaps you will need to move around to get some different angles for the package. Remember to grab a roster, especially if it is a smaller sport without a lot of information available, and shoot the scoreboard throughout your recording to make sure you know the game situation when you go back to the station or editing room.

STUDIO CAMERA

In the studio, a camera operator generally has their camera already in place and set up. In this environment, a camera operator might be asked to change set pieces or set up a studio for a particular show. In addition, shows might need to pre-record certain elements or other items of production.

While some studios still employ full crews to run the in-studio cameras, the trend is towards robotic cameras. This has resulted in the need for more specialized skills in order to operate these cameras, as well as impacting the number of studio camera operator positions available.

SPECIALTY SHOOTS AND EQUIPMENT

For sporting events, the types of specialty cameras are growing in number and complexity. While these cameras and their rigs often require specialized training, they also provide opportunities to work on shows. Some of the newer technologies are only run by people employed by the company themselves. Some examples of these specialized cameras are Jibs, Steadicams, Robotics cameras (Robos), and POV cameras (such as GoPro).

SHADING VIDEO

Also related to the camera department, but living in their own section of the production workflow, are video operators. Folks who work in video are responsible for the technical quality of the video coming into the truck or studio.

Video operators perform a function called *shading*. This involves remote control of the iris of a camera as well as making sure all the cameras have the same color regardless of their make or model. This job often involves using high quality monitors and video scopes to match these signals.

While they are not seen, without their expertise in the world of video signals, the pictures that make it to viewers' homes would be less spectacular.

GETTING BETTER AT WHAT YOU DO

So here we are near the end of the chapter. You have been reading a lot about theory and technique, the heart and soul of starting your journey to being a sought-after camera operator. However, if you just read about doing camera, you would be missing a key component: actually picking up a camera and recording some video! Imagine if all you did was read recipes about making a cake, but you never fired up the oven, cracked an egg, or tried your hand at frosting. Reading from a cookbook doesn't make you a cook, just like reading about camera technique won't make you a cinematographer.

Greg Farnese says the best way to break into the industry is to get your hands on equipment. And after a lot of practice and critique from trusted friends and professionals, you will be ready when the call comes in. When Farnese has an idea for an interesting shot, he will find time to practice that shot, whether during batting practice, warm-ups, or any time before a game. When his confidence gets high enough that he can perform the shot in a live situation, he will alert the director or the replay operator and, when the situation appears, his camera will launch into action. He is always thinking about coverage and new ways to tell a visual story without being too complicated.

For Todd Palladino, he improved his skills by doing any job he could on his way up the ranks. He did it all, he says, because he wanted to see the big picture. Whether he was a utility, assistant camera, or directing a small commercial shoot, he learned about how all the pieces fit together. Those experiences helped when he became a full-time camera guy to understand his role and how he fit together with the rest of the production.

So, get out there and start recording! You can find a lot of opportunities to get reps with a camera. Record a friend's intramural team, offer to be the team videographer for a summer swim team, or look for a local rec league. Someone will welcome your efforts to record themselves, kids, friends, or teammates and you will get repetitions on the equipment. Think about how you can get thoughtful feedback from folks in the industry, read books about cinematography, and practice, practice, practice. If you take the time to thoughtfully go after your passion to use a camera, over time your skills will improve.

POINTS FOR DISCUSSION/ACTIVITIES

**POINTS FOR
DISCUSSION
11**

1. Make a list of five to ten memorable sports moments. See if you can find video of those moments. How do you think the visuals helped cement these moments in history? Would these moments be as memorable without video?

2. Why do people think operating a camera is easy? How could you make an argument that operating a camera is actually quite difficult and requires a great amount of skill? Can you think of a few examples of activities that on the surface seem very simple, but in fact are quite difficult to master?

3. Why is the relationship of a camera operator to a director so important? What are ways a camera operator can help to make this relationship better?

4. What might be a few differences between an experienced director and a novice director in terms of how a camera crew might help them?

5. What are three main ways you can control light on a video camera? Why is it important to understand how these controls work? Why not just use "auto" mode? What is a situation where "auto" mode might be the best choice?

6. What does "FWIGS" stand for? (Remember the last "S" stands for two different things!)

7. What does the term "depth of field" mean? What are three main ways we can control the depth of field of a shot?

8. What are the different terms we would use to talk about moving a camera? Why is it important to know and use these terms?

9. What is a "utility" on a TV crew?

10. Using a video camera, record a sporting event and edit your footage into a 60-second recap of the event. Challenge yourself to not use any camera movement. No pans, tilts, zooms, or any moving of the lens or camera. This will force you to trust you can compose a nice shot in the frame.

11. Without a tripod, record footage of a sporting event. How can you make the camera stable on your shoulder? How would a larger, heavier camera versus a smaller, lighter camera change your strategy for recording? What would you do to plan your coverage of the event?

12. Go to a sporting event and instead of recording just the action of the sporting event, focus on the crowd, color, and pageantry of the event. How does this change your approach to recording?

13. Record an interview with an athlete. Go to a practice or a game and record B-roll. Edit together the interview using the B-roll to cover transitions between sound bites.

FURTHER READING

Television Production Handbook by Herbert Zettl

Cinematography: Theory and Practice: Image Making for Cinematographers and Directors by Blaine Brown

The Five Cs of Cinematography: Motion Picture Filming Techniques by James Mascelli

The Shut Up and Shoot Freelance Video Guide: A Down & Dirty DV Production by Anthony Q. Artis

Video Production Handbook by Jim Owens and Gerald Millerson

FURTHER
READING
11

Chapter 12

AUDIO

The crack of the bat. The rising voice of the excited announcer. The group sigh or adulation from a sellout crowd in the middle of a playoff game. The song that has carried a team through to the championship. The sights of all these moments are only partially complete without the audio that goes along with them. The sounds of an event can give the audience a greater sense of the space of the event and add many layers of dramatic quality to the overall storytelling nature of sports.

THE ROLE OF AUDIO

Whatever we hear from an event is in the domain of audio: announcers, music, sound effects, the crowd, or anything that makes noise. The role of audio during an event or show is critical because it adds to the content that is presented. While the medium of television is thought of as primarily visual, the sound that accompanies the pictures is another character or voice that helps tell the story of an event. The people running the show behind the scenes have critical jobs to bring those sounds to life and deliver them to the ears of the viewers or listeners.

As the main audio engineer in charge of the audio mix, known on the crew as an A1, your work will start before you ever arrive at the truck. Most likely, you will get a survey of the show from a producer and/or a tech manager. This will provide key information about the type of event, how many announcers, the type of remote truck you will be working, and many other key details. Hopefully, much of this information is familiar. You might notice some of your audio assistants, known on the crew as A2s, as names you recognize and begin to visualize the layout of your audio board as well as potential issues with setting up.

When you arrive, you have a few brief meetings with the truck engineers and your A2s and the equipment starts to be set up. In a few hours, you will fax out the tape room and graphics for their audio sources. Then a producer, director, or associate producer will work with you to complete the pre-production needs for the show. After an hour's meal break, you are in your audio booth, ready for the show to begin.

As the director calls for the open to roll, you are keeping track of many, many sources. Announcers, crowd microphones, music that you roll, graphics swooshes, and taped elements. You mix these sources together, bringing some levels up, and some down to create an artistic mix of sounds. The viewer at home enjoys all these elements in watching the action, listening to the announcers and the entire show.

After the sportscast fades to black, you might have to feed some post-game sound or small package for the Web. Then you work to help strike the truck and put everything back in its place for the next show.

AUDIO PERSONNEL

The main audio person during a sportscast is known as the A1. This person is the lead audio engineer and they lay out the audio design, check all signals for technical accuracy, and work with the rest of the truck to make sure they are sending and receiving the correct audio signals. On a live event, the A1 will often set up the audio console, including all the patches that need to be in place for all areas of the truck. In addition, an A1 will be in charge of other members of the audio crew. From A2 to utilities to parabola operators and sub-mixers, the A1 needs to have a handle on all sources coming into the truck as well as the people who are assisting to set up that equipment.

The main assistant to an A1 is called, oddly enough, an A2! These audio technicians are usually the people who are setting up microphones before a live event. These microphones include the announcer, crowd, and effect microphones. After setting up, the A2 will work with the A1 to test and troubleshoot all the audio signals from the venue. When the show begins, the A2 is often responsible for helping to set up microphones on guests who are being interviewed. In addition, the A2 will play a critical role in helping to troubleshoot audio issues for the A1 while the show is in progress. For example, an announcer microphone might go bad or an effects microphone might go out, and an A2 will have to figure out during a show what is wrong and attempt to fix the issue without disrupting the program. An A2 will earn great kudos for being able to be calm under pressure and work to solve issues quickly.

Utilities, sometimes called A3s, are the next group in the audio setup. These folks will generally help set up the world of audio, hold mics (such as a parabola on the sideline of a game), and then help to break everything down when a game is over.

NOT JUST AUDIO, *GOOD* AUDIO

As we mentioned in Chapter 11, the essentials of audio recording are not very complicated. For example, taking a microphone, plugging it into a camera, and holding it in front of someone's face to record them talking is not something that requires certification from any government offices. However, to be efficient and aware of all the pitfalls that might await you when you bring that audio back to the station or send the signal back to the truck takes a lot of practice and learning from other people and, likely, your own mistakes.

One of the best pieces of equipment to combat recording sub-par audio are headphones. Many people have fancy iPod earbuds that they can pull out of their pocket and use. These might work in some cases but they are far from being the best choice. Over-the-ear headphones that can block out all outside noise allow you to focus entirely on the audio you are recording. Using over-the-ear headphones or an earpiece that is fitted for your ear can let you hear hisses or hums from a bad cable, the buzzing of a fluorescent light, a leaky toilet, or anything that is not pristine audio.

Without headphones you might be able to observe an audio meter bouncing around what appear to be audio signals, when in fact that might just be the delightful bouncing of some inaudible buzzing or crackling of a bad microphone or faulty connection somewhere in your flow of audio. Without headphones, you are simply guessing that you are recording good audio. By comparison, this is like operating a camera and not looking at the viewfinder, or trying to edit with the monitor off, or typing a text message without making sure autocorrect didn't change your words, or . . . well, you get the idea. The simple rule is: wear headphones. Please. You'll thank us later.

Good audio will isolate the sound you want to record without any extra noises. If you want to hear a bat crack or a quarterback yelling signals, you will want to be able to control those noises discreetly from any other audio signal. The audio that occurs naturally in any environment is called *ambient* or *natural* sound. Often, people will simply abbreviate natural and refer to this as "nat" sound. Nat sound is a way to greatly enrich your production. For example, if you are producing a package about the new lacrosse team at your college, getting good nat sound from a practice can be a great way to transition from a sound bite of the coach to sound bites from the players.

Levels

When you record an audio signal, you will most likely and hopefully have some type of audio meter to check you are recording at the proper level. Unless you have a reason to try to mix levels as you record them, you are better off capturing audio at the proper level so you can mix it later. In a live production environment, the job of the audio mixer will be to check the level of every source using a mixer, which we will talk more about later in this chapter.

Depending on the sophistication of your audio meter, your ability to judge levels of audio can range from a decent guess on a level that is not very discretely labeled (often consumer-grade camcorders are guilty of this) all the way up to discrete and detailed digital audio meters. In any case, you should learn the proper recording level of your device and you should get familiar with the markings on your audio meter *before* you take it out in the field and record audio.

Different devices will label levels in different ways. Sometimes they will use colors, the top of a green area is good, yellow is possibly too loud, and red is in danger of not recording a good signal. When you record an audio signal too loud, you will run the risk of distorted audio or the signal simply cutting out altogether. Other meters might use numbers, although those are not uniform across all meters. Sometimes, the ideal level is marked as 0 db, sometimes –6 db and sometimes it is some other completely different scale. Again, you should refer to the manual or ask a fellow operator what the correct level should be *before* you go out into the field. (And since we have stressed the word *before* twice now, that must be important.)

■ Being a Good A2

Randy Flick and Rick Smith are veterans of audio production. Flick and Smith have worked all over the world on a variety of sports from WWE and HBO boxing to a myriad of professional and college sports teams on national and regional networks. Both have a lot of insight about what it takes to succeed early in your audio career as well as how to be effective members of a freelance crew.

As the main audio engineer, an A1 has the job of carrying out the audio plan for a show. The setup inside the audio mixing room of a studio or production truck is a major job. Often for a freelance production of a sporting event, the setup of a show happens on the same day of that event. For the A1, the audio assistants, or A2s, are key members of the audio team. How can they be best prepared for the job?

Flick and Smith say that knowing the basics is the most important thing. The skills of an A2 include setting up microphones and protecting them from weather or foot traffic that might damage or destroy equipment. An A2 needs to know how to set up a variety of announcer booths including headsets. An effective A2 will also have the proper tools to do their job. This includes basic tools to take things apart, such as screwdrivers and pliers, as well as basic voltage meters and something to listen to and test an audio signal.

For Flick, an A2 needs to have a wide variety of talents to be effective. An A2 is an extension of the A1 because they are outside the truck, setting up and testing equipment as well as keeping an eye out for potential problems with the audio setup plan. Often, an A2 is a local hire and over time they will gain certain insights into certain venues. An A2 can be a very valuable source of information for the A1 in terms of common microphone placements and nuances of a specific venue.

Flick and Smith also place great value on the ability of an A2 to troubleshoot. Over the course of a live event, many things can and do go wrong. Troubleshooting and working under pressure are very important because an A2 will be an extension of the A1 on the show. The main audio engineer is often in the truck setting up, testing, and running the audio board. Thus they are not available to go out into the arena or venue and help fix issues. A quality A2 will be able to fix things on their own or take instruction and be able to go out and replace equipment or figure out an alternate plan. Of course, in many situations there are truck engineers or other maintenance personnel to handle large issues, but an A2 needs to know how to fix the smaller issues quickly and efficiently.

Getting involved and learning the nuances of the live production workflow is also very important. Flick and Smith both recommend getting "near" the equipment any way you can. You are not going to be hired as A2 without any experience; however, if you are patient, getting hired as a utility for shows is certainly possible. If you are interested in audio, after your main area is set up, you might have some down time. Flick and Smith say that is an excellent time to observe, ask questions, and over time, perhaps get some hands-on training in setting up equipment.

On a freelance crew, trust is an important part of the puzzle. Most shows involve a group that might not know each other very well, yet they are expected to gel and come together in a matter of hours, know their roles on the show, and produce a live event. People on the crew need to trust each other's ability and understand their skill level and experience. Getting a chance to be near audio equipment and then paying attention and asking questions can help you develop that trust over time because the people who are trusting you are the people who have taught you. Smith talks about the importance of getting into the pipeline for freelance work, whether you are interested in audio or any other production role on a crew. You have the ability to shift to other jobs once you are in the pipeline, Smith says, but you have to make sure you take advantage of the early opportunities even if that means dropping whatever you are doing when those first few calls come in. Obviously, if you are not in the pipeline, you can't go anywhere.

INTERVIEWS

For interviews, mic placement is one important consideration for getting the best sound. For a lavalier microphone, you want to place it about a hands-width from the speaker's mouth. For handheld microphones, the interviewer will likely be working the microphone back and forth from their questions to the interviewee's answers. When you have multiple people being interviewed—perhaps a group of players after a big game or a coach and player—the interviewer will have to be careful to keep the microphone close to the person who is talking. If you are conducting the interview yourself and asking questions, you will need to work the microphone from yourself to the person answering and allow a beat, or slight pause, for your question to end and their answer to begin.

As the interview is happening, depending on how many people are available, you might be responsible for monitoring the levels of the interview. As the speaker talks, you will need to ride these levels to ensure the recorded material is loud enough to use later. *Riding the levels* means you are making tiny adjustments if the speaker gets louder or softer as the recording progresses.

MICROPHONES: A BEGINNING

Whether you are in the field or the studio, microphones help to capture sound for recording or for being incorporated into a live event. You will need to select the proper microphones to do the job. In selecting a microphone to use, many factors come into play, but the main ones are pick-up or polar patterns and the style of microphone coil that converts voice into an electrical signal. The subject of microphones is a deep subject and to become an expert requires substantial study and hands-on practice. In this section, we will give you the basics you will need to know to get you started. At the end of this chapter, we provide resources for further reading if you are interested in audio equipment and production.

Pick-Up Patterns of Microphones

Pick-up patterns for microphones indicate how a microphone "hears" sound. In other words, a microphone can pick up a sound signal from certain directions. Typical pick-up or polar patterns are omnidirectional, bidirectional, cardioid, ultracardioid, and hypercardioid. Which pick-up pattern should you use? The answer will depend on the sound or area of sound you are trying to capture.

An omnidirectional microphone will pick up sound equally from all directions. While this is a good general-use microphone because you can get good ambient sound from an entire scene, you have the disadvantage of not being able to focus the pick-up of sounds from a one particular area. One example of the use of an omnidirectional pick-up pattern might be to get general ambience of a crowd or perhaps if you are recording B-roll of a practice and you want the overall cacophony of sounds of the area.

A bidirectional microphone will pick up sound from two distinct directions. Some reporters will use a bidirectional microphone for interviews, to pick up their voice asking the questions as well as the voice of the person they are interviewing.

By far the most common microphone pick-up pattern you will use is the type that captures sound from one direction. With the setup of omnidirectional and bidirectional patterns from the previous paragraphs, I know you want this type of pick-up pattern to simply be called "unidirectional." However, what happens in physical space is that microphones designed to pick up sound in one direction actually still pick up sound a little behind as well. If you were to look at this pick-up pattern from the bird's-eye view, it will resemble the shape of a heart . . . but no, they don't call this pick-up pattern heart-directional. Instead, using a Latin root word for heart, *cardio*, the pick-up pattern authors from history decided to call these sort-of unidirectional but a little bit behind the microphone patterns that kind of look like hearts . . . *cardioid* pick-up patterns!

Cardioid pick-up patterns are used mainly because they can pick up sound from one direction. In addition, they also make microphones that can capture sound from one direction AND from far away. These pick-up patterns are narrower, but allow you to capture sound from a discrete source. These are called hypercardioid and ultracardioid microphones. For example, if you are trying to get a bat crack from home plate, but you need to set up a microphone several feet away, you will use a hypercardioid microphone, also known as a shotgun microphone. If you are trying to capture sound that is very far away, such as a quarterback way across the field, you would use an ultracardioid microphone, which is commonly known as a parabolic microphone.

Types of Microphones

The two main types of microphones you will use are dynamic and condenser microphones. Dynamic mics are great to use out in the field. They do not require any power, either a battery or from the camera, and they are rugged in terms of being jostled around in the course of normal use. Often, a handheld microphone will be a dynamic mic.

Condenser mics can capture a higher quality sound than most dynamic mics. A few drawbacks of condenser microphones are the need for a source of power as well as being a bit more fragile than dynamic mics. The source of power might be a battery or they might draw power from the camera or audio board. Typically, lavalier microphones are condensers.

Mixers

In the world of audio, you will often have more than one source of audio that you will have to record and/or mix together. By mix, we mean to blend together multiple sounds at different levels and have them heard at the same time.

On a live event, an A1 will work with a mixer that takes all the sources from various departments and sources around the truck and inside the venue and controls their level that will leave the truck for the audience to hear. For example, we might have an announcer talking, the sound of the event happening, the crowd cheering, the music, and the graphics all making noise at the same time. Obviously, if we hear all those sounds at the same volume the listener would hear a jumble of madness and would not be able to discern what was happening. Instead, if we can control each individual sound and the loudness or softness of those sounds, audio engineers can create a pleasing mix where certain sources are louder or softer than others. Every sound available to the A1 will be assigned to a fader on the mixer and they will open or close those sources depending on the situation. The bigger the event or show, the more complicated and advanced the audio mixing console. For audio engineers just starting out, you might not operate a giant professional mixer, but knowing their function and purpose would be a good way to begin your journey.

Another mixer you might come across is for recording multiple sources when you are in the field. These field mixers might serve a few purposes. If you are using a camera that only has two channels of audio, and you have more than two audio sources, you might use a mixer to combine those multiple audio sources and mix them in the field onto those two channels of audio. Some cameras or recording decks have more than two channels of audio. In those cases, the mixer might be used to record each unique source onto its own audio channel. Then, you can bring the recording back to an editor or mixer who will take those unique channels and mix them together. This could happen in a variety of ways but likely that mixing will happen in an audio room, with software such as Pro-Tools or within some video editing software.

Mult Boxes

A mult box is a piece of equipment that is a hub for several people to get access to an audio source at the same time. For example, many times at a press conference, there will be a coach and a few players sitting at a table that several media outlets are there to record. You can imagine the chaos and confusion of having ten different people trying to get all their microphones set up and moved around for each speaker. Instead, what often happens is that the audio from the speakers is sent to a mult box. Then, each media outlet can simply plug into one of the several outputs on the mult box to record their own audio.

WE'VE ONLY JUST BEGUN . . .

In 1970, the Carpenters sang, "We've Only Just Begun" . . . OK, so that might be a little dated, so you can substitute "Counting Stars" by One Republic if that helps. In any case, the best way to learn the technical aspects of audio is a mix of observing and studying methods, reading and analyzing theory, and lots and lots of hands-on practice. Different microphones, pick-up patterns, audio consoles, analog versus digital, signal paths, and mixing are all part of the complex topic of audio. This section is meant as an overview of the general things you will need to know. To learn more about this topic, the best way is to get your hands on the equipment and try to record great sound. In addition, we provide great resources at the end of this chapter to help you get more information about microphones. The more you read and practice the art of audio, the better prepared you will be to advance your audio knowledge and produce wonderful audio tapestries.

POINTS FOR DISCUSSION 12

POINTS FOR DISCUSSION/ACTIVITIES

1. Why is audio such an important component of sporting events? What does audio add?
2. Could a sporting event be covered without audio? Why or why not? How would that make a difference for the viewer/listener?
3. What is the main job of an A1?
4. What are the main responsibilities of an A2?
5. What are important tools for an A2 to have at all times? Why are headphones good for anyone to have if they are capturing audio?
6. What are some good techniques for recording an interview?
7. What are the most common pick-up patterns? Give two examples why you would use each one.
8. How can you get "near" audio equipment early in your career? Why is this an effective strategy?
9. If you were going to set out microphones to capture crowd noise for a baseball game, describe your plan to lay out microphones. How many and what types would you use? Where would you put them?
10. If you had to interview several members of a team, what would be a few strategies you could use to capture good audio?

FURTHER READING

Master Handbook of Audio Production by Jerry Whitaker
The Mixing Engineer's Handbook by Bobby Owinski
Audio Production and Postproduction by Woody Woodhall
The Location Sound Bible by Ric Viers
Producing Great Sound for Film & Video by Jay Rose

Chapter 13

EDITING, REPLAYS, AND POST-PRODUCTION

TAPE, BUT NOT TAPE

A long time ago, in a television galaxy not so far away, the world of television was live to the world. Anything you saw came directly from performers and the tubes of cameras and out of broadcast antennas to your living room. The only way you could record, archive, or playback a production was to use celluloid film. Then, in 1956, a company called Ampex created two-inch videotape that altered the television universe. With the invention of videotape, television gained the ability to record programs for playback. About a decade later, editing became possible with videotape and a whole new avenue of manipulating images became possible. Many of the skills practiced by film editors became possible with videotape. Over time, people developed techniques and equipment to further refine the videotape editing process.

Fast-forward half a century, and the folks from the world of film decided they wanted a cheap way to create edit decision lists for the editing of film. By using digital techniques, film editors were able to save time and money by digitizing their film and creating multiple versions of their cuts without actually slicing their precious original negatives. Over time, the digital world of editing film began to creep into videotape editing.

Today, most cameras are tapeless and record to a hard drive, SD card or some other digital media device that creates video files. These files are then transferred into a video editing program such as Final Cut Pro, Avid Media Composer or Adobe Premiere. Then, the files are edited and exported out for playback in the show!

NETWORKS, SERVERS, AND FILES, OH MY!

In the early days of television production of sports, everything was live. The advent of videotape allowed for recording and playing back segments and eventually certain plays. Over time, the size of videotape shrank from the original two-inch tape, down to half-inch tapes. Over the past decade, the use of physical tapes has slowly begun to fade. They haven't completely disappeared mainly because of the large volume of archived footage that still remains in use for current productions.

Non-linear networks are taking over the production environment whether in a remote production truck or a studio setting. Many "tape" rooms are now populated with non-linear disc recorders instead of tape machines.

Tape machines had a huge limitation. When you were recording, you could not play anything back. When you were playing something back from your tape machine, you could not be recording any action. This caused a constant strain between being in record or cueing up your machine trying to show replays while not missing any important action. Imagine a football team running a no huddle offense or a basketball team running and gunning fast breaks up and down the court: a tape operator is constantly forced to take the chance that they might miss some important action during the replay they are cueing up and playing.

Servers have the benefit of being able to record material and playback highlights at the same time. The limitation of a server is linked to the size of the hard drive, which might limit the amount of recording space but in most cases there is more than enough memory to record several camera angles of an entire event. During the course of an event, operators keep track of good angles and can playback a series of plays instantly. In addition, operators can call up plays using time of day or with a clip number.

These machines often have the ability to edit clips together in a basic editing form using simple cuts, dissolves, or wipes. The highlight packages are edited on the fly, during the course of action during an event.

■ About EVS, aka Elvis

Prior to 2000, if you walked into a tape room in a mobile production unit or a studio situation, you most likely saw some kind of a physical tape machine. By that we mean BetaSP or ¾-inch or maybe even a hulking one-inch tape machine would be used to play back and record material as it was being produced. As we mentioned earlier in this chapter, tape machines have the limitation of only being able to do one thing at a time. A tape machine can either be recording or playing back, but it cannot do both at the same time. This could be "Heartbreak Hotel" if you were replaying something from a tape machine and something happened live because you would not be able to replay that action. I know, I know, like you, I would also sing "Don't Be Cruel" as well for the folks who had to use this technology.

Enter Elvis . . . wait, you are thinking of a white jump suit and "Hound Dog?" Let us explain.

In February 1994, EVS Broadcast Equipment SA was founded. The company developed technology to allow the digital recording of pictures on hard disks (disk recorders) for broadcasters. While the technology of recording on hard disks was not new, EVS made a name for itself by producing technology that worked within the live event environment. After making a splash at the 1996 Olympics in Atlanta, the world of television production was "All Shook Up." Now, a replay operator could be playing back a highlight and the hard drive would still be in record. As long as you had the right source going into your machine, you would never miss a thing.

OK, OK, so what's with all the Elvis songs? Well, over time, the people who used EVS Broadcast Equipment decided the boxes of hard drives and controllers could use a little nickname. And the jump from calling the machine an E-V-S made the short leap to being called an "Elvis" all around the production world. And as more and more people used the machine, they "Can't Help Falling in Love" (stay with me, there's only a few more songs left in this set . . . er sidebar . . .).

Now, when you go into most mobile production units as well as a studio environment, you will likely see several EVS machines. They are also usually networked together so that what you record on one EVS can be played back on any other machine. An Elvis also allows for very quick editing of clips with simple transitions such as dissolves, wipes, or cuts. While you can't match the fancy and robust editing of a high-end editing system, you don't need anything fancy in a live production environment. For example, a team scores three quick baskets and the opposing coach calls a timeout. As the commercial break approaches, you can call up those three baskets that just happened and play them back in an instant. The Elvis calls up clips right away without having to cue up a tape by rewinding to a certain spot. Then, in the break, the Elvis operator can use multiple angles of the baskets from two or three different machines and edit together a quick highlights package in less than a minute and have it ready coming back from break.

The EVS is so prevalent in the production environment because it is reliable at making the production flow more efficient. The speed of calling up clips—whether they are pre-produced elements, such as commercials or player packages, or moments that just happened—and the ability to edit clips together rapidly have combined to make Elvis a mainstay of modern productions. No longer stuck with the "It's Now or Never" mindset of a tape machine, Elvis helps people sing about their "Burning Love" of this technology and its huge impact on the production world.

WORKING THE MACHINES

In a live production truck, the people who work are often still referred to as "tape" operators, even though, as we mentioned, they don't usually touch tape or operate tape machines. They are also frequently called "Elvis" operators, not because they can croon or swivel their hips, but because of the brand of replay machine that is very popular in the industry. (Made by a company called "EVS"—more on that in the box.)

These operators usually serve to run replays and edit packages. The packages might be pre-produced elements before the game starts, or in-game packages showing highlights of the event as it unfolds. In any case, these folks are busy! Often they must keep track of two, three, or four camera angles at a time, and "sell" the producer or director on which is the best angle to see the exciting action that just unfolded. They make their bones by being quick and reliable in terms of cueing up the action and paying attention to details in the flow of the game that others might miss. For example, an announcer might be discussing how a pitcher is gripping a certain pitch and a tape operator might have an excellent angle from the center-field camera that shows the grip. A quality replay operator will be paying attention to this type of detail and offer it to a producer.

An excellent "tape" person is also very organized. This means they know where clips are located. Why is this important? The flow of many events is very fast, and the ability to get to items quickly and have them ready for playback can make a huge difference as to whether a certain element can make it into a show. This organization also helps if they are editing packages. By having a system to allow for efficient labeling and placing of clips, the editor can access those clips quickly and have items ready as soon as possible.

For example, let's say you are running an EVS for a basketball game. In the first half, several players are having decent games. The home team's point guard has four assists and three good drives (seven highlights). The center has three blocks, a fast break jam, and two turn-around jumpers (six highlights). The visiting team's power forward is five for five on jump shots (five highlights) and their shooting guard has 12 points on three three-pointers and some free throws (three highlights). In addition, each of those highlights has three or four different angles available through the network of non-linear machines. Twenty-one highlights with three or four angles each could be more than 80 clips! That's a lot of action and a lot of options! Then the producer asks you over the headset to edit a package with three highlights from each team and there is only two minutes left in the half! What do you do?

This is where a little bit of planning and forethought will help you. First, you are familiar with the available angles. For example, you know Camera 2 is up top and is a tight-follow, meaning it follows the ball wherever it goes. You know Cameras 3 and 4 are handheld cameras under the baskets. And the fourth angle is from a wider slash angle from the corner of the court. Knowing this means you are going to mix up your angles, and choose the best angles for the action. We know we like to see dunks in your face! So let's use a handheld camera. We know that the block looked great from the slash camera. And the player had a great reaction to the long three-pointer towards the end of the half.

Not only are you making those decisions on angles, you have also developed a nice shorthand for noting the player and action. Maybe you use the first letter of the home team, the player's number and a short note of the action. So the home team (From a town that starts with a "P") point guard (who wears number 6) hits a three-pointer, you might label that clip P6 3, and the center (who wears number 2) dunks on a fast break might be labeled "P2 FB jam." The notes are short, yet very descriptive. And because you have used them over and over, you are quite familiar with them and find the clips very fast, add them to your edit sequence, and present them to your producer in a timely fashion.

Folks in the tape room also need to know technical standards of video. As they load items into the system, they have to be aware of video levels, color, and audio quality. With two high-definition television standards, 720 and 1,080, plus the prevalence of older footage in standard definition, the process of loading clips into the system can be a confusing and tedious process. Understanding the workflow and knowing how to recognize whether items look correct in terms of their technical merits are part of the job of a tape operator.

In some cases, an operator will not be an editor, and is only hired to do replays. These folks are called replay only or R/Os. Often this is great place to be introduced into the tape room with a little less responsibility, yet still afford that person the opportunity to get in the room and observe other folks with more experience. R/Os are paid a little less, mainly because they are not asked to edit during the show.

COOKING IN THE TAPE ROOM

Most shows have a long list of items to edit for any given show. For a scripted studio show, a team of editors (or a couple of very tired editors) work from a rundown to produce different elements for a show. In the live production environment, edits are usually simpler than what can be produced in a fully equipped edit suite. However, some larger shows will have a road edit suite that travels with the show and edits packages before and during the sportscast.

For non-linear tape operators, their edits might be a little more involved in pre-production for the show. Once the show begins, the menu of items being edited are wide-ranging and need to be produced with a high level of speed, accuracy, and attention to detail. Let's take a look at some of the typical pieces edited for shows.

Teases or Opens

Coming on the air, teases, or opens, are used to set-up the show. These can be as simple as a ten-second set-up of the teams to a highly produced, in-depth summary of a series or a season. Championship games for the major sports often have teases that are several minutes long and take weeks to conceive, shoot, and produce.

Packages

A package is an all-in-one edited piece that tells a story. This could be the story of an individual, group, team, or situation. For example, how the star player overcame financial hardship to make it in college, or how a team from last season had success despite a slew of injuries. In any case, a package typically mixes sound bites, reporter voiceover, and B-roll to convey a story. B-roll is footage that is used to add other shots to a story. For example, if a player is talking about the defense the team played in their last game, the B-roll you might see would be footage of the team making steals or blocking shots. If a coach is talking about the young players on the team stepping up in recent games, then the B-roll you might see would be footage of those young players.

Editing techniques can range from simple cuts and no music to being highly produced with extensive video effects, graphics, animations, and soundtrack. Features edited in the truck tend to be more straightforward due to technical limitations, while packages edited back at the station might have more bells and whistles added.

Packages often have a lead-in, which is an on-air talent introducing before it airs, and a tag that gives a closing thought after the conclusion of the package.

VOs, SOTs, VO/SOT

A VO is a piece of video that has a voiceover from the on-air talent as it plays. A common piece used as a VO is highlights. Highlights are sequences of plays that tell the story of part of a game (half, inning, round, hole, last five minutes) an entire game, several games, or a season. Highlights could also be used to exemplify the performance of a particular player or group of players. During a game, highlights are extremely time-sensitive. Paying attention to the flow of the game and knowing potential storylines before going into a game can be life-saving practices for editors to be able to be efficient, accurate, and fast in producing quality highlight packages. Sometimes highlights are intended to be voiced-over by the talent. Increasingly another element editors are asked to produce are rollouts to break or for the end of the show. In some cases, an editor will cut with a particular piece of music and no voice will be included. These tend to be a bit more artistic and, while they might tell a subtle story, rollouts are often used to show the emotion of the players, coaches, and perhaps fans of a particular event. The style of rollouts is dictated by the producer and director. They might have very specific instruction for a rollout, but in some instances leave the process entirely up to the editor.

Typically, an editor will have a timeframe to make the highlights fit. For example, a producer might ask for a 30-second highlight from the first half, or the game from last night. The editor might get a list of plays or a rough script to use, or they might work with an associate producer or assistant director to figure out highlights. When getting off the air at the end of a show, rollouts will likely have a specific length allowing a producer to end the show cleanly and link up with other network programming.

SOT stands for "sound on tape" and typically refers to a sound bite. This means a person speaking on the screen. Usually, the editor will give a little bit of video pad so the director can roll this piece of video and get it on air without missing the first bit of sound. SOTs can have B-roll and might include more than one speaker.

VO/SOTs are pieces of video that combine the above elements. Typically, an on-air talent will have a script and a specific time to read over the VO leading into the SOT. In some cases, several VOs and SOTs might be edited together and an on-air talent will have to read several voiceovers leading into sound bites. When possible, most producers will try to pre-tape more complex VO/SOTs to avoid having an on-air talent having to hit several marks in a live situation.

Sponsored Elements

A growing trend in sportscasting is the increasing amount of sponsored elements. These can take the form of billboards, commercials, or sponsored highlights or statistics. For example, a car company might sponsor the "Drive of the Game" that will feature a drive to the basket or an overnight delivery service company might "deliver" the "Stat of the Day," which might be some particularly interesting statistical tidbit. These become crucial elements in the show because they often come with specific graphic or audio elements that need to be produced and shown during the course of the sportscast.

An editor will need to be aware of these elements and have them loaded into their machine for use at a moment's notice in the show. While a producer will often make some selections for an editor, a great strategy is to make some "soft" selections to be prepared for these requests.

Re-Airs, Collapsible Shows, Fixes

After a show airs live, the event might still have some life by being played a few more times. For example, major boxing events that are shown first-run as a pay-per-view event are often re-aired a few times. An editor might be asked to make some changes for several reasons after a show is over. The graphics might need to be changed or the overall length of the show might need to be shorter to fit into an allotted time on a channel. In other instances, a mistake might need to be fixed to correct a factual error or technical glitch.

Other shows might be recorded in pieces or with several discrete camera angles recorded with the intention of putting a show together entirely in post-production. For example, in the case of poker or other events that go on for hours, a producer will enlist an editor to cut out the long stretches of inaction so only the bits that have enticing action are part of the final show.

■ The Editing Process

When editing video, learning the process can save you valuable time in finishing your project. Similar to many of the roles and techniques described in this book, this box shows one approach. If you edit many projects, over time you will develop a strategy to go from raw material to finished piece. This is one way to begin the journey and a general approach to editing.

Whether you edit by yourself or with a producer, you will be in a much better position if you can make some decisions before you ever fire up your machine. For example, you will need to know the determine length of the piece, delivery method, potential audience, when the piece needs to be done, and what material you have. You might also need to consider if you have to create or have someone else create graphics, acquire rights to music or sound effects, if you are going to have someone sweeten your audio mix, or any other post-production treatment of your piece.

The next phase to consider is ORGANIZATION. Yes, in all caps. We won't tell you there is a single correct way to organize your material before you begin, but we will tell you that not having your material organized is a great way to set yourself up for chaos. By organization we mean labeling your clips and having a logical file structure. If you can't find your files, then that will make it very difficult to use them!

Getting your footage, graphics, music, and any other material ready to edit will involve logging and then capturing the material into your editor.

Logging is looking at every frame of video, listening to music and audio, and generating a log of the material. A log is a detailed description of the material. If you are logging video, you will generally write a timecode (imbedded within the video) and a short description of the footage. If you are logging a sound bite, you might transcribe the audio word-for-word or you might just write the general idea. The log exists to help you be more efficient as you edit. If you have already watched all the footage before, you will be able to make quicker decisions during the editing process.

Capturing involves the process of taking your material and getting it ready to edit with your software. This process will create a file that is friendly with your editor so you can make edits. Some folks will make a distinction between capturing footage and digitizing footage. These terms are making a distinction whether or not the material is digital in the first place. If you have an analog piece of material, say a printed photograph that you want to scan or a piece of film, then technically you would have to digitize that material to use on a computer. If you are capturing something, then it is already digital and you are just bringing it into your editing system.

Today, another option with video and audio are cameras that record to some type of card or hard drive. In these cases, you will be importing files. In any of these cases, the technical side is a very deep subject that involves an ever-changing menu of formats and encoders. We would encourage you to look at the technical manuals associated with your camera, computer, and software to determine the most efficient way to bring your footage into your computer. And when in doubt, Google it!

The next step in the editing process is potentially endless! In this next phase you actually put together your material into a rough cut. From this rough cut, you refine your edit by adding transitions, fixing audio levels, and adding graphics or other special effects. Usually, you will go through several rough edits before you arrive at your final cut. The common difficulty is knowing when your project is finished. Especially for young and inexperienced editors, the challenge will be to know what is good and what still needs fixing. As we have suggested in many places in this book, this will be your chance to call in your expert connections, colleagues, and friends. We tend to advise folks to avoid parents, because they are not the greatest critics and they tend to love everything you do. Compliments are great for your ego, but usually not so great for improving your end product.

After you get your final cut locked in, you will have some more fine-tuning to do. This is where you will color-correct and work on your final audio mix. On some larger projects, specialists handle these functions. These are experts at mixing audio tracks or making sure that video levels and colors are fine-tuned to perfection. Once you get these nuances perfected, you are ready to export and deliver!

The Melt

At the end of most live events, a producer will ask the tape room to create a melt. A melt is simply all the best plays, shots of players and coaches, and color from the game as well as any other pieces the producer might want to keep for future use. For example, many producers melt complete packages, highlights, sound bites, and other material produced in the field just in case they need that material for something else further down the line.

The biggest challenge in creating this melt is deciding what to keep. Obviously, you can't save everything, but how fine a line do you draw regarding what to save? Is that single from the second inning important to save? Perhaps it drove in an early run, but the final score was 17–15 and in the grand scheme of things it didn't play much of a factor . . . however, it did produce a run, so do you need it or not? And how many angles of each play that is a save should you put on the melt? For example, a player who scores 45 points and made 17 baskets: do we need all five angles of all 17 baskets? The short answer is probably not, but some producers will ask you to err on the side of putting too much on the melt. They would generally rather have a few extra angles rather than be missing a critically great angle.

When the world was using videotapes, the process of melting was a long process. Each angle had to be played and recorded in real time. With the advent of non-linear production techniques, this process is much different in most cases. The melt is a matter of file management and hard drive space. Many producers will ask for a lot of footage, knowing they can either get another hard drive, which at this point is not a huge expense, or simply delete files they no longer need and condense their material. We will discuss the topic of archiving large amounts of material later in this chapter.

Technique First . . . but Don't Forget the Equipment

In essence, when you are working in the "tape room" or in an edit suite, keep in mind you should learn technique, not software . . . but then learn software, too! The technology is changing so rapidly that as soon as anyone puts ink to paper or bit to the screen, the landscape has already changed. The key for a successful "tape" operator is to understand the technique of how to tell a story. This can mean having a sense for when to slow down or freeze a replay or when to include a cutaway shot of the pitcher reacting to giving up a long home run. Editing and replays are part of the overall storytelling process of the sportscast, and adding to the narrative is an important skill.

Having made that point, of course, you can't tell your stories if you don't know how to work the equipment! It will certainly help you to be successful if you can get your hands on a machine in the hours leading up to a production—this will give you the opportunity to press the buttons, turn the knobs, and see how the thing works. In addition, ask questions, take notes, and observe. You will make mistakes, especially in the live environment, everybody does. The key is learning from those mistakes and being flexible enough to learn new techniques, pieces of equipment, and standard operating procedures. Most productions are very similar, but they often have little specific details that are important to learn and remember. Does the director like to start replays in a freeze or already in motion? Do you put a team animation on the end of packages or does that come from the technical director? Do rollouts get music? Should sound bites have a second or two seconds of pad at the beginning? These are just some of the details that can help save time and help you do your job effectively.

Finally, getting lots of different experience is a great way to get better. If you are always on the same local show, using the same machine, you will be great at that machine on that local show. Stepping out of your comfort zone not only helps you grow as a technician and operator, but also gives you views to how other folks do their job. Observing other operators is an outstanding way to pick up new tricks and to share some of your own.

POINTS FOR DISCUSSION/ACTIVITIES

1. What is a melt and why is it useful?
2. Although many people still use the term "tape room," what is the current form of media used for replays?
3. Watch a sporting event on television. How are replays used to tell the story of the game? Are they used to go to commercial break? What about between innings, periods, or at halftime? Are there other times where pre-taped elements are used during the show?
4. What is an Elvis? How did that technology change television production?
5. Research current video editors (you might want to start with Avid, Final Cut Pro and Adobe Premiere, but there are many others). What are the differences in price and features? Are there any free options?
6. What are some online video delivery options? Go beyond YouTube, and see if there are other video hosting sites.
7. How have Instagram and Vimeo changed the delivery of video? Can you find examples of these forms of video delivery being used in the world of sports by teams, players, fans, or other organizations?
8. Look at different examples of interviews and packages from sports television networks. What style do they use? Is it serious and dramatic or light-hearted? How do they use B-roll, graphics, music or other elements to build the story?
9. Why is organization important when editing a project? How would you organize your project in terms of file structure?
10. What is logging? Why is that a key part of the editing process?
11. Using still images, edit together a short commercial for your favorite sports team. Use an upbeat piece of music and export your video to the Web.
12. Record an interview and edit together the best sound bites. Use B-roll to cover where you put the sound bites together.

FURTHER READING

In the Blink of An Eye by Walter Murch
On Film Editing by Edward Dmytryk
Editing Digital Video: The Complete Creative and Technical Guide by Robert M. Goodman
Cut by Cut: Editing Your Film or Video by Gael Chandler
Grammar of the Edit by Christopher Bowen
The Technique of Film and Video Editing by Ken Dancyger

Chapter 14

GRAPHICS AND DESIGN ELEMENTS

GRAPHICS AND THEIR RAPID EVOLUTION

Many moons ago, graphics were shot with white letters on a black board and superimposed over video. These primitive and simple elements have given way to graphics machines that can animate complex titles, incorporate moving video and sound. The modern graphics operator needs to have a skillset that includes design, computer network and database integration, as well as attention to detail to work in a high pressure and time-sensitive environment. The volume of graphics that are incorporated into a modern sportscast range from something as simple as a lower third with the name of a player and their position and jersey number, to full screen animations that are able to key out over video.

THE GRAPHICS CREW

The folks in the graphics department are usually a team of at least two people. This area is easily one of the busiest parts of the production from the time of crew call until the show fades to black. The graphics crew has a lot of information to convey and build in a short amount of time. The people who work here and succeed are well-organized and good under time constraints.

The graphics coordinator (usually an associate producer) works closely with the producer of the show to build a list of potential graphics. This person will have the latest statistics and information to make sure that anything presented is accurate and up-to-date. With larger sports and leagues, this information might be readily available and delivered electronically. For a smaller sport, for example a high school contest, the information might be less available and not updated on a daily basis. A font coordinator needs to know the story lines before the game to prepare the information for building graphics, and they also need to be able to keep up with the stories of the contest as it unfolds. They will need to work with the operator as well as listen to the producer, director and announcers to keep up with the show. This can be quite a challenge!

The graphics operator can also be referred to as the "Duet operator" or "Hyper X operator" because that is the machine they are using. As an operator you will be responsible to create and deliver all on-screen graphical elements. One of the biggest challenges in this position is the high level of technical and artistic skill needed to be an effective operator. The programs in use by the industry are not your typical Photoshop or AfterEffects, although knowledge of those programs would help as well. As we note in the box, learning the machine takes some innovative strategies and determination. A graphics operator will also need to have skills in database management. Often a league or venue will have a database that updates in real-time and integrates into the graphics machine. This allows the operator to call up a graphic that can automatically be populated with information. For example, a graphic for a player might have their name and spaces for their points and rebounds in the current game. When the graphic operator calls up this graphic, the machine will go out and communicate with the database and automatically populate those spaces with the current stats. If a player drives to the basket, drops the bucket and gets fouled, then seconds later they will be standing at the free throw line. With the help of the database, the player's information is ready as soon as the stat is updated. This allows the graphics team to be very efficient and quick in regards to calling up graphics.

In addition to the coordinator and operator, often a few other folks are a part of the team: the statistician and score bug operator. This of course depends on the size of the show, the budget for hiring crew, and other factors.

A statistician will keep track of a variety of statistics during the show. This person might serve a dual role of helping the announcers and the graphics department. Often, they will give the information to the graphics team in the truck and, after the graphic is built, will give the information to the announcer so they have some frame of reference for the note that is appearing on the screen. The "stats" position might keep items such as balls, strike, and overall pitches in baseball, or points off rebounds in basketball, or average starting line of scrimmage in football. Quality statisticians come prepared to watch the key stats of a game yet are flexible to take instruction from the producer or graphics team to keep track of the items that relate to the storylines of the game.

Prevalent on many sportcasts is a graphic that is on the screen for a majority of the game. The score bug gives the viewer a constant reference for the score and where the game action is in terms of inning, quarter, half, set, or whatever segment the game is being played. While this graphic is sometimes populated automatically by a data feed,

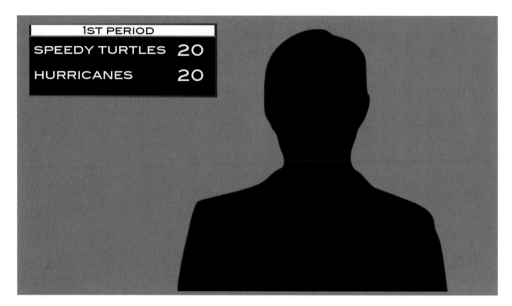

A score bug

the score bug operator works to make sure the information is accurate. On some score bugs, an operator will be responsible for adding certain pieces manually. For example, sometimes a score bug will have a sponsored element, provide the current team on the floor, or let folks know that a penalty has occurred. These are triggered manually by the score bug operator. Another common function of the operator is to change the size and position of the score bug. The score bug might shift from a position at the top left of the screen and transform into a larger score going to a commercial break. Again, this is manually triggered by the operator.

■ The Evolution of the Graphic Operator and Designer with Craig Wilkie

Craig Wilkie is an accomplished graphics operator and designer. He has worked in production trucks for hundreds of events and has designed several on-air graphics packages for a variety of clients. We spoke to him about the evolution of television graphics and some strategies for career development.

When Craig Wilkie was a junior as an undergrad in college, a speaker came to his class to offer students the opportunity to work the telecast at the local racetrack. While a hundred or so students were offered the opportunity, only Wilkie and two other students took it. When he got there, Wilkie was able to try a variety of different production positions, including technical directing, camera, tape, and graphics. While all the jobs were interesting, Wilkie found a passion for graphics and he has been developing his skills ever since.

About 10–15 years ago, graphics machines were not very advanced. They basically did one thing: added text or simple graphics to the screen. They were essentially simple machines that were pretty close to consumer electronics. With some time in the chair, and a little bit of instruction, one could master those early machines.

Over the past 10–15 years, however, Wilkie says graphics machines have become much more sophisticated. Beyond simple text and graphics, these machines incorporate video, audio, and multiple data streams. An operator needs to understand not only the software, but principles of graphic design and some computer networking. The learning curve is very steep and one faces an almost constant development of new technology, software, and workflow.

We asked Wilkie about how a person early in their career who is interested in graphics would approach learning this position. He says that the challenge will be getting in front of the actual machine because they are not easily accessible unless you are at a college that has the equipment or know someone at a local TV station or production facility.

The good news is that the opportunities to learn are available if you have the right approach. Programs like After Effects as well as a wide array of online tutorials can give you the basics of motion graphics and design. Wilkie suggests finding ways to get "near" the machine as a means to getting some time with these machines. By this he means, you might look for work that is associated with a TV production, perhaps the utility position (mentioned in Chapter 11), and in your down time, ask someone to let you sit at the keyboard and learn the machine.

As for a learning approach, Wilkie cautions against just learning the buttons to do very specific actions. Instead, he suggest coming up with an idea that you want to see, or trying to design your own graphics package, coming up with a bigger goal and then trying to create that idea on the machine. Learning the process of starting with a blank screen and creating something will lead you to a lot of questions that you will have to find the answers. These answers lay in a variety of places including other operators, the Internet, and from your own playing, analyzing, and solving.

These small projects might seem like they are not relevant by themselves. However, Wilkie has found these small projects begin to add up over time and will add to "tools to your toolbelt." He has had many instances where he has been asked to build something on a graphics machine, and he harkens back to a problem he has already solved by learning the machine with his strategy.

Eventually, Wilkie found that people came to him when they had problems that others couldn't solve and he had plenty of practice looking for and finding solutions. He does not attribute this to some innate graphics ability, but rather this skill developed over time. In some cases, it might just be a keyboard shortcut that saves a few seconds. But those few seconds, over the course of a live event, could make the difference between a graphic making it to air or taking too long to build and missing the chance.

Some keys to Wilkie's success over time have been relationships with other operators and his approach to being more than just a great operator.

The relationships with other operators pay dividends in a few ways. For one, Wilkie is willing to share the tips and tricks he has learned and in return he receives valuable information from other operators. They all might share information about a certain show, producer workflow, the layout of a truck, or some new piece of technology. This is a two-way street that makes both Wilkie and the folks in this network stronger.

In addition, Wilkie has gone beyond being a world-class operator and has taken the time to learn the design side of the process. To be a television graphics designer takes several skills. First, you need to understand the technology involved. This includes computer-networking skills, file and database structure, and the code involved in making the software go. In addition, you need to be able to design visually pleasing graphics that pay attention to the look of a channel, team, or network as well as color theory, layout, and graphic design.

In Wilkie's opinion, people tend to focus either on operation or design, but rarely both. A lot of time and effort is required to bring both of these areas along at the same time. However, these skills can complement each other. For example, as an operator, you understand the importance of usability and you can incorporate that knowledge into your design. As a designer you will know the potential of the machine and can create a package with the operator in mind. In addition, having both of these skills will increase the opportunities for employment; because you will be relevant to several different clients.

WHAT WE SEE

What appears on the screen from the graphics team has a jargon that lets everyone know what is on the way. This can impact how long the graphic will be on the screen, how to frame a shot, the source, and how to transition to and from the graphic. The way people refer to graphics reflects the simple and direct language you will find throughout production jargon. As with many areas in the production flow, people need to be on the same page and know what is coming, so using the correct terminology consistently allows people to gain a wealth of information in a short amount of words and time. The following is a brief description of the major types and styles of graphics that appear on a typical sportscast:

Lower Thirds (L3rd or L3)

A staple of sportscasts. These graphics are called lower thirds because, oddly enough, they tend to either cover the lower third of the screen or at least are placed in that general area. Lower thirds are great to use when you need to convey one or two pieces of key information such as a player's name, position and a key statistic or two.

Full Screens

When a graphic covers an entire screen, this will be referred to as a full screen. These graphics are useful to highlight more complex information. Although you have the entire screen for your graphic canvas, you should still not try to cram more than four or five pieces of information on a single full screen graphic. The two main reasons are time and

A lower third

readability. During an event, you will rarely have time to read a full screen for longer than five to seven seconds if you are lucky. In addition, too much information on a full screen will appear cluttered and confusing. If you find yourself running out of room, create a second or third full screen to show your information.

Sponsored Elements/Billboards

One of the key functions of graphic elements is to provide corporate logos for sponsored elements throughout the show. This requires folks to be certain the logos and colors used are accurate and up-to-date. Businesses and companies often pay large amounts of money and a tiny two-inch square logo can cause hours of apologies and corrections and loss of revenue if they are not correct.

A very specific type of graphic element is called a billboard. These often have some type of voiceover associated with them in the vein of "This sportscast is brought to you by . . ." Again, these are often company logos and require an attention to detail to make sure they are correct in terms of color, aspect ratio, and anything else the client has requested.

CHANNEL/SHOW STYLE GUIDES

A style guide is a list of rules that accompany a graphics package. Stations and leagues will often be very specific about how graphics are built and presented. A specific logo

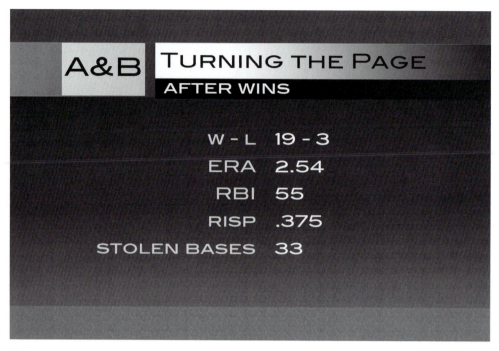

A full screen

or a particular bar or anything that goes on the screen in graphic form will have a rule or guideline associated with it. These can be as simple as a color choice, or as complicated as which animation or sound effect goes with a particular graphic. This is usually a document in printed form with a wide variety of examples for coordinators and operators to reference. When new graphics packages are rolled out, sometimes stations or leagues will hold a training "summit" to show folks how to use all the elements.

POINTS FOR DISCUSSION
14

POINTS FOR DISCUSSION/ACTIVITIES

1. Watch a sportscast and observe the use of on-air graphics. How are they used to enhance telling the story of the event? How often are they used with mostly numbers versus words?
2. How have graphics machines advanced over the past 10–15 years? What are the range of skills you need to be a successful graphics operator?
3. Look at the score bugs for a few different live sportcasts. What information is included? Do they ever change over the course of the game? What information is added or subtracted in different situations? Where are the bugs placed?

4. Using a motion graphics program, design a simple graphics package for a sportscast. Include at least a lower third for a name, a lower third for statistics, a full screen page for graphics, and some type of score graphic. If you don't have access to a program, you could download a free trial of some software or even sketch your ideas out on paper.

5. If you are interested in learning more about a professional grade graphics machine and software, describe a strategy for getting behind a keyboard. Who could you get in touch with to ask some questions? What companies might be interested to have you as a guest?

6. Why is it important to develop your skills as an operator *and* a designer? How can this help your career development?

FURTHER READING

Motion Graphic Design: Applied History and Aesthetics by Jon Krasner
After Effects Apprentice by Chris Meyer and Trish Meyer
There are many online tutorials for various graphics programs, such as Lyric, Duet, and Hyper X to name a few, that you can watch to get more familiar with that software. As we mentioned in this chapter, getting near these machines will often require finding a station or mobile production company that will allow you to get some time in front of the machine.

FURTHER
READING

14

Chapter 15

DIRECTING AND THE FLOW OF THE CREW

INTRODUCTION

When you sit down in a concert hall before a symphony orchestra performance, you often hear the very dissonant sound of different instruments. The clarinet might be rolling up and down scales, a violin section might be running through some plucking of strings, the timpani drum is tuning, and overall everyone is on their own page, getting ready in their own way on what seems like a hundred different pages from a hundred different books. What happens when the conductor arrives and simply taps their baton? Hopefully, the orchestra unifies into a single unit and prepares to make a cooperative journey through several pieces of music.

Before a sporting event, you will also find a group of people getting ready in what can seem like very different and seemingly chaotic ways. Cameras are rolled out in pieces and assembled in their positions, the audio engineer will be playing music, testing microphones and setting levels, the technical director will be running through different transitions, graphics are being built, and the tape room is editing and loading their room with a variety of images. A director will eventually be the person weaving together all these different people and pieces of equipment and, along with the score provided by the producer, conducting a piece of sportscasting that will bring together everyone on the crew into a symphonic collaboration, complete with swells of emotion and the narrative of the event.

WEAVING A TALE, TELLING A STORY

The goal of a director is to tell the important story or stories of an event. This involves a variety of strategies to get the most out of a crew, location, and the set of technical equipment at their disposal. Often a crew is a mixture of freelancers and staff employees who might only work together for one day. The director must find a way to communicate the mission of the show within very tight time constraints. In other cases, the crew might work together all the time, and then the challenge might be how to keep the crew attentive and fresh in their approach to the day's activities.

In many cases, the producer will have a plan for the show, including storylines and other narrative elements for a director to use. These elements might include graphics, edited pieces, statistics, sound bites, or other pieces that might come to the production all ready to go, or the producer might need something created on site.

A director will need to combine the members of the crew and the technical equipment, and make aesthetic decisions to bring these elements to fruition. In addition, as the show progresses, a director will be responsible for making many decisions, often with only seconds to decide what is coming next. In a live event, a director will make hundreds of decisions that will help tell stories.

The producer, the members of the crew, and everyone involved with the production will be waiting and listening to a director to know what to do and when to do it.

THE LANGUAGE OF DIRECTING

Directors have a very specific way of talking during a show. If you were to listen to their voice over a headset during a production, it might not sound like anything special. However, the words they use and the way they speak are very intentional.

The challenge for a director is to communicate clearly with a large number of people and often with more than one person at the same time. For example, if the on-air talent is leading to a sound bite, the director will need to figure out a way to tell the technical director (TD), audio department, stage manager, talent, tape room, cameraperson, and graphics all at the same time. Everyone will need to be in perfect coordination to get from the talent on camera to the tape and back again so the viewer at home doesn't notice the switch. For example, the TD will need to know when to take the sound bite on air, the audio person will need to know when to fade out the announcer and when to fade in the taped piece, and the stage manager will need to let the talent know when they are clear and when they will need to speak again.

The reason a director can make all that happen at the same time involves a conscious decision to use quick, clear, precise, and predictable language for the crew. They will try as often as possible to give each command a "ready" command before giving the "action" command. For example, when asking the TD to change cameras, the director will say "Ready Camera 2," and then when she wants to switch to that camera, she will say "Take Camera 2." One of the interesting benefits of speaking this way is that she is using the least amount of words to make something happen and, by announcing over the headset what is coming next, the director also lets the camera operator and audio person know to be alert for the change as well.

Talking to multiple people at once can be difficult, but by using a consistent vocabulary and predictable commands, a director can execute difficult transitions from one element to another without any trouble. The goal of a director is to guide their crew through a production with clear, concise, and timely directions. When directing in a studio environment, a director will give a ready command and then an action command for something she wants carried out. The ready command says what is coming next, and the action command states what is happening now. For example, "Ready Camera 2, Take Camera 2" will cut to Camera 2.

List of Common Director Cues

Take: A cut to a source.
Mix: A dissolve to a source.
Fade: A dissolve that generally implies to or from black.
Add: Dissolving on a graphic.
Lose: Dissolving off a graphic.
Open: Bring up level of a microphone or other audio source.
Close/kill: Turn off the volume of a microphone, etc.

Pan, Zoom, and Other Camera Directions

Cue: (1) Tell someone to speak; (2) To put something in a certain spot such as a tape or a prompter, as in "cue the tape to the head" or "cue up the third story."
Roll: Play a tape. Also "roll record."
Track: Bring up the volume of an audio source.
Standby: Letting everyone know that the production is ready to start. When a director says this, if someone or some piece of equipment is not ready, this is everyone's chance to say they need a minute, or to ask for clarification.

Some Items a Director will Talk About

Camera.
Graphics/super.
Talent.
Microphones.
Music.
Tape.

Commercial.
Black.
Bars.

A director can also combine many actions into her ready command and then it is implied that everything will happen when the command is given, for example: "Standby to fade up on Camera 2 with music and graphic in 5 . . . 4 . . . 3 . . . 2 . . . 1 . . . and fade up . . ."

This command is a cue for all three things to happen at once, fading up on the camera, adding the graphic, and fading up the music.

■ Working with People

The challenge of directing a show involves making several technical and creative decisions with relatively short amounts of time to make those decisions. Directors often talk about the need to connect with and develop respect between themselves and the crew as a key element to having a successful production.

Marc Payton, Suzanne Smith, and J.R. Aguila are all veteran directors with many years of experience directing live events. Each of them speaks about the importance of the "human resources" aspect of their job. Each of these seasoned directors has strategies for working with the crew to maximize effort and respect, and successfully navigate a live show environment.

For Smith, who has directed football shows for CBS, during the course of the show she knows the moments are coming when something either goes wrong, or the situation is so fluid and happening so fast that the quicker she and the crew can react, the better. The key for Smith is talking to the crew when they arrive on location, at the camera meeting, and even during the show. Building trust and, over time, respect helps in those tense situations where everyone needs to be on the same page, with a common goal to bring a moment to life. In some cases, Smith is working with essentially the same crew from week to week. In that case, she has the benefit of knowing the crew very well. However, sometimes one or two members of the crew are doing a job they are not familiar with or are not very confident. In that case, Smith will do what she can to put them in a position to succeed. Smith remembers that we have all been new to a position or task.

Smith tells a story of a cable puller who finally was called upon to run camera. They were very excited and nervous. Even though the crewer was nervous to put someone without a lot of experience on her show, Smith was confident they would do fine because she had previously observed this person not just showing up to do their job, but also bringing information and curiosity to the show. They asked good questions, and even offered information about where the team entered the field. Smith shares information from her own experiences, and knows they will help each other. In addition, the good attitude of this person early in their career was a good fit for the crew. For Smith, skill level does not always trump the dynamic of the crew.

Marc Payton spent a lot of time working various positions on live event crews before he became a director. Doing those jobs and observing other people doing their tasks allows him to understand what he is asking people to do. For Payton, directing is 20 percent craft and 80 percent working with your crew. If the crew is on your side, sharing your vision, and not afraid to try their best, then you will be in a great situation to succeed. The craft of directing can essentially be learned. You can learn the right words and through experience know the mechanics of directing. The respect and trust between director and crew is built over time. Payton says any show is a group effort. No one role is more important than another. The entire crew shares the giant pie of success of a live show. When the show goes well, people who know and trust each other create the end product together.

J.R. Aguila, who has directed a variety of sports for Comcast SportsNet Philadelphia, says the utopian situation is a crew with people who know the sport as well as you do, understand the important moments, and are people you have worked with often. As Aguila went through school and early in his career, he paid a lot of attention to the people around him and how they did their jobs. He brings this knowledge with him when he works with a crew. Aguila has many goals when he meets with his crew, including sizing up their ability and experience and letting folks know his expectations for the show. When the crew can anticipate their role in a production then that will save critical time later in the day. For Aguila, the moments of an event are fluid and mere seconds can make the difference. These seconds can be in the form of short commands for the TD, or having a graphic loaded going to break, or how replay sequences will be rolled.

With many different skill levels for a variety of shows and a myriad of events, all these directors want to set their crew up for success. Each of them talks through the different situations before the show. For example, when the game winning field goal is about to be attempted, a director cannot stop and tell the four, eight, ten, or however many camera operators there are what they need to frame up and capture. That situation and many others are covered pre-show. Aguila cautions that if you have to take the time to call a camera operator into a shot, then the moment is likely gone.

DIRECTING DECISIONS

We have discussed how a director gets from one thing to another, but that is only a small part of a director's job to tell a story. How does a director decide where to go, when to go, and maybe even more important, where *not* to go, and when *not* to go to a shot or replay? These decisions must be made confidently and often with very little time to think about all the options. Especially in a live environment, a director has to keep the flow moving. A basketball game will not stop so a director can figure out a good camera for a coach's reaction nor will a talk show be very efficient if a director has to keep stopping to figure out how to cover the guests answering questions. A director must have a plan going into the show.

Often, the phrase that pays is "plan for what you can, prepare for what you can't." In essence, this means for the parts of the show that you control, perhaps the pre-game segment, or anything that is tightly scripted, you should be able to predict with reasonable certainty what is going to happen. Therefore, you can plan for these situations. A director can rehearse these portions of the show and tweak or fix parts that might not be working. In other instances, for example during live game action, you are not going to know what is going to happen. The quarterback might throw an 80-yard bomb, but he also might be sacked for a huge loss. In these cases, you need to have a plan because you can't reasonably predict exactly what is going to happen. A director will plan for as many contingencies as they can predict will happen. What camera is responsible to get the reaction of the defensive player who makes the sack? What music will roll when the commercial break comes after the touchdown? How will the TD get into and out of replays, split screens, or other elements of the show? Planning for what they can and preparing for what they can't allows a director to be ready for as much of the show as possible.

So, having said that, directors need to plan and prepare for as much as possible. There will also be times when a director will need to break from his plans and either take a chance on something a bit different or adjust for some contingency that wasn't evident when the show was broken down. For example: using a camera from behind a hitter to show a historic home run, isolating a certain microphone to get some interesting natural sound, or using a split screen to compare something from earlier in the day to a current condition.

DIRECTING LIVE EVENTS

Live events have a great sense of uncertainty and thus provide a great challenge to a director. How can a director tell a story without knowing what is going to happen? What activities can a director do to put themselves in a position to succeed? How can directors meet, assess, and work with a crew that he might never have met before today? How does everyone, from the producer to the technical crew to the on-air talent, get on the same page and cover a live event?

With the goal of telling the story or stories of the event in mind, the setting of the event becomes critically important for initial decisions a director must make for a live event. For example, if a director is preparing for a football game, decisions about camera placement will differ greatly if the game is in a professional football stadium with established camera positions versus a high school stadium that will require lifts to get the necessary cameras into position. The way a director learns about a particular venue is by conducting a site survey. A site survey is a walk-through of not only the venue where the event will take place, but might also involve available spaces for trucks, locations for crew meetings, meals, satellite trucks, or any logistical aspect of the production. If the budget allows, a director might take a trip with the producer and other members of the production crew to get the lay of the land. In other cases, a site survey might be a much less formal affair conducted the night before or the day of an event. In any case, this will allow a director to know more about a particular venue, which will inform decisions regarding setting up the show, such as where the talent might be located, camera placement, or concerns related to covering the event.

Production Meetings

While the site survey will inform many decisions, a director will most often need to work with the plan developed by the producer to cover the event. As we discussed in Chapter 10, this plan can involve everything from the timing of how the event will begin, potential elements that can be rolled into the show, pre-production needs, or perhaps the general tone of the overall production. For example, an event might have historical significance that might overshadow the result of the game itself. Perhaps a player is wrapping up a storied career, or a stadium is hosting a final game before demolition. In these cases, the result of the game may or may not be important, but a director will make decisions based on this information and set up accordingly.

A producer's plan might offer a lot of details in terms of how a director will plan or prepare, but in some cases, a producer might not have a lot of information coming into a game. In any case, a director can prepare for the event by doing research on her own. He/she should know details that can help tell the story. For example, the players, teams, league, and other information could inform a director's decisions. As we keep saying, the goal is to effectively tell the audience what is happening and why certain elements of the game are important. If a director doesn't know the potential stories, then logically he couldn't tell them!

Armed with all this information, directors are in a bit of an odd position. They know the stories, they understand the potential and limitations of the venue and they are well versed in the producer's plans and the overall theme of the event including pertinent information about players, teams, or the town where the event is taking place. At the same time, a director works in a control room and sits in a chair, often very far from the action. So how does she take this information and tell the story? Obviously, as you have read through this book, you know that everyone from the on-air talent to the technicians and production assistants are waiting for instruction to put these ideas into motion. As you saw early in this chapter, the language of a director is very specific and meaningful to all the folks working with them. With only their voices, directors conduct a symphony of individuals to perform a well-orchestrated performance from all members of the crew.

This process begins with a meeting with various members of the crew either en masse or in small groups. The production meetings, rehearsals, and camera meetings involve going over information to lay out the production plan and prepare the crew for what is likely to happen. Again, we find a director planning for what they can and preparing for what they can't, only this time these plans and preparations take place overtly for the crew to learn about expectations and ask questions if necessary.

A production meeting often takes place with the director and producer going over the overall flow of the show including the pre-production schedule, the production plan, post-production needs, meal information, and the plan for striking or packing up the equipment after the show has wrapped. This production meeting ideally includes the entire crew and provides a chance for the various departments and crew members to ask questions and get answers face-to-face in a less stressful environment than in the heat of a production. On some shows, this might have to take place over headsets or in smaller groups with the producer and/or director. This might be due to time constraints, logistical limitations of meeting spaces, or perhaps the crew is familiar enough with the show that a short talk over headset can effectively disseminate information. Some production meetings are so specific and detailed that a producer or director will provide a production packet of printed information that tells everyone on the crew what is expected in a particular situation.

For example, on a national telecast of a football game, if 20 cameras and eight tape operators were guessing what they should be shooting and recording, how could a director accurately predict and call for a certain shot or replay? Instead, production meetings allow for a clear plan to be in place for most of the most common occurrences of an event. In some cases, a crew member might have a different idea about coverage or a way to make a process easier for everyone and this is the chance to discuss those ideas. In the middle of an event, with so many moving parts flying all around, the discussion and implementation of new ideas becomes a difficult and risky proposition. Which of course, in some cases, is exactly what happens because something out of the ordinary occurs! However, starting with an established plan is a great way to get everyone on the same page.

■ Working with a Producer

Working together with a producer is a key function of a successful director. The directors we heard from earlier in this chapter, Suzanne Smith, Marc Payton, and J.R. Aguila, all have strategies for successfully collaborating with a producer. Most of the following thoughts have a common theme. Knowing a producer's plan and understanding potential storylines are key ingredients for a director to be successful during a live event.

For Aguila, the producer will give the overall plan of the show and the director will take the production in that direction by making certain technical and creative decisions and communicating with the crew. For a sportscast to be a success, the producer and director need to be on the same page. Aguila has studied live event production his entire life, from watching games as a child up through his formal training. His decisions are based on keeping the viewer at home in mind. He is trying to convey the story of the game to both the seasoned fan and viewer all the way over to someone who might be new to the sport. Aguila keeps in mind that folks have been watching sports on TV longer than he has been on the planet and thus doesn't need to reinvent the way people watch all the time. That doesn't mean he doesn't try new things, but with the help of his producer, Aguila can take smart chances.

For Marc Payton, a live event is akin to editing a movie in real time. The producer is someone who is formatting the show in a variety of ways including setting up storylines, working with the talent, and determining replays. As a director, Payton has the task of how to implement the format and how to tell the stories of the producer. Again, being on the same page as the producer going into the event can help them work efficiently.

For Suzanne Smith, being in synch with the producer is key to having an effective show. The producer decides on where the show is heading and what storylines are to be told, says Smith, and the director decides how they will get there. The less time they spend having in-depth conversations during the show means more time to get to certain stories.

The Camera Meeting

A particular production meeting that often takes place is a camera meeting. A camera meeting is most likely a face-to-face meeting with the director and camera operators. Camera operators serve many important functions for the production including being the eyes of the director in the venue. Thus, good communication between the cameras and the director is critically important. This meeting allows the director to explicitly convey the flow of the show and how she would like cameras to cover certain elements of the action. Often a director will go through each camera position and explain their responsibilities for the show. One camera might need to be wide at all times to show the entire field, other cameras might need to be constantly hunting for color shots, and others might receive a list of particular players to isolate whenever they enter the field of play. Again, this is an opportunity for communication, discussion, and clarification of anything that a camera operator might not understand. Many directors will provide sheets with numbers and pictures of players, coaches, or other important figures associated with the event that a camera operator might need to identify in the viewfinder of their camera. Even on shows with camera operators that are familiar with a certain director and their show, this meeting will still take place, although the length of the meeting will likely be shorter and information shared will likely be briefer, keeping the lines of communication open serves everyone.

After a meal for the crew, everyone settles into their positions and the clock begins an unforgiving countdown to the show hitting air. Ready or not, the event will begin and the director will need everyone focused and ready for their assigned tasks. These moments leading up to the show are often when a director will rehearse several elements of the show. Rehearsals allow for everyone to get into the flow of the production, practice transitions, camera shots, play pre-recorded elements for talent, or take care of any unfinished pre-production. Most directors will rehearse some part of the show. Some directors will rehearse many times, make adjustments, and keep rehearsing until they are confident they can get it right. The moments leading up to a show allow a director to shift into yet another role they serve on the crew.

One of the best traits for a director to possess is the ability to coach and develop members of the crew who might be in the beginning stages of their career or be unfamiliar with a particular sport or piece of equipment. A good director will identify a crewmember that might need some extra attention and use rehearsals and pre-production time to work with that person. This could take the form of talking them through the framing of a camera shot, properly cueing and rolling a replay in tape, or calling up graphics. Directors who develop and work with their crew, even under the pressure of live production, will enjoy the benefits of this mentorship. Directors who belittle someone who is inexperienced will tend to make that person gun-shy and nervous. Who can operate successfully under that pressure? An even better question is who would want to work under those conditions? A quality director strives to learn the strengths and weaknesses of everyone on the crew and works with those folks to make the production as successful as possible.

In addition to communicating with the technical crew and producer, the director also needs to pay attention to the on-air talent and work with them to enhance the production. Obviously, the on-air talent are talking directly to the audience, so hopefully they can work with and not against the flow of information. In some cases the director will lead the on-air talent, and in other cases the director will need to follow what the announcers are discussing or describing and attempt to give a camera shot or replay to support what they are talking about. With the help of a producer, who will often talk to the talent via talk-back, the relationship between director and announcers can be a fruitful one.

As mentioned earlier in the chapter, live events will offer a director some of the most challenging decision-making circumstances. A game can change in a matter of seconds, and the director needs to be ready to assess the situation quickly, communicate quickly and effectively, and then get ready to do it all over again on the next play! This skill comes not only from experience but also from visualizing different scenarios and preparing for them. What camera sequence will tell the most effective story? Will the producer and talent be expecting a graphic? Should we see a cutaway of a dejected member of the losing team? How will the show go to and come back from commercial breaks? Preparing for what you can't exactly predict will pay huge dividends when a director faces these situations.

In a live event situation, a director has a lot of responsibility before, during, and after an event takes place. They need to be aware of the content of the show as well as the technical quality of every element of the production. These technical elements might include video levels, audio clarity, or accuracy of graphics. The director will invariably need to troubleshoot something during a show. A situation might be as simple as a lineup change that needs to be communicated to the audience right at the beginning of the show, but it might be more complicated and require quick thinking.

One example of needing to think and act quickly came during a baseball game we worked in Oakland, CA. In the middle of the third inning, the switcher dies and we are stuck on Camera 3. Instead of having seven cameras and graphics and tape and all the other sources normally available, we now only have one . . . and that camera is high up on the first base line. The director, thinking quickly, leaves his seat, runs back to the truck engineer, and begins cutting the game from a router in the back of the truck. A few minutes later, the switcher is reset, and they can operate normally. To the viewer at home, while it wasn't perfect, it wasn't a complete disruption of the game.

DIRECTING SCRIPTED SHOWS

As with live events, scripted shows require a director to communicate with a crew clearly and consistently. Unlike a live event, most scripted shows have a large portion of their content predetermined. Thus, when practicing "plan for what you can, prepare for what you can't," a scripted show should be much more predictable for a director.

With a scripted show, the director will be depending heavily on a producer to provide a format for the show and timing information for segments and packages. In addition, a producer will likely provide graphic and music cues for a director to use, although the implementation of these elements might be a collaborative process between the producer and director. For example, during a highlight package, a director might choose a cut of music to go underneath, and then decide when to add a score to the end of the highlight. A producer might provide certain information, but a director might need to improvise how to incorporate that information into the show.

A director still might need to make adjustments on the fly in a scripted show environment. If a show is heavy, in other words is running too long, a producer might need to adjust the order of show elements or remove certain elements of a show, and a director might need to make these changes on the fly or with very little notice.

In addition to straight scripted shows, a director can be asked to navigate through some form of a hybrid show that mixes elements of live events and scripted shows. For example, a sports talk show might have topics for each segment with specific roll-ins to augment the discussion. In this case, a director would know specifically a little bit about each segment, but would need to cut the show based on the discussion of the host and guests of the talk show. This would differ slightly from a live event because, in theory, a director can direct a guest as to where to sit or which camera or person to direct their answers towards. In general, a studio show provides much more control for the director than a live event where the production is at the mercy of the sport or event being played.

OTHER DIRECTING POSITIONS

Technical Director

The technical director, or TD, usually sits right next to the director and operates the video switcher for the show. On some smaller productions, the director and TD are the same person. On a live event crew, a TD is usually the one who communicates with the crew when the director is absent. The TD will sometimes handle running pre-production, but in essence is in charge of cutting different video sources that are seen on-air by the audience at home.

Modern switchers have the ability to play video and audio. Many TDs find themselves playing back elements that were traditionally rolled in tape, such as commercial billboards, station promos, and other transitional elements. In addition, the TD is often a key person in pre-production, using the switcher to add graphics to edited packages, providing effects to footage, moving or resizing images, and performing a variety of visual manipulation of items used in the production.

The TD position requires a high technical skill level and, in the freelance world, the ability to work an ever-changing variety of switchers. A TD also needs to be able to focus on the instructions given by the director and, on occasion, help a director by taking a camera or other video source in a case where the director either misspoke or perhaps made a mistake. This will usually happen with a TD who has worked with a director many times before.

In terms of career paths, many directors come from the TD position, so this is an excellent place to try to get to if you aspire to be a director someday. The TD chair is an excellent view for many of the technical elements of the show.

Assistant/Associate Director

Often times, a director will need some assistance in keeping track of the timing of the show. This could be the timing of commercial breaks, talking to master control about when a break is rolling, or the length of packages coming from tape or graphics. The person often given these timing tasks to help a director is the assistant or associate director, often simply called the AD.

An AD usually has one or more stopwatches in their near vicinity, and counts out of taped elements, commercial breaks, and sound bites. The AD might also help with pre-production if the director is meeting with the cameras or talent before a show. Along with the TD, an AD is a key assistant to a director successfully navigating a live or studio environment.

SUMMARY

Any production has a variety of positions and personalities pushing and pulling in many different directions. Without a plan of attack and clear voice leading the way, any production will likely sink into chaos. The director is the person providing the clear guidance and path for a crew to follow to effectively tell the stories involved in a production. A director speaks in clear and consistent language so he or she can be predictable to everyone involved in a production. Directors must be able to make informed and quick decisions over and over during any production. Live events provide more fluid and unpredictable situations than a scripted show, but both are likely to call on a director to navigate through some situation that needs immediate troubleshooting. Good directors take inexperienced crew members and work with them to make them better and reap the rewards of this mentorship not only on the current show, but future shows as well. Directors work closely with technical directors and assistant/associate directors to bring a show to life.

A director is tasked with telling stories by working with the crew and bringing stories to life. Finding the right words, pictures, and sounds, and getting those elements to the audience is the big challenge. Through production and camera meetings, rehearsals, and consistent and calm directing throughout a show, a director can bring the stories home to the audience as if they were sitting in the arena.

POINTS FOR DISCUSSION 15

POINTS FOR DISCUSSION/ACTIVITIES

1. If you could only use your voice to give directions, imagine getting a group to complete a task such as cooking dinner, moving all the furniture out of a room, or building a house. What kind of language would you use? How could having a meeting before beginning your task help clarify your instructions later?

2. What other jobs are similar to the role of director? How do these roles handle conducting several other people simultaneously without having the entire project descend into chaos?

3. How does a director tell a story with the different pieces available? How do you think they effectively combine pictures, sound and text to tell these different stories? What do you think would be the hardest part of using these items? What do you think would make the process of storytelling easier?

4. Watch any live sporting event and analyze the direction of the show. Pay particular attention to how the show is cut together. Are there reaction shots after big plays? Do they cut away from the main action often or rarely? What is the pace of the show? Fast? Slow? Does it depend on the action during the event?

5. Why is consistency important for directors? What might happen if a director didn't use the same language or cadence for delivering commands?

6. Script out what a director would say in the following situations (remember that a good director will use ready commands to let people know what is about to happen. Make your best guess about the number of cameras you have, placement, as well as graphics, tape machines, and talent):

   a. The opening of a show right before the first pitch, kickoff, drop of the puck or tip.

   b. Before during and after a homerun.

   c. The end of a basketball game that is coming down to the final shot.

   d. The final play of a football game with the game on the line.

   e. A post-game wrap up following an exciting win.

7. To practice using director language, you can play the "game of ball." This is a very simple game where two people roll a ball back and forth and try to score a goal. The game is less important than just having some kind of action in front of you. To do this exercise, ideally you have at least two cameras hooked into a switcher, a TD, and a stage manager and everyone is on headsets. Setup a studio with at least two cameras and two players standing next to chairs, or milk crates or cardboard boxes or anything that can serve as a goal. The game action is two minutes, and players gently roll the ball back and forth trying to score goals. Very simple, and they are more like stage props than athletes trying to gain international fame playing the game of ball. The stage manager should keep time in the following manner: 30 seconds pre-game to introduce the players. Then they play for two minutes rolling the ball back and forth, and then a 30 second post-game for the winner to be announced.

The director should have a quick camera meeting with the two (or more) camera operators and discuss coverage for the game. The coverage plan will be up to the individual director. Some questions that usually need to be answered might include: Who will be following the ball back and forth, who will get each player before and after the match? You can cover the game however you like, but we should at least see the ball rolling back and forth.

If possible, you should record different directors covering the game of ball in their own way and then you can compare different styles of directing from within your own class.

The benefit of this exercise is to give you a sense of covering an event (and we admit that this is not the most exciting game). From this simple coverage you can connect to how you would cover other sports. For example, in basketball, you always want the option to see the game action. Therefore, one of your cameras would always be high up to give you that angle of coverage. Then what would be important? A low camera? A camera at an angle from the corner of the court? Thinking about coverage and telling the story of whatever event you will produce can help you start to make some pre-show directing decisions. The game of ball is an exercise to help you start that journey.

FURTHER READING
15

FURTHER READING

Television Production Handbook by Herbert Zettl
Directing for Television by Brian Rose (a little older, but great information and technique from seasoned TV directors)
Directing Television: A Professional Survival Guide by Nick Bamford
Studio Television Production and Directing by Andrew Utterback

Chapter 16

THE DEMO

As high school and college students prepare for careers as sportscasters, whether in front of or behind the camera, this should be one of the central questions you ask yourself daily: "How can I produce the elements necessary for a good demo?"

Demo is short for *demonstration*—that is, a brief sampling of your abilities as a sportscaster. If you don't have a demo, how can you show a news director, sports executive, station manager, production manager, or other potential employer you can do the job? Aspiring television and radio sportscasters of all types need a demo. Certain "above the line" production personnel such as directors, producers, and some technical directors or editors occasionally require demos, while "below the line" personnel such as camera persons, audio technicians, and others often do not (more on demos for production folks later).

GENERATING DEMO MATERIAL

The eternal paradox for those trying to break into sportscasting is generating examples of good work, even though you might have little or no professional experience. There are a number of ways to produce material for a demo at the high school or college level. They include, but are not limited to:

- projects from regular coursework
- student or community radio and television productions
- any self-produced materials
- work that is produced during internships

The projects you produce for college coursework or for television or radio stations that are student or community run could supply you with enough material for your demo. That material would include standups, reporter packages, anchor, play-by-play, sideline and/or sports talk segments. If not, you may have to improvise and produce demo-worthy material on your own. Aspiring reporters for both television and radio might attend certain events open to the public such as news conferences or "cover" hard news. In that case, be sure you are properly credentialed and that you inform all concerned—from club, school, or other personnel to the principals you are "covering"—that you're just doing this for your own demo. The same is true if you're generating material for a feature story or "covering" a sporting event.

Interns at local radio or television stations are often given the opportunity to produce work themselves, either for the station's air product or offline. Offline opportunities can come any number of ways. For example, if you're in the field with a station's reporter, see if you can't record a standup after the reporter is finished. Oftentimes before, after, or between news shows, interns will be allowed in a studio to record anchor segments. Production folks often have the opportunity to perform a whole host of hands-on duties.

"I was an intern my sophomore year at a station in Syracuse, New York," says Brian Feldman, now a sports anchor, reporter, and videographer for KMOV-TV in St Louis. When you're an intern, if you're really nice to them—don't bug them too much— you can ask [whoever you're working with] 'can I just shoot a quick standup?' Or when you're done with your internship at the end of a semester, a lot of stations will let you sit on the set and anchor after the six o'clock newscast is done. I actually did that multiple times so the news director [of that station] could see how I looked on their set. It doesn't matter if you're applying to that station [where you are an intern]. It's simply a way to look good on a professional set. Even if you do work at a campus station, it may not look as good with the lighting and the set in general."

Aspiring sports anchors and reporters will need access to equipment, including some combination of a camera, tripod, portable lights, microphone, digital recorder, audio/video editing software, and a studio to produce either audio or video work. High school or college undergrads should be able to use the equipment normally available to them for school or student station projects. Graduates might be able to go back to their alma maters and utilize their resources at little or no cost. Purchasing some or all of this equipment and studio time is always possible, but finances are often an understandable issue. Borrowing a camera from a friend might be a solution, although new and used so-called "prosumer" high definition cameras are available for reasonable prices. Local cable affiliates in your town, community or school district might be in a position to offer the use of their equipment and studio at little or no cost. If you can't get a studio, an anchor segment can be recorded in a basement with reasonable sound-proofing in front of a green screen. Just add a "news set" in post-production using available software. Radio anchor/reporters can do the same thing, creating small studios at home with some well-placed soundproofing, a microphone, and editing software. Radio "sportscasts" can be scripted and recorded onto a computer.

Play-by-play broadcasters, with the permission of high school or college athletic directors or the public relations folks from sports teams, can take a digital recorder to an event and "broadcast it." And if you're denied a seat in the media area, just buy a cheap seat and sit somewhere in the stands where you hope you're not bothering other fans. Hey, in some cases, they might even like hearing your commentary!

■ Getting Creative by Adding Your Own Soundtrack

Phil Giubileo is the voice of the Bridgeport Sound Tigers of the American Hockey League. When he auditioned for the job, he wasn't allowed to just send the club his demo. Rather, the team specified exactly what type of demo he needed to make. Here's the story in Giubileo's own words:

> When I interviewed for the position in Bridgeport in the spring of 2006, I was handed a DVD of an old Sound Tigers game and was told to call a period of that game and submit it as my demo.
> The game that I was asked to call was a good two years old. As you might expect, calling a game off of a TV into a recorder, without any game notes, etc. would be difficult. I was simply given a media guide from that particular season, but by no means was that adequate (or accurate) enough to work with.
> By scouring the Internet for information, I actually tracked down the stats of the two teams up until that point of the season as well as the box score from that night. I was even able to locate basically what we today would call our AHL Media Kit, which is generated by day, but usually once that day ends, the information isn't readily available.

Armed with the proper information, I was able to prepare for the broadcast as I normally would. But I had another issue to work through. The DVD that the club gave me contained the game call of the previous announcer who was fired. As a result, I would have to turn down the sound so that I could call the game. Without any crowd or background noise, I would have been left with a pretty lifeless environment. It would sound flat when recorded because it's difficult to feel like I'm at an event when I'm watching this on a muted television in my living room.
What I ended up doing was actually recording ambient crowd noise off of my NHL 2005 video game from my PlayStation 2. I recorded about 45 minutes of natural sound and burned

it onto a DVD. For the "broadcast," I used my home mixer to run the natural sound into the mix in real-time so that I could hear it in my headset as I called the game. The result was a rather realistic sounding call, as well as a way for me to feel like I was at a game, as opposed to calling it off of a TV. There's something about having a crowd in my headset that helps me tremendously.

When listening back to my demo, it's apparent that I used a crowd track. The hiring folks knew that they gave me a DVD with someone else's commentary on it. But I'd like to think that it still helped the overall sound enough to give the team an idea of what they were hoping for when they asked me to go through this exercise, which was to illustrate what I would sound like as the "voice" of *their* team as opposed to listening to some demo clips while broadcasting the games of another team.

Aspiring sports talk show hosts can create a program from scratch. Try to access studio time through your college radio station, (unless they already have a talk show that you can host), a station where you are an intern, or the local public or community radio station. Schedule times with friends and family to "call in" and ask a question or make a comment. If you don't have access to a studio, record a podcast with an in-home studio that can be created with a microphone, a little soundproofing, and a phone patch into your computer.

John Kincade is a sports talk show co-host on the *Buck and Kincade Show* on 680, The Fan in Atlanta. He says podcasting is a great way to generate examples of your work for a demo.

"Oh, absolutely," says Kincade, who also does sports talk on ESPN Radio. "Anything that gets you more 'reps,' anything that gives you an idea of what it's like to provide content, to be able to go through the motions of putting on a show. Even if nobody's hearing it, *you* are hearing it. Because I guarantee you, *you* will listen to your podcast and you'll go back and say, "ooh, I hated how that sounded" or "that wasn't good" or "I found out after seven minutes I was hemming and hawing and I need more content." I think it's a great method. I used to do shows into a tape recorder. It's a way that anybody can get better. I don't care if you're at my level or you're just starting out."

For those in production, much of what we've told the performance folks is true for you. Examples of your craft will come from coursework, student or community television and radio stations, or other material you can somehow generate on your own. To that end, finding opportunities to get experience other than school or internships is as simple as looking all around you. You can approach a little league, church league, or even the intramural program at your school. There are events happening virtually every night of the week at ball fields, gyms, or pools. Once you get permission from the right people and they know it's simply an internal, learning experience for you, just shoot and edit. You will only be limited by your imagination. Pick up the weekly paper in town and find the roller derby team or ballroom dancers or martial arts studio. The list of people who would welcome some form of production utilizing their content is virtually unlimited, although be sure to remind them this is just a teaching tool for you. For them, it will be like getting a haircut at a barber school. In some cases you might get a great haircut, while in other cases, well, you might not.

Once you have one of these volunteer projects in place, you will need to figure out what you are producing. Something small and manageable would probably work best. If you are working alone or with one or two other people, you should be very realistic about how much you can take on. This means you might try to produce highlights or a game story for one or two games, *not* an entire season of highlights. Use the opportunity to work whatever skill you are trying to improve. This might be camerawork, audio design, graphics, or a combination of several areas. Some examples of work produced would be an interview with B-roll of one of the players, an audio-only piece with sounds of the game, or a mini-documentary that follows a player or coach throughout their day of preparation for the big game and the game itself and short interview after the game. Again, the advice here is to be ambitious but realistic about what you can produce.

Your Work Must be Your Work

Whatever demo you decide to produce, whether you're talent or production, you personally need to be responsible for as much of the material as possible. Of course on a substantial television or radio production, others are expected to be involved. However, if you're an aspiring television or radio anchor/reporter, you should shoot all interviews and footage as well as script and edit any packages *yourself.* That goes for the editing of the actual demo reel as well. News directors might ask you if you indeed did the shooting, scripting, and editing yourself because you will probably have to perform the same duties once you get the job. It's the same for play-by-play announcers who might have shooting or editing as attendant responsibilities.

While you're urged to produce demo material that is of the highest possible quality, do not use any material that is misrepresentative of your work. For example, if you're an intern at a station, don't take someone else's reporter package, add your voice or standup, and try to present it as your work. This is a form of plagiarism. If you're an intern and you use that station's studio set or microphone flag, make it clear you did the work as an intern and nothing more. Anything else is called lying.

EIGHT IS ENOUGH

Once you have gathered the material for your demo, you will no doubt agonize over what elements to use and in what order to use them. But the most important thing to remember is that a potential employer will frequently make up his or her own mind about you after viewing that demo for approximately . . . eight seconds . . . if that!

It's why you start your demo by putting *your best stuff first*. That is, the one piece of video or audio that will make people want to see or hear more.

Typically, many in the industry will recommend you start your demo with a montage—that is a segment of your best material, about 45 seconds to one minute in length, composed of clips of around eight to 12 seconds each. This will provide the viewer with a quick look at the overall depth and breadth of your abilities. After that, the demo should contain longer segments to show your ability in specific disciplines or simply your performance over a sustained period of time.

Here's a look at potential demo elements, including their order on the demo, broken down by discipline:

TV Sports Anchor/Reporter

- A 45-second to one-minute montage of unique and creative standups, anchor lead-ins, live shots, interview questions
- Two 90-second to two-minute reporter packages, preferably one hard news and one feature
- Brief one- to two-minute continuous, unedited anchor segment including on-camera lead-ins, commentary if you have it, and highlights voiceover
- Any other elements that display the uniqueness of your talents totaling 90 seconds to two minutes, including a continuous live shot, interview, or host segment

TV/Radio Sports Play-by-Play

- A 45-second to one-minute montage of exciting, dramatic, or otherwise incisive calls
- Several longer more sustained segments, each 90 seconds to two minutes, demonstrating your ability to call the action, use unique phrases, provide timely facts, or tell stories as well interaction with an analyst. For TV, your interaction with camera shots, graphics and replays. For baseball, a good, solid, unedited half-inning demonstrating as many of these abilities as possible
- A standup open

■ Any other elements that display the uniqueness of your talents totaling 90 seconds to two minutes

TV Sideline Reporter

■ A 45-second to one-minute montage of standups, live shots, interview questions
■ Two to three minutes of unedited, live standups and interviews in various scenarios and locations
■ Any other performance elements that display the uniqueness of your talents; additional standups if applicable

TV Sports Host or Studio Analyst

■ A 45-second to one-minute montage of show open, interview question, commentary, interaction with guests, and interaction with other show elements such as video, graphics, etc.
■ Several two- to three-minute, unedited segments including show open, interviews, commentary, and interaction with guests and show elements
■ Any other performance elements that display the uniqueness of your talents

Radio Sports Anchor/Reporter/Sideline

■ A 45-second to one-minute montage demonstrating the full depth and breadth of your talents including quick hits from anchoring, live reports, features, and interviews
■ Several two- to three-minute, unedited segments expanding on these same elements
■ Any other performance elements that display the uniqueness of your talents

Radio Sports Talk

■ A 45-second to one-minute montage of commentary and opinion including, but not limited to, exchanges with callers, interaction with broadcast co-host, interviews, breaking stories, and depth of knowledge
■ Several two- to three-minute, unedited segments expanding on these same elements
■ A 90-second to two-minute sportscast of current sports news displaying solid, unique writing and creative use audio such as sound bites, play-by-play, etc.
■ Any other performance elements that display the uniqueness of your talents

PRODUCTION DEMOS

The challenge of presenting the work you have done as a technical member of a crew is being able to separate what you have done from the overall production. For example, if you are trying to get work as a technical director (TD), showing someone a segment where you cut cameras, ran an effect from the switcher, and inserted a graphic isn't going to get you a job. As we discuss in great detail in Chapter 17, much of your ability to prove yourself comes from peer and supervisor recommendations.

However, there are some positions where it would be appropriate to provide some of your material as a demo reel. These positions would include camera, editing (especially in terms of feature pieces or complete programs) and graphic design.

ALL DEMOS

Regardless of what you want to highlight, whether you're on-camera or have behind-the-camera skills, there are several aspects that relate to all demo reels:

- If there is a glaring mistake on a particular element, even if the mistake was some-one else's responsibility, you should *leave the entire element out* of your demo. While the mistake may not be yours, it may prove distracting. Furthermore, the prospective employer might infer that if you allow a sub-par element on your demo, your judgment might not be the best; that you might be willing to allow mistakes like the one in your demo to go out over the air
- Speaking of other people, your demo is meant to highlight *you* and no one else. So, say you have a segment where you have a co-anchor, try to keep the on-camera seg-ments to yours only (unless you have some interaction with your co-anchor where you have a starring role). Also, if you're an anchor leading into someone else's reporter package, just include the first few seconds and the last few seconds of that package before editing the next element in your demo
- In the case of other demos—such as those for play-by-play, host, or sports talk—interaction with a partner or guest might be critical to displaying your skills in that area and should probably be included
- Be ready at all times with individual demo elements filed in computer folders so you can custom-make a demo "on-demand" depending on the job description
- Include a video slate with your pertinent contact information (name, email address, and phone number) at the front and end of your demo
- If you don't have a .mov, mp3, or similar file, you can email a link to your demo from

  - an online video service such as YouTube or Vimeo
  - an online audio service such as Sound Cloud
  - your own webpage (see more below under "Personal webpage)

- While links are the recommended format, if you are producing a demo CD or DVD, *neatly* label both the disc and the box with your pertinent contact information (there are plenty of CD/DVD labeling programs available)

- Don't "over-do" the demo with enhancements like animated introductions, special effects between segments, or music beds. Let your work be judged on its own merits
- Again, don't use someone else's work—that's called plagiarism
- Again, don't try to impress prospective employers with microphone flags or CD/DVD labels from commercials stations, sports teams, etc. This is misrepresentation at its worst and experienced professionals will see through it
- Get a few people you trust (industry professionals, professors) to give you feedback on the demo
- When in doubt, leave it out

PROFESSIONAL OPINIONS ON DEMOS

The preceding information on demos has been gleaned through the authors' combined half-century's worth of sportscasting experience. But these are just *our* opinions. Take note of the variety of opinions from across the industry spectrum, answering the question "what makes a good demo reel?"

Brandon Mercer, News Director, KTXL-TV, Sacramento

Make it really long. Give me an hour. Why would you have any cap on the length? What I do is, I watch the first ten seconds . . . maybe . . . nah, I watch the first *five* seconds. If it's good in the first five seconds, I keep watching. Then I'll watch another 20 or 30 seconds. If it's still good, then I just let it play. Sometimes it ends after two minutes and I say, "what was that, you have nothing better?" But if I see something go on for like ten or 12 minutes and it's great content after great content, I know they can do the job well. And give it to me as a link to a website—I throw DVDs away.

Chris Lanni, News Director, WJAR-TV Providence

I look for energy and enthusiasm, your knowledge of the topics that you're covering. Writing to video. Creativity. Something that makes you stand out. A lot of times, it has to do with presentation, so I look for creative live shots or standups or the proven ability to react on the fly to an unexpected situation.

I prefer DVDs or online clips that start with a reporter standup or anchor montage that give me a feel for who

Brandon Mercer, courtesy of Zohreen Adamjee

this person is and what kind of on-camera energy they have, followed by longer form storytelling packages to be sure they can craft a compelling story. Following that, long-form anchoring. Make sure your best stuff is up front. Ideally a good length is probably three to four minutes.

Ed Kilgore, Sports Director, WGRZ-TV Buffalo

My opinion of that has changed over the years. I used to just send the best sportscast I had and hoped it was a perfect one. And then I realized that anybody who pops a tape in, within ten seconds, you're either dead or alive. They [news or sports directors] may not like the way you part your hair, the pitch of your voice, you have one eyebrow that's higher than the other . . . whatever. I know from being in a position to hire people, if I didn't see in ten or 15 seconds, if I wasn't immediately attracted in some way, I just wouldn't waste my time looking at the rest of it. So, put your very, very best stuff first. The first thing you want to see is a variety of settings like a live shot where you're ad-libbing—you're not looking down at notes but you're eyeballing the camera and you're talking in a conversational, energetic way.

Jerod Smalley, Sports Anchor/Reporter WCMH-TV Columbus, Ohio

I sit and watch demos done by young professionals, either right out of college or two to three years out. The one thing that stands out to me is creativity, but not over-the-top creativity. You know, you're not putting on a puppet show—which by the way has been done! I've seen some ridiculous things on demos in an attempt to be unique, to be memorable. You *do* want to be unique. There are [also] a couple of factors out there, racial factors, gender factors. When a news director has a job opening, they might have those factors in mind as much as who is the best person for this job. So there are a lot of things (potentially) working *against* you when you apply.

Jerod Smalley, courtesy of WCMH-TV

Send your best performances and your most creative performances. Creative leads when you're anchoring. Live shots if possible. And not just standups but motivated standups—a standup that has you *doing* something, demonstrating something, being a part of the culture of that story. To show that ability I think is huge because it shows your versatility and it shows news directors they'll be able to use you in a number of different ways. I think that's the biggest skill in today's modern media, versatility. How many things can you do well.

Adam Goldberg, Director of Marketing for the Memphis Redbirds Baseball Team

The more samples of what [the applicant] does, the better. A montage [at the top] can certainly pull me in and give me a quick overview of what they do and what their style is. Personally, I only need two or three minutes. I can make a pretty quick judgment off the top and then when we get deeper into the process, I'll want to interview them to get to know them a little bit better.

Adam Goldberg, courtesy of Memphis Redbirds/ Allison Rhoades

I like to hear the banter back and forth if they have a color commentator, how they work with others or just by themselves. I like to hear the commentary during a period where the play is slow so that I know that they can keep the interest going in a down time of the game. In addition, I want to hear a home run call or an exciting play. Being in Minor League Baseball, you want to build on the excitement of the game.

I would say that we want somebody who can also talk about the promotions that we do in addition to just the game. In baseball, specifically, there are so many things that can happen. I'm always looking for someone that has an extreme knowledge of the game and is never going to be caught off-guard by anything that happens during the game.

Jason Benetti, Director of Communications and Play-by-Play Voice of the Syracuse Chiefs Baseball Club

From the knowledge I've gained from people that are in the Majors and from decision-makers in the Major Leagues that I've spoken to, it seems to me that [you put] highlights first, then a stretch of play-by-play that's a half or full inning . . . probably just a half-inning because you want people to want to listen to more rather than listen to everything you've got. Then maybe an interview as well to show how you actually interact with people.

Tom Boman, courtesy of Tom Boman

My demo is never without some humorous moments, off-the-cuff remarks, something that shows me smiling because I think people want to be able to be around their announcers. So if there's no humor in what you're doing, it might seem like you take yourself too seriously.

Tom Boman, Broadcast Manager, Learfield Sports, a Leading Syndicator of College Sports Broadcasts

If it's football, I'm looking for five solid minutes of play-by-play, ideally a singular drive if possible. That doesn't just show me how you can call the highlights, but how did that develop. Lead me down the path of the story of that particular drive. If it's men's or women's basketball, five solid minutes. And make it your best. Then after that you can give me a pre-game or post-game interview.

If you want to put a highlight reel on there, that's fine but I'll tell you, there are guys all over the country who can call highlights, but they can't necessarily call extended play-by-play.

I'm looking for the basics. Can the person do a radio broadcast? Radio is an art. You're still painting a picture in the listener's mind. With no pictures, you get to do everything. In a football broadcast for instance, listeners really only care about four things. They care about down, distance, score, and time. That's all they really care about. Everything else around that broadcast, little stories about players, insights, stats, that's all gravy. Somebody gets in their car or turns on the radio in the garage and you don't give them time, down, distance, and score within the first 30 seconds to a minute, they're going to freak out on you. Then I'm looking for fit. Do they have ties to the university? Do they have ties to that particular city or town? College fans are loyal. They want their broadcasters to be as loyal to that program as they are. You can get equal talent between three finalists. Now, what's the difference? How are they with the alumni group? How are they with speaking engagements? How are they with hosting banquets? If you're going to be the voice of a college program, you're going to be required to do a lot of things outside of the games themselves.

John Kincade, Sports talk show Co-Host on the *Buck and Kincade Show* on 680, The Fan in Atlanta

Brevity. Impactful. And when I say brevity, according to most rating services, the average listener stays on a station for around six or seven minutes maximum before they flip the station. So to me, make it brief, make it impactful and don't over-produce it. I honestly feel some demos are too slick, too over-produced, unless you're trying to get a job as a production director or something like that. Make it about what it's supposed to be about. Have impactful opinions and points of view that make you sound interesting, that showcase your voice, your point-of-view, your energy. I don't know how many times I've heard a demo and the energy level is a four. That doesn't mean you have to be screaming, but be fired up, be excited, be energized.

And never, never just email your stuff out of the blue. I know a lot of program directors that hate that. They immediately delete it. That's arrogant, that's way out of place. Do not just send somebody, unsolicited, a link to your reel in an email.

David Schuster, Sports Reporter, WSCR Radio, Chicago

Just being yourself, showing your personality. Showing you're informative. More so your personality, because anybody can script something by Googling it and reading it. But I think if you show your personality, be it audio or video, I think that comes through. So my first recommendation to anybody who's doing a demo, show what your strengths are and if your strength is your personality, make sure it comes through.

PERSONAL WEBPAGE

A number of online services provide Web hosting free of charge or as part of a bundle of paid services. If you decide to go this route, you should probably try to use your own name as the domain. Keep it simple with your demo and résumé. If you are industrious, links to other types of demos or longer segments of individual performance or production skills might be included.

THE RÉSUMÉ

While your demo will ultimately get you the job, a solid, comprehensive, and concise résumé also helps. There are as many résumé formats as there are font styles, so don't get overwhelmed. That said, here are some general rules from our viewpoint:

- Keep your résumé to one page
- Center your contact information including your name, address, phone number, and email address at the top of the page in a bolder, larger font than body of the résumé

- Under this, include an *italicized* one to two-line self-description of you as a sports-caster and as a person. This might include your experience, versatility, and special skills as a professional as well as a line about you as a person (our view is that this self-description is better than the so-called "employment objective," which might paint you as a beginner as well as pigeon-hole your abilities)
- On the left, in bold underline, should be the title "Industry, Broadcasting, or Sports-casting Experience
- Under this, indicate the entity, your title and the time period you worked. List in date order starting with latest and working backwards
- Under each of these items a brief (bullet points work well) description of your duties. Production folks should list your highest position on the project and avoid a laundry list of credits
- Each of these items should be true *industry experience*, including for college students, all internships and student-run and class productions
- If you still have room and you have run out of industry experience, list a new title on the left in bold underline and title it "Previous employment experience." List in the same reverse chronological order, including only the most important positions you held (indicating characteristics such as a high level of responsibility or personal conduct)
- The next title, "Special interests and skills," is where you can list:

    - related skills such as familiarity with computer software
    - your social media skills, including, if applicable, positive results that you've had in projects where you've utilized social media
    - unique or interesting activities or hobbies that add a dimension to your personality or demonstrate other traits such as creativity
    - charitable/volunteer work and other community activities

- The next title should be "Awards" and should include any awards that you received demonstrating industry or academic excellence or community service
- The last title should simply read "References upon request." If references are indeed requested, this gives you a chance to handpick those you think will help most with this particular position. It also gives you a chance to contact them ahead of time to warn them to expect a call, who will be calling and what you would like your reference to emphasize on your behalf
- And always remember, when in doubt, leave it out

And if it's not true, leave it out as well. Simply put, it is paramount that everything and anything you put on your résumé is *the truth*. All you need is for one person in the industry to catch you lying. One lie is not worth the effort of a cover-up. Sooner or later, somebody is bound to find out, hurting both your career and your reputation.

One other thing we recommend is sending out your résumé as a PDF file in order to prevent anyone from changing its contents or format.

POINTS FOR DISCUSSION/ACTIVITIES

POINTS FOR DISCUSSION

16

1. How might you personally produce demo material for a particular discipline even if you lack the ideal facilities and/or equipment?
2. What are the issues inherent with enhancing your demo with music, special effects, etc.?
3. What do we mean when we say "when in doubt, leave it out?"
4. Why is it important for you to produce all aspects of your demo (i.e., shoot, edit, script, etc.?)
5. Are there any disadvantages when producing demo material utilizing the resources of a commercial entity where, say, you are interning?
6. Why is it important to put your best material first in your demo?
7. Should you send your demo to someone even if there isn't a job available? What are the advantages and disadvantages?
8. What should you do with your demo *before* you send it to someone with an employment opportunity?
9. What are the pitfalls of lying on your résumé?
10. Based on the various opinions on *what makes a good demo*, how would you edit yours?

Chapter 17

CAREER DEVELOPMENT

Always do what you're afraid to do.

Ralph Waldo Emerson

IT'S OK

It's OK to be afraid. It's OK to fear the competition. It's OK to be intimidated by a business that can be cutthroat, demoralizing, and potentially demeaning.

It's OK.

Acknowledging your fears is half the battle.

Whether you aspire to perform in front of or behind the camera in sportscasting, the perils in achieving your dream can be fearsome . . .

Paranoid? Don't be. But, there is a lot of fear in the unknown. While these fears may be overstated, the ardent desire to achieve a dream can be powerful. Combine that desire with the apparent mysticism that appears to block the doorway to your dream (along with the reality that this *is* a difficult business to break into) and it can severely play with one's head.

Because of that, it is extremely important for you to come face-to-face with these perfectly natural feelings. Dealing straightaway with these emotions is really the first step toward making that dream come true. Give yourself a break, please!

The popularity of and subsequent competition in sportscasting, partly explains the mystery surrounding how to get a job in the industry. Those who are in a position to hire are constantly being inundated. A manager's email inbox might be stuffed with demos, résumés, and solicitation letters. Telephone messages often sit, unacknowledged. Oftentimes, a manager is simply too busy meeting the demands of his or her job to acknowledge in any way those trying just to get in the door.

While the halls of professional and college teams as well as television and radio stations and websites might seem impregnable to some, always remember that things frequently are not as they seem. Perhaps you have seen the movie *American Beauty*, the 1999 film awarded Best Picture by the Academy of Motion Picture Arts and Sciences starring Kevin Spacey and Annette Bening. Spacey plays a middle-aged man named Lester Burnham who becomes fed up with his suburban existence. The family living next-door to Burnham features a father, a Colonel Fitts, played by Chris Cooper and Fitts' son, Ricky, played by Wes Bentley. In the film, Colonel Fitts comes off as a stringent, former military man who's as macho as they come. Fitts' son is initially portrayed as a mysterious, reclusive voyeur who initially gives Burnham's daughter the creeps. Later in the film, the son eventually woos the daughter with his unique, sensitive, almost poetic outlook on life. While in a pivotal scene, Colonel Fitts eventually sheds his manly façade to reveal that he could be gay!

So, take heart. That sportscasting or team executive might be perceived as unapproachable, but there are ways to make contact. After all, how do you think any of the people who work in sportscasting got there in the first place?

YA GOTTA BELIEVE

The late Tug McGraw was a relief pitcher for 19 Major League seasons with the New York Mets and the Philadelphia Phillies. One day while with the Mets, McGraw emerged from a team meeting, blinked at the assembled media, smiled and promptly spouted, "Ya gotta believe."

Even as McGraw was speaking, the Mets were mired in last place in their division. This was August. By the end of the season, however, the Mets would win their division, the National League pennant, and go seven games before losing the World Series to the eventual champion Oakland As.

Ya gotta believe.

In yourself.

You *have to* believe in yourself. It is *the* primary prerequisite to getting a job in sportscasting. The right cover letter, demo, management contact, look, voice delivery, editing technique, shooting style, approach to production . . . These things don't mean anything until you *believe in yourself*. It is the first brick in the foundation, the first step in achieving your dream of working in sports television, radio, or video production. You need to know, deep in your heart, deep in your soul that you *can* do what you dream of doing. Not just performing in the job once you get it, but the formidable, time-consuming, character-testing job . . . of trying to get the job.

"EXPECT" TO FAIL

Dr. Robert C. Chope is a professor at San Francisco State University and a psychologist with the Career and Personal Development Institute in San Francisco. He wrote the book, *Dancing Naked: Breaking Through the Emotional Limits that Keep You From the Job You Want*. He says believing in yourself starts with banishing those negative thoughts.

Dr. Robert Chope, courtesy of Roberta Ann Johnson

"Counterproductive beliefs such as "I'm an idiot . . . I failed . . . I'll never get work," lead to emotional blocks, stress, low creativity, and poor interview performance. Interviewees need to free themselves from these beliefs by trying new activities. Try something that you will fail at, like golf. If people experience failure in something that doesn't mean much to them, then they won't take real disappointments so hard. Ricky Henderson holds the record for getting caught as well as for stealing the most bases. A good night for a basketball team is 60 percent from the floor . . . well that is 40 percent failure."

Failure is a regular, *expected* part of trying to get a job in sportscasting. Most times, telephone calls go unanswered and carefully crafted, heartfelt emails often end up deleted. Links to demos, if not deleted, might sit for weeks, even months, never to be clicked.

FACE REJECTION HEAD-ON

How do you continue to believe in yourself when so many people in the industry appear to be rejecting you out of hand?

Dr. Carol Goldberg is a board-certified clinical psychologist in New York. She conducts workshops to help people be healthier and more productive, using stress management, motivation, and healthy lifestyles. She says those who haven't yet built a successful track record in sportscasting can still build on their success in other areas.

Realize [you] have to begin somewhere. Most people are fearful when they start new projects. After acknowledging your feelings, move on to focus on your goals. Think of your past accomplishments. Remind yourself of what you did that helped you succeed such as talents, skills, and hard work. They are the foundation for future accomplishments.

YOUR FANS

Also, don't forget your "fans." That's right, your *fans*. These are the people who believe in you now, even before you speak your first word on air or shoot and edit your first frame. Maybe it's your parents or a best friend. Maybe it's a teacher or mentor. Hey, athletes have fans in the stands encouraging their every move. Football and basketball teams have cheerleaders. Why not you?

Dr. Carol Goldberg, courtesy of Carol Goldberg

Of course, with each fan you have, there are bound to be the naysayers, the ones who stand on the sideline, shaking their all-knowing heads, convinced you're doing the wrong thing with your life. Simply put, this is negative energy and it's not good. Let's put it this way, if you heed their advice, bail out, and go into some other line of work, how will you feel 20 years from now? Will you be sitting at some boring, unfulfilling job, daydreaming about what could have been?

For the parents, family, and friends who love you, but have only negative things to say, tell them you love them, but you have to do what you have to do in order to achieve your dream.

THE THREE PS: PASSION, PERSISTENCE, PATIENCE

> *Life isn't fair. It's just fairer than death, that's all.*
>
> William Goldman, *The Princess Bride*

Life is not a meritocracy. It's not the Boy or Girl Scouts. You don't always get a badge, patch, or some other reward for being competent, good, or even great in a particular area. Sportscasting, like any other businesses, is chock full of politics, favoritism, nepotism, dead weight, and other such characters and characteristics. Many times, the best one for the job doesn't get a sniff at the job. It's just the way it is and we all have to learn to deal with it.

An unreturned phone call or receipt of an impersonal form letter or email declining your candidacy for a job is not an indictment of you. This is about the business. There are a number of reasons you didn't get the job that had nothing to do with your or your talent:

■ Perhaps you didn't fit what the company was looking for
■ The executive who received your application might have been simply too busy to acknowledge your phone calls or emails
■ Maybe the job was given to a friend or an associate or someone on "the inside" and you had no shot at it from the beginning

Hopefully, if you were rejected, you were able to get some kind of feedback from the company or establish a solid relationship with someone for future reference.

The object is to convert the rejection into the energy you will need to pursue your goals. That "who is he to tell me I don't have the talent to make it in this business?" feeling can be converted into positive power. Once you've processed the putdown, you need to:

- internalize and rationalize it
- take a stance of aggressive, controlled, properly dispensed "I'll show him I have the talent to make it in this business!" and use it
- seize the moment to write that next email, prepare that next demo, or network to that next person who could help you to get where you're looking to go

There are three essentials that will equip you for the long haul, keep you focused, balanced, and invigorated as you look to break into the business. We call them the three Ps: *passion, persistence* and *patience.*

> *Passion enables good people to do great things.*
> Dr. Bob Kriegel, motivational coach

Passion is defined as *a powerful emotion, such as love; to have boundless enthusiasm.* When you're passionate about something, you are turned on by its very essence.

What turns you on about sportscasting? Whatever it is, hopefully you're passionate about it. *Passion* will allow you to fantasize about doing something you've always wanted to do while getting paid to do it. *Passion* will help you envision yourself a success, getting to do what you'd simply love to do, not just for the money, but for the ultimate satisfaction of doing it simply out of that love. *Passion* will pull you through the process of getting your first or that next job in the business, igniting your fire just when you thought the latest rejection letter had snuffed it out.

Hellen Davis is the president of Indaba, Inc., a management consultant and coaching company that deals with Fortune 100 companies. She is also the author of a number of books, including *The 21 Laws of Influence.* In that book, she talks about the Law of Commitment, in effect equating "commitment" and "passion."

> "The Law of Commitment is one of the most important laws in influencing people. When you're passionate about something, it comes across in your tone, in your drive, in your motivation. People pick up on that, they see it and they hear it. Then, they get that great "gut feel" about you. Most interview processes are conducted with a "gut feel" and instinct, as well as the demo and the résumé. Passion and gut are inseparable."

The next P is *persistence. Persistent* people refuse to give up or let go, they *persevere* relentlessly for as long as it takes to get the job done. Dale Carnegie, the public speaking and personal development pioneer who died in 1955, said: "Most of the important things in the world have been accomplished by people who have kept on trying when there seemed to be no hope at all."

There are many people in sportcasting who might appear to lack the inherent, natural talent to succeed but ultimately became successful because they gained entrance through sheer, unmitigated *persistence*. They crafted creative approaches and kept hammering away at their target until they hit it. Not only that, but they utilized their persistence to improve at their craft while moving up in their field.

Taking it a step further, you will not only have to *think* you can accomplish what you're setting out to do, you have to *know* it. *Foresee* your ultimate success. See yourself getting that interview or that next job. Let your hunger push you. Let your *passion* help to give you the drive you need. And, as we spoke about earlier in the chapter, utilize the confidence you've gained from succeeding in other areas while surrounding yourself with positive people who will help you to persist.

Hellen Davis sees *persistence* and *passion* as being joined at the hip.

> "I've met tons and tons of people, yet I can count on one hand the people who have the persistence to get face-to-face time with me. People will email me, they'll call me. And I'll say, "you know what, this person is really passionate about what they want, they're really committed. I think, maybe I should give them the time they want because they're committed and they've shown that in their persistence." Commitment and persistence are inseparable. If you're passionate, but you don't have persistence, you're just a flash in the pan. You don't have staying power."

The final P is *Patience*. A patient person is generally defined as someone who exhibits calm in the midst of enduring pain, difficulty, provocation, or annoyance. Someone who can be tolerant and understanding while facing a burdensome situation is someone who has *patience*.

Imagine for a moment that this search for your first or next job in sportscasting is tantamount to driving an automobile. *Passion* might be the engine, *persistence* would be the steering wheel, and *patience* would be the brakes. No race is won with the pedal always to the metal. Sometimes, you'll need to step back, step away, simply step off the accelerator.

Patience will help you regulate your *persistence*. In other words, while you're champing at the bit to make that 25th phone call or send that 25th email or text to a potential contact, your sensibility—indeed, your patience—will help you to wait a while so you don't go over the line. One thing you don't want to do is anger someone who can ultimately help you because you've been a little too persistent. If you find your potential contact or that person's assistant or secretary is getting a little testy from your persistence—indeed if *their* patience is wearing thin—it might be time to chill or perhaps explore a new approach. Patience will help you take a breath, gather some perspective and perhaps while your waiting on the sidelines, help you plan a different approach or think of a new way of reaching out and making contact with this person.

Dr. Bob Kriegel is a motivational coach who co-founded one of America's first sports psychology institutes in 1972.

> "Do it different ways. Some days it's a phone call. Other days it's an email. It's important to keep your name around them. And if you do it in unique ways, they might tend to think "this person's consistent and this person seems really interesting."

YOU AND THE PERSON IN NIGERIA

Imagine you're an aspiring sportscaster fresh out of college. You have found a website or industry publication that regularly spotlights career opportunities. You see an ad that says the following:

> Midwestern radio station looking for fulltime sports director to handle sports talk, play-by-play and morning sports reports. Cover local and nearby major college sports. Send samples to . . .

Being an aspiring sportscaster your entire life, you instantly visualize yourself in the role. Inspired, you email or snail mail your demo and résumé to the person listed. You feel as though you're talented and ready. You're definitely the person for the position . . .

While you're thinking this, so are five other seniors at your university. So is a person at the school in the next town, the next city, the next state . . . in all 50 states . . . hey, it's the World Wide Web. Even a person in Nigeria can see it.

Always know that whenever you answer an ad it's tantamount to playing a lottery. The odds are simply not in your favor when you're a blind applicant. Typically, hundreds of candidates may answer an employment ad. Sure, it's possible you could get the job, but it's also highly unlikely.

Motivational coach Dr. Bob Kriegel:

> If you answer an ad, you're just another piece of paper on somebody's desk. It's like sales. Everything is done through contacts. It's all about who you know and how to get to that certain person. You can network to almost anybody, even if it's several persons removed.

We won't discourage you from sending your materials to blind ads. It's true that people have actually become employed through them. We just don't recommend them as the *sole* means of looking for employment.

We feel your chances are made better and your opportunities are more plentiful when you know someone.

MAKING FRIENDS

Walk into a classroom, a wedding, a bar mitzvah, or any social function for the first time. No doubt you'll scan the room, eyes darting, looking for an immediate answer.

"Do I know anybody?"

To "know" someone immediately changes the circumstances for you. It presents the opportunity for you to interact with somebody, to communicate, to touch, to laugh, to feel. It's a fundamental human need. Suddenly, you won't be stuck mindlessly stirring your watered-down drink in the corner of the room.

"People," singer Barbra Streisand once crooned. "People who need people, are the luckiest people in the world."

The importance of knowing people in the sportscasting industry is frequently one of the fundamental precepts of developing a career. It's one of the fundamental precepts of life! Human beings are simply more comfortable interacting with other human beings who are familiar to them. The plurality of social networking sites, various associations, chambers of commerce, and business card exchanges corroborates the need to, as the old telephone company ad used to say, "reach out and touch someone." Family, friends, associates, even simple acquaintances are much easier to interact with—at least initially—than that stranger on the train. When people need a doctor, they ask for a referral. When they need a plumber, an electrician, or a landscaper, a friend invariably asks, "Who do you know?" When trying to break into a competitive field like sportscasting, familiarity doesn't breed contempt. It breeds opportunity.

Who do *you* know? More specifically, who do you know in *sportscasting*? The president of ESPN? The owner of a television station? A program director? A disc jockey? A sales person? A receptionist? A janitor?

Anybody? They all, in some way, could help.

BECOME AN INTERN

The kid who graduated college in 1982 may not have known many people. He just knew he loved football and he wanted to work for the National Football League. And so he put his passion and persistence to work, writing letters to the league and every one of its teams. He eventually was hired as an administrative intern in the NFL's New York City offices. After a brief stint as an intern with the New York Jets, he returned to the NFL as an assistant in its public relations department. From there, he moved up the ranks, filling a variety of football and business related positions with the league.

Finally, the kid would reach the pinnacle of his profession. On August 8, 2006, Roger Goodell was chosen to be the commissioner of the National Football League.

An internship can be your entryway into sportscasting. You will learn. You will meet people. And yes, it can lead to a job.

Internships, their types and specific duties, vary among entities. Often internships:

- are restricted to college students and, even then, frequently juniors and seniors
- are usually unpaid, instead offering college credit in return for a myriad of responsibilities
- can be restricted to more mundane tasks like getting coffee and refilling the copy machine
- include more hands-on responsibilities like writing, editing, shooting, and sometimes even performing

The depth and breadth of each internship often depends on the size of the entity and the scope of the hired staff. Suffice it to say that when economics dictates the situation, interns can be given a lot to do, depending on their willingness and their ability to do it.

"A good intern needs to be aggressive," says Chris Dachille, executive sports producer at WBAL-TV in Baltimore. "You have to take control of your internship. Don't come in text your buddies or tweet 'I'm so bored' or something to that effect. If you want to be successful in this industry, come in and—while picking your spots—ask questions. Learn what everyone does. Go out on stories. Be active. Stand out. It's very fundamental."

No matter the internship and its specifics, always know that management is watching you. Even if it's just a matter of putting paper in the printer, if you do it with a smile, they will like you. If you do it with a smile and do it without them asking you, they may soon start to think you're somebody they'd want to hire for something bigger and better.

In terms of training, there's nothing like it. When finances come into play, management might decide, "Give it to the intern," and that might thrust you into a position where you are doing what might be termed "real work." Quite obviously, this could be your litmus test, the one that might lead to an actual position of employment in sportscasting upon graduation or maybe even before it!

At the very least, even if your internship doesn't lead to a job with that particular sports broadcaster, you should be able to walk away with some solid industry contacts. So be sure to conduct yourself professionally by:

■ dressing appropriately
■ arriving early and staying late
■ asking good questions
■ performing your duties to the best of your abilities

Doing these things will often leave supervisors and co-workers with a good opinion of you. These people can become industry contacts who can help you to meet other people in sportscasting and, eventually, find out where the jobs are located.

DON'T LOOK FOR A JOB

The first aspect of getting a job in sports television, radio or video production is to *not* look for a job. That's right. *Don't look for a job.* There's pressure enough, real or imagined, attempting to find your way in. Don't start by pressuring yourself to actually "get a job" right from the beginning.

Instead, you need to make meeting people your first and *only* job. Meet as many people as you possibly can who could potentially lead, directly or indirectly, to a position in sportscasting. In the meantime you might have to take on a fulltime job to pay the bills, like waiting on tables or working in a clothing store. But your other fulltime job needs to be that of just meeting people.

"Meeting people is huge," says David Schuster, sports reporter for WSCR Radio in Chicago. When I first broke in, I was working in an entity where we recorded scores for people who would get them over the phone. Yet while I was covering events for them, I was meeting people along the way, whether in person or talking with them on the phone. Eventually I impressed people and they remembered [me]. These days, when young kids come along and I meet them, I watch them very closely to see if they are impressing me. And I will remember that. If I'm impressed by them I will recommend them to somebody else."

Networking *is* work. But if you really want to break into or advance in sportscasting, there is no room for complaining about having to work *and* look for a job at the same time. No grousing about having to try to meet people during the day, then earn money at night and on weekends while your friends go out to socialize. *Now* is the time to sacrifice, to put in the time and spend the extra hours necessary to get what you want! There'll be plenty of time for going to the movies and hanging out with your buddies. When the time comes, they'll want to hear all about your new job in sportscasting.

"When I was in college, I never attended a party," says Jim Nantz of CBS. "I worked every day, volunteered for every radio, television, newspaper . . . anything. And I had a negotiation skill that never let me down. I always got what I wanted because my negotiation was 'I will work for free.'"

START MAKING YOUR LIST

Your initial list of contacts with direct or indirect knowledge of sportscasting can include:

- college professors
- your university's alumni
- classmates
- contacts made during your internship
- anyone you meet through your membership in an industry group or association
- referrals through friends and family

Acquiring contact information from your college is as simple as contacting your university's career development or alumni offices, or a simple search on Twitter, Facebook, or the World Wide Web.

Once you acknowledge a potential contact, record each person's name on an excel spreadsheet or even a 3 × 5 card. Take note of everything you discover or already know about the person including:

- how to spell and pronounce their name
- where they work
- their exact title
- anything else that might help you make a friend (nothing is too trivial!)
- who referred you to this person (this is key—be sure to record *that* person's name and information as well)

THE KEVIN BACON GAME

Starting with these contacts, you should be able to develop a self-sustaining network that can provide advice, counsel, and, ultimately, reliable first-hand information on immediate or potential employment opportunities. This will ultimately give you a leg-up on the competition, discovering where the jobs are before they hit the industry websites or publications. Imagine having someone who has worked for a particular television or radio station or sports team taking your materials and hand-delivering them to the person who will ultimately hire you, giving that person his or her own personal endorsement of you at the same time!

The networking concept is borne out by the game "Six Degrees of Kevin Bacon." This game holds the premise that the actor Kevin Bacon can be connected to any other well-known actor by connecting him through no more than *six* other films. For example, Katharine Hepburn was in the 1994 movie *Love Affair* with Tom Signorelli. Signorelli was in the 1996 movie *Sleepers* with Kevin Bacon. That gives Katherine Hepburn a Bacon number of two.

No, you're not Kevin Bacon, but the same premise can hold true for *you*!

PLAY GOLF

Career development in sportscasting is like playing golf. When aiming for the green, success is oftentimes in the approach. And so you need to craft your approach to networking into a fine art.

Your best initial approach is often an email or letter, even if it's to reintroduce yourself. That said, you might need to call to acquire the right information for that contact. If you happen to get connected directly to the desired person when you call, don't panic! *Be prepared.* If necessary, have something scripted (but don't be a monotone telemarketer and simply "read from the script"). Have some prepared notes and simply greet the person and if necessary, remind them of your connection to them (former student, intern, friend of a friend, association member, etc.). Tell them you were going to drop them a line and that you were calling to get their contact information. The person could oblige your request and quickly hang up the phone or keep you on the line and chat away. If a conversation ensues, we'll tell you what to say later in the chapter.

Chances are though you won't get that person on the phone. More than likely, you'll get a receptionist, secretary, or administrative assistant or someone who just happens to be passing by. Whoever answers the phone, again, *be prepared.* Just state your business and be sure to confirm the exact spelling of his/her name, the correct pronunciation, the email and/or street address and if possible, a direct line to his/her office for the future. The incorrect spelling of a name, title, or one mispronunciation will send the wrong signal!

THREE LINES

The temptation is to send a heartfelt, passionate, comprehensive, multi-paragraph, multi-page email or letter when trying to initially engage your contact. But as eager as you are to impress that contact—to tell why you'll be the best, most talented sports broadcaster they'll ever hire—it's often a wasted effort. It is extremely rare that an email or letter alone nets someone employment. And as we've detailed, people involved in sportscasting are often very busy.

Generally speaking, the email or letter you write should be, give or take, just three lines. *Three lines.* Write just enough to say who you are, what you want, and what you intend to do about it.

Line one should remind the person how you're connected to them. Perhaps a person has referred you to them or you were a former intern or student.

Line two should state your purpose, something like "I am exploring career opportunities and would like to meet with you/speak with you by phone/begin an email correspondence with you," whatever the case may be.

Line three should state that you intend to follow-up this communication in the near future.

■ The Advantages of Snail Mail

While email has become the preferred method of correspondence (texting is probably a little too personal early in the process), we often suggest the use of snail mail when reaching out to someone, especially for the first time. Of course it might take a few days to be delivered and it will cost you the price of a stamp, but it is increasingly becoming a *unique* way of corresponding with someone—and unique is always good when trying to get that person's attention. Ask yourself how many emails someone typically receives in a day versus how many hand-delivered US Postal Service letters they get. It certainly can be more special to receive one letter than one of the dozens (hundreds?) of emails that land in an inbox on a daily basis.

■ Schmooze, Schmoose, or Shmooze

Call it being nice. Call it being friendly. Call it being a *schmooze*.

The dictionary might spell it *schmooze, schmoose,* or *shmooze. Schmooze* is Yiddish, the centuries-old language that combines Hebrew, German, and elements of several other languages. *Schmooze* literally means to chat or to talk. But taken in the vernacular of American culture, one dictionary defines *schmooze* as "to converse casually, especially in order to gain an advantage or make a social connection."

In order to gain an advantage or make a social connection. Isn't that what you're trying to do? Make a connection?

Schmoozing helps to form relationships. It's the quality you need to have when following up that three-line letter or email; how to further deepen and enrich your connection with that industry contact. It can also be helpful with someone who can *help* reach those contacts such as a receptionist, secretary, or administrative assistant. It's how you might get them to cooperate with you regarding their boss or co-worker, whether acquiring contact information or how best to get them to come to the phone or to schedule an appointment. *Schmoozing* is, simply, a good quality to have. It's you being nice to people, whether taking an interest in their life, their career or sincerely inquiring about their overall well-being. You can *schmooze* with someone when meeting them as an intern, while at an association meeting or during an informational interview. *Schmoozing* in an email or letter might be a little tougher, where frequently the tone or intended meaning of words can't be conveyed as accurately. Nonetheless, *schmoozing* will come into play as you continue to deepen the relationship with your contacts.

SIX WORDS YOU SHOULD NEVER SAY

It's become a stock phrase. Your attempt at trying to make or solidify a contact goes unanswered. Forlornly, you throw up your hands and utter the dreaded . . .

"They never got back to me!"

To that we say, always assume people will *never* get back to you. That's right, *never.* If you assume they will never get back to you, you will never be disappointed and you will always be ready to take the initiative and make the next move. Remember we said earlier in the chapter, in your original three-line letter or email, make that final line say, "Kindly expect me to follow-up with you in the near future." This should always be your thinking because *you* are looking to establish a relationship; because *you* are trying to get them to give you their time, their expertise, their friendship. And so *you* have to be the one to drive the process.

Follow-up can take many forms. It can be:

- another email, letter, or a phone call
- you asking someone who knows this person to intercede on your behalf
- a well-timed visit to an association meeting where this person is the featured speaker
- a follow-up correspondence with a co-worker or associate of this person with whom you've already been in touch

Motivational coach Dr. Bob Kriegel says that developing the right approach for some-one you've never met might also require some research.

> You have to really know [them]. It's like selling. You have to know everything about [your customer]. You have to understand not only their job, but also their personality. If you can, talk to people who work for the person you're trying to contact. Look them up on a website. Check their history. Find out their birthday. Find out what he or she likes or dislikes. It shows you're interested and it shows you want the job.

Whatever the circumstance, don't forget to record each and every attempt at contact, including what type of contact was attempted, the result and when it occurred. It will help you to manage your efforts so you don't end up becoming a pest.

"There's a fine line between being persistent and being a pain," says Chris Lanni, news director at WJAR-TV in Providence Rhode Island. "I appreciate persistence to a point. [Acceptable approaches] differ from news director to news director. The occasional phone call is fine. The occasional email is fine. But if you find yourself calling multiple times per week, there's a good chance you're going to shoot your job hunt in the foot."

YOU'VE GOT MAIL

Nothing is more heartening than to work very hard at something and seeing a result. In this case, a returned phone call or email from an industry contact you have long pursued.

Your reply, be it an email, letter, or phone call, should be personable but also to the point. If their reply to you seems to indicate they are happy to hear from you and their response is detailed and inquisitive, feel free to keep your response on those terms. If they are more brief and to the point, that is your cue to be the same.

Your goal is to establish a relationship on some level. If it turns out to be written correspondence, so be it. If it's by telephone or at some point a personal "informational interview" can be arranged, even better. Whatever the method, it's now your job to perpetuate that relationship. Do this through honest questions about their job or soliciting their opinion of your work by getting their feedback on your demo, writing, or other samples of what you have done.

▪ Breaking into freelance production

You just graduated from college after completing several years of study. With your diploma in hand, a great cover letter and résumé and a wonderful demo reel that is carefully crafted with your best student work, you decide you are ready to make a splash as a member of the production crew for a live event or studio. Steve Paino—president of Total Production Services (www.tpsweb.com), a company that provides production support for live TV events, including staffing services for television crews—offers some advice about a few options to make a successful start toward that goal.

For starters, Paino will let you know right up front that your journey from fresh college grad to fulltime remote television freelancer is not a quick process. He says the usual path to becoming a member of most technical crews is to try to become a *utility*. On a production, utilities are basically there as assistants for many different folks. They might help set up a booth, run cables, or load boxes on carts to be delivered around a venue. During a show, they will pull cable for handheld cameras, run water out to folks, or anything that can help support the show. After the show, a utility will be asked to help strike and put away all the equipment. Sounds glamorous, right? Paino says he gets hundreds of résumés that seek these positions and most of them come in and immediately get tossed away. The reason is that the number of folks trying to break in far outnumbers the positions available. This doesn't mean you can't eventually make it on to a crew, but it does mean that you need to have a solid approach to get noticed. And remember, this process is just to get into the utility rotation, not the camera, audio, or replay position you might really be interested in. But first things first.

Get Noticed

The journey begins with some experience. This can be in the form of a small college or larger high school webcast. Anything that shows you might have an inkling of what is happening on a remote broadcast.

You also need a great cover letter that ideally would state in the first sentence, "with my vast experience in mobile television . . ." Short of that, you will want to be able to talk about the two or three internships you have completed with a regional sports network. Without these types of résumé items, you are two years behind your peers from similar backgrounds.

Paino emphasizes that "you cannot get discouraged by the three, four, five, 12 times you get turned down. You won't be rejected 12 times in a month, but over the course of a year, you will not always get the job. But you can't give up on the process."

Vitally important is to understand when you should be sending in material and trying to break into the system. Crewers like Paino don't hire a crew a month before an event. Shows are booked three months or more in advance in most instances. This means the NHL and NBA seasons are being hired in August. College football begins the hiring season in June and college basketball in October.

Paino recommends a "three-pronged" approach to just getting your name on the list. He says you should snail mail, email, and then a week later make a phone call to follow up. You should be careful not to be annoying, but you need to give a crewer something that rises above the noise of the other 100 résumés that also arrived that week.

If your résumé makes it off the dead pile, you will not likely be given a spot on the utility list. In fact, Paino talks about tiers of his utilities. First, he is aware you exist, but isn't going to call you first. Your best option at this point is to offer to shadow a utility for several shows. After showing this initiative, you might rise to the level of getting four to six shows . . . in a year. The next level would be getting 15–20 dates a year. Paino's A-list utilities work 80–100 dates a year.

Develop

So how do you go from just being someone who Steve knows exists to a consistently hired utility? Take advantage of your time. Paino says, "once the cameras are set up, they just sit there. A motivated utility will hop on a camera and practice." If you are working shows on a consistent basis, this will be your opportunity to develop relationships with other crew members. Most of them will be willing to show you the ropes and explain certain pieces of equipment. Along with the experience you gain from setting up and breaking down over and over you can, over time, gain a basic working knowledge of the mobile television production environment.

When a utility shows motivation and takes advantage of opportunities, people will notice. Paino will get a call from a member of the crew and hear about a certain utility's skill level and that they are ready for the next challenge.

Opportunity Knocks

So when and where do you get your chance? Again, this is not a quick process. Going from an anonymous résumé to a viable utility is likely a year to year-and-half process and that is if you are able to show you are ready to work.

Generally, the scenario is a Saturday in the winter when pro and college sports are in full swing and Paino is in need of 60 camera operators, but he can only find 59. That is when a utility will get a chance to show off the dividends of all that practice and motivation. Then, the process will begin again for the utility-turned-camera-operator in terms of maybe four to six jobs a year as a cameraman, then maybe 10–15 the following year and on it grows.

Reputation

A key element in all of this is the relationship you develop with your fellow crew members. They are often the ones who sing your praises or lament your faults. Do you show a good work ethic? Have you made good connections with members of the crew? Paino is not at every show he crews, so the feedback he gets is very important. And when a freelance technician is looking for work, the recommendation of a crewer can go a long way.

ACT LIKE IT'S A JOB INTERVIEW

Meeting face-to-face via the aforementioned "informational interview" is probably the best way to make a good contact. You can do this if the person is a reasonable driving distance away. If it's several hundred miles or even a train or plane ride away, try to schedule other informational interviews in that same area to make the most of your time and money.

"If somebody's in town or if they're from my market I will almost always meet with them," says Ron Harig, news director at KOTV-TV in Tulsa, Oklahoma. "Whether they have a job or whether I know anything about them or not, just because you never know what you may find. So, if it's convenient and they're in town and I have time, I'll visit with them. But it's best to be honest up front. 'Hey, I'm looking for a job, can you give me a few minutes of your time?'"

If you are able to book an appointment, double-check all of the information: the exact location, a cell phone number in case you get lost, etc. (this will potentially send good signals to your contact that you are thorough!). Send your contact a thank you via email or snail mail reconfirming details of your visit. In fact, this is a good time to remind you about *gratitude* every step of the way. After a returned correspondence, after a phone conversation, after giving feedback on your work, after anything they've done for you— be sure to send some sort of note of thanks or appreciation.

Informational interviews are basically informal chat sessions that take on a characteristic or tone that is dictated by the parties involved as well as where and when it takes place. Some might last 15 minutes, be restricted to someone's office, and end with an amicable handshake. Others might last half a day and could include an extensive "interview," a tour of the broadcast entity, and even coffee or lunch.

While we define informational interviews as *informal chat sessions*, don't be naïve. This is an opportunity for you to meet someone in the industry who might directly or indirectly help you launch or further your sportscasting career. Given those circumstances, treating your session more like an actual *job interview* is the best strategy. As the well-known axiom goes, "you never get a second chance to make a first impression."

DRESS THE PART

The first thing is another well-worn aphorism, "dress for success." This includes for both sexes:

- Personal grooming such as hair-styling/cutting
- Minimal jewelry
- Easy on the cologne/perfume

For men:

- Trimmed or no facial hair
- Suit or sport coat and tie
- No jeans
- Shined dress shoes

For women:

- Business suit or a blouse and skirt

Please ladies, nothing alluring! While you may attract the attention of your host, it will be the wrong kind of attention. It's important that you send the right signals with their first glance at you—that you're there to do business, not funny business.

BE EARLY

Before you leave the house, be sure you have the exact directions. Confirm building locations, exact floors, suite locations, etc. Arrive early. If you're, say, more than five to ten minutes early when you do arrive, find something to do. The bottom line is, there is no excuse for being late. *None.*

Take some sort of business brief with you containing your demo, other examples of your work, your résumé, and anything else you think might be applicable to your budding professional life. If there's an organic moment, you can ask them to take a look at your materials and leave them as a calling card. Ask your host to take a look at them and to provide feedback, which you will solicit at some future date.

THIS IS BUSINESS

When you arrive at your destination, be business-like. Firm handshakes with a liberal sprinkling of "pleased to meet you" for everyone you encounter. Careful to try to remember names if you can, even if it's not the person you originally came to meet. You simply never know . . .

Again, the actual agenda will pretty much be up to your newfound friend. Whatever the venue, your job is to be in listening mode. That is, allow the person to begin the conversation and you can react accordingly. Don't look at this as an opportunity to "sell yourself" per se. Remember, you're just making friends.

As your visit is ending, begin to ensure the future of your relationship. Establish those ground rules by asking if you can keep in touch with him or her periodically. Ideally, they might also be able to refer you to one or two other people in the business who would be open to you getting in touch. This way, you've accomplished two things by the close of your visit: 1) you've established a solid industry contact who, in the future, could provide anything from career counseling to solid employment leads, and 2) you've made the process self-sustaining by acquiring additional, potential contacts.

Finally, shake hands, thank the person by name and tell them you look forward to staying in touch. And don't forget the thank-you note, and perhaps make it something handwritten that's delivered through snail mail.

WASH, RINSE, REPEAT

After you leave, take a deep breath, smile at the good job you did and take heed of the positive accomplishment of making a great contact within the sportscasting industry. Then, at the soonest possible opportunity, record everything about your visit (in the same vein as you recorded the information about your earlier telephone calls). This will give you fodder when making that follow-up call for feedback on your demo.

From here on, it's up to you to stay in touch with the person. With each contact, reaffirm your connection and your intent to stay in touch. Each time you connect, confirm the ground rules such as whether your should continue to follow-up with a phone call, email, or some other form of contact as well as how often you should reach out.

Hopefully, each contact you make refers you to at least one or two others in the business. Your job is to essentially repeat the process, from initial contact to ultimately developing a professional relationship through email, social media, snail mail, phone, or an informational interview.

Ultimately, through this network of contacts, you are led directly or indirectly to an internship, an entry-level position, or even something more akin to your lifelong dream— an actual, real live, *job*.

■ Apply for the Job You Don't Want

The competitive nature of sportscasting makes it advisable to apply for the job you don't necessarily want. Play-by-play announcers may want to apply for reporter/anchor positions as a way to get started in the industry. Those looking for a television sportscasting job may first want to apply for a position in radio. In fact, we recommend that all aspiring sportscasters consider applying for employment opportunities in *news*! (Just be sure you demo has elements reflecting your abilities in these areas.)

There are a myriad of reasons for trying to break into news. That is, newscasters have to perform many of the same functions as sportscasters. Both have to do:

- interviews
- script
- voiceover
- editing
- live shots in the field
- broadcasts off of a teleprompter as an anchor
- stories that follow the general journalistic precepts of clearly and concisely communicating accurate facts in an interesting way

Many of the same fundamentals apply on the production side, specifically producers, directors, writers, camera, and other disciplines.

In other words, as they say in football, there is no substitute for "getting your reps."
Transitioning from news to sports can happen in any number of ways:

- Smaller market stations frequently have designated news people "crossover" to cover sports stories or anchor the sports segment
- Sometimes news people apply for openings in sports at their own station and make the transition right there

- Once you're in sports, applying for play-by-play positions becomes easier
- It's not unheard of for news people to freelance as play-by-play announcers, even in the smaller markets

In other instances, people are hired by broadcasting entities in other departments such as sales or human resources and make the transition to sportscasting that way. Some sort of previous sportscasting experience or experience concurrent with that non-performing position is usually a prerequisite. But the fact of the matter is, the "get your foot in the door" philosophy often rings true.

"Would I hire someone with a news background to be a sportscaster? Absolutely," says Peggy Phillip, the news director at KSHB-TV in Kansas City, Missouri. "Anybody who's got a passion for it is somebody that we would consider if we had an opening. The thing about sports that differentiates it from news is sports is where the emotion is. That's where the guts of who we are as people . . . we're competitors. Sports allows us to relive our youth and to be in the moment."

NBC sportscaster Bob Costas adds another dimension:

> In general I think, having some kind of reference beyond sports is useful. Not that it's going to come into play all that often, but I think if you have some sense of the world around you, you never know where that might come in handy and add a little texture to a sportscast and differentiate it from what's out there. So reading something besides the sports page or watching something on TV besides the games I think actually is a good thing.

■ Become a Small Fish in a Big Pond and a Big Fish in a Small Pond

Visualizer two college seniors. One of them is trying to break into sportscasting as a performer, the other on the production side. Chances are the aspiring production person will end up at a regional or national sports network or a major market station *before* the up-and-coming performer. Part of that is the ratio of production personnel to performers at a large market station or network. But also, production people can be groomed from lower-level jobs such as production assistants, whereas the vast majority of performers need to get their on-air experience in some of the smaller markets.

Here's one strategy for getting to that larger market entity sooner or more easily. Try becoming a small fish in a big pond and, at the same time, a big fish in a small pond—and hopefully the ponds are within driving distance of each other. For example, let's take a top-ten market such as Atlanta. About a two-hour drive south of Atlanta is Columbia, Georgia, market #127. Picture yourself as a sports reporter or anchor in Columbia while, at the same time, having an association with a larger Atlanta station. Perhaps your contract would allow you to act as a stringer or maybe you'd simply have a low-level, part-time position with the Atlanta entity. The beauty of this plan is that you're getting your on-air experience at the smaller outlet while holding down a lower-level position at a much bigger station or channel nearby. Doing this will allow you to be in front of or have greater access to those who are in a position to hire, perhaps putting you in a better position to get to that higher market.

CONGRATULATIONS, NOW WHAT?

Those drafted by a professional sports league are normally all smiles on the podium; wearing the cap or jersey of the team that drafted them; shaking hands or hugging the league commissioner; feted by family and friends who hope to share in some of the fame and fortune to follow . . .

But what that draftee should be thinking is, "wow, now I have really to go out and *perform.*" That should be your thought after getting your first job as a sportscaster. Acknowledging the pressure to perform, how to perform to the best of your ability, and how to continue to get better.

For sports anchors, reporters, hosts, play-by-play announcers, and production personnel, feedback is sometimes sporadic or non-existent. News directors and other supervisors are busy people who sometimes might only reach out to you when giving you an assignment or criticizing a mistake. The general manager for that Minor League Baseball team or athletic director from the college might be willing to share an opinion, but what about their true "broadcasting" expertise?

What you need is a real, honest evaluation of your work. It's important to approach your news director and see if you can't schedule feedback sessions at regular intervals. If you cannot make this happen, there are other sources of expertise. Former professors or fellow professionals would be good to reach out to. Sending samples of your work might also serve the duel function of cultivating deeper relationships as you constantly seek career opportunities down the road.

■ One Broadcaster's Thoughts on Agents

This question was posed to a broadcaster: Do you have an agent and if so, how do you know when it's time to get one? Here was the response:

> I do not [have an agent]. I've thought about it for a long time. I know a lot of people who either had or have agents. For those who do, there have been some good and some not so good experiences. I had been told to look for an agent between my second and third jobs.

When first starting out, there's not a lot of money to be made so agents aren't really necessary, nor might they be interested in you because there's not much money for them to make. You simply can't make a lot of commission in a small market. That said when moving to a larger market or a network, a good agent will get a demo looked at by people who I can't get myself. If you're applying to market 150, they will most likely look at your demo without an agent. The higher you move up, the harder it is to get somebody to look at your stuff. I'm starting to think about it. To pitch a network, an agent can get that done. If you're just looking for negotiations or coaching, you can get that in other places. The agents have relationships with network types.

DON'T EVEN BRING YOUR EGO TO THE DOOR

Our own self-love draws a thick veil between us and our faults.

Lord Chesterfield

Ego has been on the minds of philosophers and psychologists for centuries. The reason is its inherent power and the subsequent damage it can do to an individual when left unchecked.

Your ego can get you in trouble before or after you get the job. Your activity in social media, for example, can help to satisfy your ego, but inappropriate postings or comments can come back to bite you, especially when it comes to prospective or current employers. Be careful.

When blinded by ego, people can sometimes act irrationally. They give less thought to how they're performing in their job and more thought toward whom they have to compete against. They get distracted by conjuring ways to hurt the competition instead of just doing their job. Ego can also cause you to shift blame to others, as is the case with performers who will often call out production people on the air about some sort of technical snafu.

Whether it's through prayer, meditation, or exercise, whether it's through friends or just some personal philosophy, your ego has to be left at the door, or—as the heading suggests—don't even bring it to the door. This is not easily done. As a sportscaster, particularly someone in front of the camera, your ego is always being fed. It's a fire; you should try to keep it at a pilot-light level.

After you get the job, work on keeping it by doing the best you can, by culling all of the resources necessary to make you the best you can be. That means when you receive the feedback and criticism that we just talked about, accept it with an open mind, an open heart, and true gratitude. Some of that feedback is bound to make you a better broadcaster. And if you think the criticism is specious, just grin and bear it.

Always keep in mind you are part of a team. News directors, talent, editors, camerapersons, team general managers, and athletic directors will make suggestions on how you should do your job. Again, receive it all with an open mind and gratitude.

As we said earlier in this chapter, life (sportscasting included) is not a meritocracy. People will always be going for your job. Get used to it. Have faith in your own abilities as a performer or member of the production team. Keeping an open mind to that feedback and criticism will help, but also the work ethic and determination to always try to get better, to think outside the box, to—within reason—be open to trying new and creative ways of doing the same thing.

Always keep in mind, before you complain, before you lose your temper, before your let your ego get the best of you and you do something irrational . . . you're covering sports and getting paid for it.

Vin Scully, entering his 65th consecutive year in 2014 as the voice of the Los Angeles Dodgers, sums up breaking into sportscasting this way:

> Don't get discouraged. It's tough. It's very difficult. And as far as sportscasting is concerned, with the advent of the former player [in the business], that cuts the jobs in half. But even so, if that's your dream, you have to give it your best shot. Wherever you start, go! Continue to try to get to whatever you think is the top. It doesn't have to necessarily be the Major Leagues. As long as it fulfills your dream, I think you're going in the right direction.

As the Chinese proverb says, "The journey is the reward."

TRY THESE

TRY THESE
17

1. Make a list of what scares you about trying to break into broadcasting and how you might deal with those fears.
2. Make a list of your accomplishments, your strengths, and your good qualities.
3. Make a list of friends, family, and professional people you might call to start building your network.
4. Choose a person in the business and outline a strategy for how you can get to know them and get them to know you.

5. Just for fun, choose a famous person and, through the game Six Degrees of Kevin Bacon, outline a strategy for networking to that person.

6. Make a list of some of the things you can do as an intern, other than your assigned duties, to make you more valuable to a company.

7. Write a three-line letter or email that introduces you to someone you've never met.

8. Go through the actual process of making an industry contact and record every move you make.

9. Arrange for and go on an actual informational interview.

10. Dream a little and create the "perfect job" you'd like to be in ten years after graduation and plot a possible career path for getting there.

Chapter 18

FINANCE

WHY DO I NEED TO UNDERSTAND?
CAN'T YOU JUST PAY ME?

I can see your look very clearly as you opened the book to this page. Unless your brain is wired a certain way, your eyes start to glaze over as we enter into the realm of financial models and economic food chains.

You have visions of your freshly pressed suit and your well-written open to the show, or the call for the game-winning home run/touchdown/shot/goal. Or, you have been practicing your camera skills with pans/zooms/tilts, or how to organize clips, run the switcher, make the opening graphic or mic up the coach for the interview. In your mind you have signed all the tax papers, direct deposit is ready to go, and you have already earmarked the take-home pay from the first check for a tiny party with friends to cele-brate breaking into the business.

Yet before we release you into the wonderful wild world of sportscasting, we present—like a heaping plate of steamed veggies—a chapter about the business of sportscasting. Somewhere in your brain, you know this chapter is good for you, but you can't quite place why you should care. Why should you care about the business side of things when you are very focused on getting your personal career development on track?

The basic answer is simple. To thrive in any system as an individual at the ground level, you need to understand the system from 30,000 feet. The pieces of the production puzzle fit together like cogs in a machine and that same metaphor works when you add more pieces to the puzzle. The actual sportscast being produced, whether that results in a live event, a studio show, a documentary, or a podcast, does not exist in a content vacuum. The costs of putting that sportscast together—from the tens of thousands to produce a live event, or the handful of dollars paying for the laptop, Internet connection, and recording software for a podcast—are not insignificant. Knowing how the money flows allows you to have a greater scope of the landscape and thus a wider range of targets to aim for your career to land, develop, and flourish.

So, grab a little salt, or maybe you prefer a bit of cheese on your veggies, and let's feast on the beauty of finance in sportscasting.

FOLLOW THE FLOW

In spite of ups and downs with economies around the world, sports seems to be relatively immune. Broadcast rights fees for various sports and leagues continue to rise at a steady pace, and show little sign of slowing down. In addition, more and more sports networks are popping up to cover, analyze, and discuss the action. To understand why this has been happening on a consistent basis, we need to look at the major players involved in this process. The shape that begins to form is a triangle of three main groups. Broadcasters (and we use that term loosely to encompass over-the-air, cable, and various other distribution methods), corporations and businesses, and fans form around sports leagues and teams to drive the business. Some areas of this relationship bear more financial burden than others, but they all exist in concert with each other in a symbiotic relationship. Each benefits in different ways from the other partners and none could exist and thrive without each other.

Sports Leagues and Teams

At the heart of the sports world are the leagues, teams, and participants that practice, play, and provide the content for everyone else. The economics involved with the leagues are massive, whether we are talking about the NFL or college athletics. The money for leagues, teams, athletes, and coaches flows in from many different revenue streams. Fans, broadcasters, and companies all contribute funds in a wide variety of ways. The contributions can be everything from ticket and player jersey sales to sponsorships and broadcast rights fees.

When you look at the *Forbes* top 50 most valuable franchises you find three soccer teams with worldwide appeal, Real Madrid (worth $3.3 billion), Manchester United ($3.165 billion), and Barcelona ($2.6 billion) at the top of the list. The New York Yankees ($2.3 billion), Dallas Cowboys ($2.1 billion), and New England Patriots ($1.635 billion) are next on the list and represent marquee teams in American sports. For team sports in established leagues or conferences, the popularity is translated into cash through broadcast rights fees, merchandise, and other revenue generating operations such as ticket sales and other game-day operations.

For individual sports such as golf, tennis, or auto racing, an entity such as the PGA, USTA, or NASCAR will serve as a unifying body to provide competitive structure, scheduling, and payments for performance, in addition to maintaining rules related to competition or punishment for violation of those rules.

Overall, in 2013, the teams in the top 50 of *Forbes'* list are worth an average of $1.64 billion; a 16 percent increase from 2012.[1]

Broadcasters

First, let us agree that the term "broadcast" is meant as a general and not literal term. The days of major networks simply sending out a signal over-the-air and being received on televisions and radios has grown into a complex delivery system that expands the over-the-air delivery method to cable, satellite, Internet streaming, and even social media to get content in front of an audience on screens and speakers of a wide shape and variety.

While the essence of the coverage is to tell the story of the game, the athletes, and the subplots around the game, the broadcasters also have the added challenge of being financially viable. Without the business side of the equation, broadcasters could not afford to produce events. That doesn't mean that the artistic elements involved with producing the games should be ignored, but the balance needs to be carefully maintained.

Part of the financial equation involves the money paid by broadcasters for the right to show certain leagues on television. The amount a network will pay to get access to games has been rising since they began negotiating these contracts. For example, in December 2011, Fox, NBC, and CBS all extended their NFL contracts that were set to expire after the 2013 season. Michael Hiestand of *USA Today* reported the nine-year extension that runs through the 2022 season increases the amount those three major networks spend to a total of $3.1 billion annually. That amount represents a 60 percent increase from the expiring deal.[2]

While the amount might vary depending on the sport or league, broadcasters will pay these rising fees for several reasons, including the live and exclusive nature of sporting events. People tend to watch sporting events as they happen, so being able to show a sporting event live represents a very valuable piece of programming to a network. In an age when most programming can be viewed on the audience's schedule through DVRs or streaming video sites, sports remains one of the few pieces of programming that is viewed first-run as it happens. In addition, in a sport such as professional football or Major League Baseball, only so many teams exist, and those teams only play a finite number of games. You can't simply write an extra episode of a game. You need to be there at kickoff, or tip off, or the drop of the puck to see the action.

While the money leaving broadcasters is rising at a steady rate, they have a fighting chance to make profits through the money they receive from the viewing public and advertisers.

For example, a cable station that has a strong viewership, such as ESPN, can demand money from cable providers to allow their station to be on their cable system. And the larger their audience, the more a broadcaster can charge for advertising on their channel.

Corporations, Businesses, and Advertising

Another piece of this puzzle are the entities that are paying to sponsor these sporting events. Advertising plays an important role in the flow of money. The money from sponsors funds teams, leagues, and broadcasting. The return on their investment comes in the form of revenue generated from brand awareness for the audience of the events.

You see advertising in many forms in the world of sportscasting. They can be the title sponsor of the arena, or have signage on chairs, stairs, or dasher boards. In addition, they might buy ad space in game programs or pay to be the title sponsor of an entire event. For example, Mountain Dew was the presenting sponsor of an extreme sports tour that aired on NBC. They paid between $8 million and $10 million for the right to have their name associated with the event.[3]

For broadcasters, advertising is a major source of revenue that helps to offset the cost of paying rights fees and producing coverage. Kantar Media reported that advertisers spent more than $74 billion for commercials in 2012. In terms of sports advertising, Kantar reported that for postseason play in the NFL, NBA, MLB, NHL, and the NCAA Men's Basketball Tournament, the total ad revenue was more than $2.9 billion. For March Madness alone, the amount spent on ads was more than $1 billion. While the numbers are staggering and growing, the important fact to glean is how these funds help to keep the financial ball rolling and allow broadcasters to keep producing content.

Fans

Completing the circle are the folks who go to the arenas and fields as well as watch and listen to the games. Fans are the ultimate consumers of all the content produced, purchased, and advertised. They drive the financial bus in terms of buying the tickets, paying for cable, eating the food, wearing the merchandise, and buying the goods and services of the corporations and businesses. They are also the market for where you will be plying your trade, whether in front of or behind the scenes.

■ The Relationship Between the Business and Production Sides of the World

Norby Williamson started in the mailroom at ESPN. Over time, he has risen through the ranks and for a while was a producer for the "worldwide leader in sports." He has worked on a variety of shows and productions over time and has a strong passion for the artistic and storytelling side of the sports broadcasting business.

In his current role as executive vice-president, programming and acquisitions, Williamson remembers his time as a content producer, but now has a keen eye and sensibility about the financial side of the equation. He believes that understanding the flow of money is important for someone entering the business of sportscasting, but that the level of understanding is a relative measurement. Williamson believes that the financial part of the business doesn't need to be your primary focus. He talks about the old school of thought that if you are creating content, you shouldn't care about the business side. That kind of thinking was relevant when the delivery of sports was fairly straightforward. A network would buy rights to the game, then sell advertising to offset the cost and help a large, national broadcast network make money on the endeavor. The climate of sportscasting is much different now.

Williamson believes the better you understand the overall business, the better position you will be in to do your job. And as you rise through the ranks, the percentage of how much of your day-to-day life depends on the understanding of the business side of the production will change. When you are a production assistant, you might be focused on 2 percent of your world in relation to the business side, and 98 percent is concerned with content for the show. As you rise to different levels in the production, your awareness and understanding of the flow of money will need to increase.

Regardless of where you are working, understanding how the content that is created can be monetized is important to growing the business and the brand of yourself and your sportscasting entity. And even though you might be spending 98 percent of your time working on content and ideas, you still need to have an idea that you are working in a business in the back of your mind. For example, if you are producing a show, and you have a sponsored element in a show, you need to understand how and why that is important to incorporate into the show. In essence, understanding the financial flow from a macro level can help you operate in your particular job at the micro level of an event.

Another balance that companies need to find is the amount of money spent to put on an event. For example, the cost for Fox to put on the World Series in two different cities is tremendous in comparison to a local cable production of a high school basketball game. While there are some upfront costs in terms of equipment or delivery (for example a T1 data line), Williamson talks about the tremendous advances in technology that have brought the costs down in terms of equipment. The return on investment is a consideration that can be affected by several factors. As a network, ESPN needs to make tough decisions on how many resources are used for a particular production. In some cases, it can spread out the overall costs to help benefit production that, if they stood on their own, might not have the same resources available to produce an event up to the high standard of ESPN. For example, if ESPN is covering several games, it might get a break in cost from a mobile television company. Or, the cost of a graphics package that might cost thousands of dollars to produce can be spread out over several events and distributors to help reduce expenses over time. ESPN has partnered with colleges and universities who are able to make some initial investments in the technology (such as graphics machines or fiber to deliver the content) and they are able to be viable partners for ESPN to produce content *and* help reduce the cost to ESPN to produce events. ESPN has the ability to provide some basic production support, for example an ESPN-themed graphics package, commercial advertising, and the distribution through a very reliable and high quality Internet stream. This partnership can greatly reduce the cost to ESPN to put on the event, while the school gets to promote sports, such as lacrosse, baseball, or volleyball that might not get coverage if the schools did not participate.

The greatest cost involved in producing content is the rights fees that networks pay. In spite of dips the economy might take, the cost for rights fees have always gone up. Williamson says there are several factors involved to explain this phenomenon. First, as the world of broadcast and cable television continues to change, the value of a live audience continues to be high. Sports are one of the few programming choices viewed more live and less on demand or on a DVR. Ratings show that sports are a popular form of entertainment that generates consistent revenue. With this success comes awareness and creation of other networks. With these other networks comes competition. And the competition to get access to the limited amount of professional sports creates a bidding process. In addition to the bidding, the actual value of rights fees are not necessarily what people *should* pay. Rights fees are worth what people are *willing* to pay.

CONCLUSION

Understanding the financial side of sportscasting gives you a valuable perspective. As you begin and develop your career, as you seek, apply for, and get jobs and cultivate opportunities you might not even know exist, understanding the flow of money will allow you to negotiate and navigate through the business side of sports. Yes, the art of telling sports stories is the main reason we get into this business, but at the end of the day, we must also remember that this is a *business*.

For example, Danny Lawrence wanted to create a company that could compete in the sportscasting marketplace. Instead of trying to compete with ESPN, Elmrox is using digital platforms to engage in thoughtful debates about sports. It cannot afford to be a high-light show and pay all those rights fees. Instead, it will create content that will appeal to a wide variety of audiences, from politics to entertainment and also sports. Using social media and other available digital platforms, Elmrox is attempting to enter the world of sports in a very non-traditional way. Whether it thrives or not will be a result of how well Lawrence and his company can read and adapt to the marketplace.

As the world of sportscasting evolves and changes, the opportunities you might find have not even been created yet. This could include different platforms for delivering content, and increasing use of mobile devices for the audience to watch that content. By understanding the basics of the business side and keeping up with the latest trends and news, you will be better suited to have a successful career in sportscasting.

POINTS FOR DISCUSSION/ACTIVITIES

POINTS FOR DISCUSSION
18

1. Why is it important to understand the flow of money as it pertains to sportscasting?
2. How does money flow to a sports team from a broadcaster?
3. What are emerging technologies that might impact the business of sport? (For this question, you might do a simple Internet search to look for "sports and business" or "sports and technology").
4. What are some ways media outlets, teams, and players are capitalizing on novel ways to deliver their content to fans? How do these delivery methods make money? Do they charge subscription fees? Advertising? Are they simply there to drive fans towards purchasing items such as tickets or merchandise?
5. How do you think the business of sportscasting might change over the next 10–20 years?

FURTHER READING

FURTHER READING
18

The Business of Sports by Scott Rosner and Kenneth Shropshire
Sports Television: The How and Why of What You See by Dennis Deninger
The Business of Sports: A Primer for Journalists by Mark Conrad
The Business of Television by Howard J Blumenthal and Oliver Goodenough

ENDNOTES

ENDNOTES
18

1. Kurt Badenhauden, "Real Madrid Tops the World's Most Valuable Sports Teams," *Forbes*, July 15, 2013. www.forbes.com/sites/kurtbadenhausen/2013/07/15/real-madrid-tops-the-worlds-most-valuable-sports-teams, accessed October 25, 2013.
2. Michael Hiestand, "New NFL Deals Go Up 60%," *USA Today*, December 14, 2012. http://content.usatoday.com/communities/gameon/post/2011/12/new-nfl-tv-deals-bonanza/1#.UnP_TpRa3y8, accessed November 1, 2013.
3. Chris Smith, "The Dew Tour Changes, But Mountain Dew Remains a Top Action Sports Brand," *Forbes*, October 19, 2012. www.forbes.com/sites/chrissmith/2012/10/19/mountain-dew-gains-untold-action-sports-legitimacy-with-dew-tour, accessed November 1, 2013.

Chapter 19

CURRENT TRENDS AND FUTURE POSSIBILITIES

Around the middle of 2013, ESPN made two, significant announcements. First, the self-proclaimed *Worldwide Leader in Sports* stated it would lay off an estimated 400 employees. Around the same time, ESPN said it would discontinue its foray into three-dimensional broadcasting (3D).

The layoffs came in the face of ever-increasing rights fees the network continues to pay in order to repel potential competition from the likes of CBS, NBC, and Fox, all of which have their own national sports networks.[1] ESPN dropped its 3D service after finding, in its words, "limited viewer adoption of 3D services to the home."[2]

Economics and technology are two of the most critical issues affecting the future of sports programming on the national level as well as with regional sports networks (RSN) such as Yes Network in New York and the NBC and Fox RSNs around the country. Financial and technical questions also abound at local television news stations, where management has to decide how much—if any—local sports reporting to include in their nightly newscasts. All of these entities are paying particularly close attention to the future of digital content and the portals that deliver this information. They are also aware of how fans are not just viewing or listening to the sporting event on television or radio, but also interacting with "multiple screens" that are covering that event at the same time.

THE FUTURE OF RIGHTS FEES

As you've just read in the previous chapter, the rights fees paid by sports networks to leagues, conferences, and schools for the right to televise games are the primary fuel for the sportscasting engine. These fees have increased to historic levels. In just a 20-month period that ended in November 2012, Comcast/NBC, ESPN, Fox Sports, Turner, and CBS agreed to spend $72 billion for the TV rights to professional, Olympic, and college sports well into the next decade.[3] Regional sports networks are following a similar path. In 2013, the Los Angeles Dodgers were anticipating a new 25-year, $7 billion deal from Time Warner Cable, believed to be the most lucrative for any single sports team in history.[4]

In order to continue to pay these fees, the networks have turned to advertisers and the cable and satellite companies that carry the networks. The cable and satellite companies then pass the increased costs to carry sports networks onto its customers. National and regional sports networks are the most expensive channels on most bills.[5] As of 2013, the average household was spending about $90 a month for cable or satellite TV with nearly half of that amount going towards the sports channels packaged into most services. Over the next three years, monthly cable and satellite bills are expected to rise an average of nearly 40 percent, to $125, according to the market research company NPD Group.[6]

Even the broadcast TV networks such as ABC, NBC, Fox, and CBS, which historically distributed their channels free on cable and satellite-TV systems, are now charging what are called "retransmission fees," which are also passed on in subscriber's bills. These fees are included under the provisions of a 1992 federal cable law.[7]

THE FANS ARE WATCHING

You might say fans are watching, *therefore* rights and subscription fees have been going up. But you might also say that fans are watching *despite* the fact that rights and subscription fees are going up. ESPN reported that more people watched college basketball on its network during the 2012–2013 season than at any point in the channel's history.[8] In 2012, more than 200 million Americans watched that summer's London Olympics, while in the same year, NBC's *Sunday Night Football* was the top-rated primetime show during the fall TV season. In fact, ESPN Sports Poll conducted a survey and found that more people preferred watching sports on TV than going to a live event.[9] In 2012, the Nielsen research firm estimated that people spent about 20 percent of their TV viewing hours watching live sports programming, a share that is expected to rise.[10]

Because fans are watching, advertisers are also willing to pay. In June 2013, during the Sports Business & Technology Summit in New York, advertisers trumpeted high-rated, live sports programming as a great investment. "Advertisers follow the eyeballs and right now there are a lot of eyeballs for sports," said Jon Diament, executive vice-president of ad sales and marketing for Turner Sports.[11]

AND SO IT ALL WORKS

According to early 2013 estimates by two financial firms, SNL Kagan and Barclays Capital, ESPN generates substantial income thanks in part to its monthly subscriber fee of $5.06, by far the highest fee for any cable TV channel. In fact, according to the same estimates, dedicated sports channels account for four of the top ten cable network subscription fees.[12] The average RSN collects between $2 and $3 per subscriber per month, more than most other channels, making them high-revenue generators as well.[13] And because the model works, the main suppliers of content for these channels—the teams, leagues, conferences, and schools—would appear to have every incentive to continue to leverage the situation, seeking more and more dollars as rights become available.

IS THERE A SATURATION POINT?

The elephant takes turns taking a seat in the offices of the sports channels, then in the halls of the teams and universities. Acknowledging the elephant is to rhetorically ask, "is there a saturation point?" Is there some moment in time where the fan will say "I won't pay any more to see my favorite team or alma mater on television?"

Rick Burton, courtesy of Andrew Burton

Rick Burton is a professor at Syracuse University. He says:

"There have been a lot of people, including me, who've said [rights fees] can't keep going up, but they have. So I don't think we've reached the ceiling, nor do I think there's been any indication—at least from the growth properties—that we've reached the ceiling. I think the reason they've continued to go up is that sports programming is pretty unique. It's live, unscripted drama where no one knows how the game is going to finish or how the season is going to end and anything can happen in that two-hour block. And while more women are watching sports than ever before—which certainly contributes to the growth of rights fees—men have not turned away from sports, so it continues to be a cost-efficient way to speak to them."

Neal Pilson, the former head of CBS Sports and now a consultant, sees it this way:

"So long as sports drives new business and as long as sports is premier programming for the American public, and so long as Americans continue to support it by watching it, buying the products of its sponsors, and continuing to pay their cable bills, then this escalation will continue. What we have here is competition unlike anything we have seen before in the sports marketplace.[14]"

THE FUTURE OF LOCAL SPORTS ON NEWS PROGRAMS

According to a survey conducted in 2006, sports directors, anchors and reporters at local television stations in the top 50 markets in the United States believe their segment on the local television newscast could become extinct. The survey was conducted by the Center for Sports Journalism at Penn State University. The respondents were 216 sports directors, anchors, and reporters. Many respondents believe their role is diminishing and that someday sports may not be part of the local television newscast.[15]

While the survey was conducted eight years ago, concerns for the continued existence of local television sportscasts persist. The advent of national and regional sports networks, the Internet and social media, and a sizeable number of news directors who simply don't value sports have all contributed to this issue. According to a March 29, 2012, article by Jane Kwiatkowski in the *Buffalo Times* newspaper headlined "Tough Times for Local TV Sportscasts," a number of stations were noted to have downsized or totally eliminated their sports departments.[16]

Ironically the founder of ESPN, Bill Rasmussen, says the value of local television sports is not lost on him. "I think those stations that just walk away from sports are using ESPN as an excuse," says Rasmussen, who founded ESPN in the summer of 1978.

"ESPN can't give the local sports in Grand Island, Nebraska, or Lake Charles, Louisiana. Even in the larger markets where ESPN has a local presence, the local high school and college kids are a big deal and I would hope there will always be room on stations across the country for those sports to be aired."

"When I started in television in Springfield, Massachusetts, the ABC station there did not do any sports. They said "we can't afford it." And that was back before ESPN. But the other station [in the market], because they had sports, they were always far and away the number one station, and a lot of people said that was because they could catch the local high school scores or whatever the local sports flavor was."

SHORT, SHARP, STRONG . . . AND *LOCAL*

Peggy Phillip, news director at KSHB-TV in Kansas City, thinks producing good, local sportscasts in the future will be a matter of work ethic as much as work product.

> "I'm going to tell you, I think lazy sports guys caused this [decline in sports reporting] to happen. They became irrelevant in some markets. I have worked at television stations where there isn't a sports department and I've worked at television stations in major sports markets like Baltimore where the sports department was eliminated. The problem is that when sports is nothing more than a series of video clips of home runs, those sorts of things will not keep sports relevant for today's audience because there are a million other places where people can get that."

> "If a local sports department wants to remain relevant they have to go and find stories that can't be found anywhere else. That local story that ESPN doesn't have, that's hard work. Then, when you have only two minutes at 6 pm and two-and-a-half minutes at 10 pm, it's hard because you don't have a lot of time. So you have to figure out how to tell great stories quickly. That's why I always say that with "shorter, sharper, stronger sentences" you'll be able to tell great stories in a minute-and-a-half."

The L word, *local*, seems to predominate among professionals when discussing the future of local television sportscasts.

Chris Dachille, Executive Sports Producer, WBAL-TV, Baltimore

> "I think the future . . . as long as you key in on your audience, I think you're servicing what folks want. And the folks want their teams."

Chris Lanni, News Director, WJAR-TV, Providence, Ri

> "The future, I believe, is in hyper-local sports reporting. If a viewer wants the latest Red Sox score, your local station isn't necessarily their first choice. But it's up to the local television stations to provide sports coverage that you can't get anywhere else. That requires hyper-local sports coverage. The *human* aspect of the hyper-local sports story."

Dennis Smith, retired News Director, WLBT-TV, Jackson, MS

> "You have to make sure that what you're putting out over the air is going to draw a fair amount of interest on all levels, with all people. Too much of what you see on the air locally is just the same old thing."

■ How Much Money You'll be Making

It's hard to predict salaries for the sportscasting business in the future. But it's relatively safe to say you'll be making a lot less than your college friends in other fields, at least when you first start out.

According to a survey conducted jointly by the Radio Television Digital News Directors' Association (RTDNA) and Hofstra University, the average starting salary in 2013 for new sports reporters with no previous fulltime experience was $22,000 a year. Not only was it the lowest salary among the other 14 or so positions in the newsroom, it was about *half* the yearly salary for new 2012 college graduates in fields such as business, computer science, and education.[17]

Aspiring play-by-play announcers can expect a similar starting salary as the "number one" announcer for a lower-level, Minor League Baseball team and perhaps a $400–500 per month "stipend" (including an apartment) if you're hired as that number one's "broadcast assistant." Play-by-play or a production position for a one-time only event on small market television or radio might carry a fee of $75 or lower per game.

As you move up in market size, so should your pay. According to the survey, the average sports anchor in 2013 made $58,000 per year while the average sports reporter pulled in $38,300. Play-by-play and production salaries also rise commensurately as you move up in market size. In radio, the sports reporters earned more on average than sports anchors $59,500 per year to $36,700.

Six-figure salaries are attainable in the larger markets and network levels for many of these positions (including ones not mentioned in the survey such as sports talk and sports show hosts, sideline reporters, game analysts, producers, and directors) while event or studio crew members such as photographers, editors, and floor directors can make out well on a per diem basis. For freelance technicians such as technical directors (TDs), audio mixers, camera operators, replay/tape operators, and graphics, the level of production and union rate cards are major factors in how much you will make on a daily basis. A ballpark figure for major markets is about $350–400 per day for a ten-hour day for most technical positions. This figure will fluctuate based on your crew position and the size of the show. For example, a TD is generally a very important position in terms of getting a show on the air. So, regardless of the size of the market, most TDs can command a good rate for a day of work. By comparison, the difference in rate between a camera operator in a major city for a professional sporting event versus a minor league or small college event can be as much as $200 less. Some areas are controlled by unions in which case the event doesn't matter, the rate is the rate. If you have to travel to work an event, most companies will give you a per diem of around $40–50 in expenses for every day you travel to work plus a certain amount per mile if you have to drive your own car.

That's the good news. The reality check reminds us that sportscasting, like many other businesses, is a pyramid. The higher you go, the fewer higher-paying jobs that are available.

For more information, the RTDNA/Hofstra survey can be viewed at www.rtdna.org/article/tv_salaries_fall_radio_stagnant.

THE FUTURE OF NARROWCASTING

As we discussed in Chapter 1, ABC, NBC, and MLB joined forces to start The Baseball Network in 1993. It would become the first network to be owned by a professional sports league. The Baseball Network would ultimately fail a year later due to the baseball strike started in August 1994, but the concept of single-sport, single-conference, indeed single-team or school networks has taken hold.[18]

The Golf Channel was started in 1995 and 19 years later has never been more popular.[19] Other channels covering the NFL, NBA, NHL, auto sports, soccer, and tennis, just to name a few, have since followed. In 2007, the Big Ten Network became the first major college conference to launch its own network. The Pac-12 has a collection of seven regional networks that covers conference-related athletic events. The Southeastern conference and ESPN have announced plans for a joint venture, which will include a television network and digital platform launching in 2014.[20] And the Atlantic Coast conference, perhaps eyeing the dollars earned by Big Ten schools, is researching the feasibility of launching its own television network.[21]

But the creation of future, similarly themed networks of this type might hinge on the success of ventures like the Longhorn network, a partnership between the University of Texas, ESPN and IMG College, launched in 2011. One of the big issues with the Longhorn network is cable and satellite distribution, or perhaps more accurately, the lack thereof.[22] In fact, the Longhorn network is not alone in this issue with other RSNs also having the same problem.[23] Adding a channel to its lineup can affect the price a distributor charges its subscribers. Thus, the matter of carriage joins that of rights fees as another issue facing the future of the industry.

Of course as we have seen, the fans have been pretty much willing to pay the price.

MEDIA CONVERGENCE AND ITS EFFECTS

A person has just covered a sporting event and he or she does the following:

■ Writes a story on the game for the entity's website
■ Supplies video and/or audio of game coverage including standups and interviews
■ Appears on the post-game show for the channel that televised the game
■ Tweets out their perspective on the game

Is this person a sportscaster or a print journalist? The answer is *both*.

Through much of the twentieth century, the boundary line in sports coverage was clear. There was the print media and there was the electronic media. Now, sports journalists can often be painted with a broad brush and described loosely as *content providers*. That content is provided across a number of different media platforms. The blending of these media platforms has been described by some as *media convergence*.

Convergence definitions vary, but in most versions it is the blending of old media, (e.g., traditional media such as magazines, newspapers, television, cable, and radio) with new media (computers and the Internet) to deliver content.[24]

John Pavlik, professor and chair of the department of Journalism and Media Studies at Rutgers University, provides a similar definition. He defines media convergence as the coming together of computing, telecommunications, and traditional media.[25]

And so as the *content provider* for this blending of old and new media, you need something that sportscasters often refer to when discussing the athletes they cover: a multiple skillset. That was strongly pointed out to you in Chapter 5, where a sports anchor/reporter urged you to acquire multiple skills (shooting, editing) when preparing for that first job. As it relates to media convergence, the ability to write long-form (newspaper style with quotes), post Web content and handle social media obligations are all strongly recommended proficiencies for sportscasters.

TV EVERYWHERE

Another result of media or technological convergence is the streaming over the Internet of live video that had been almost exclusively reserved for the bigger television screen. Streaming allows viewers the opportunity to view events on their computers or on-the-go via their mobile components. Every major, professional sports league in North America streams games over multiple platforms, a trend started by Major League Baseball in 2002.[26] During the 2012 London Summer Olympics, NBCUniversal made every single Olympic event available live by way of television or streaming, with most of the content delivered via the so-called second screen. The digital coverage served up some 159.3 million video streams, 64.4 million of them live.[27] ESPN touts its WatchESPN service as "bringing you 24/7 live programming from your favorite ESPN networks on your computer, smart phone, tablet, Xbox 360, and Apple TV." The network claims 40 million subscribers to the service with a goal of doubling that in the near future.[28]

But the overriding issue with streaming is a concept known as "TV Everywhere," in effect a uniform, industry-wide, authentication process that would allow producers to protect their streamed content. While development of TV Everywhere has been slow, programmers agree it needs to happen sooner rather than later. NBC Sports Group chairman Mark Lazarus says "The TV Everywhere aspect of our business, specifically around sports and live events, is an important part of protecting the pay TV ecosystem. All the distributors and all the programmers should be moving towards a way to protect the value of that system so we can continue to pay the rights and build our high-quality content."[29] ESPN president John Skipper calls it a "lead priority," saying "finding ways to make authenticating WatchESPN as easy as possible is what's keeping me up at night."[30]

■ The Fan and his Digital World

"The fan," says Rick Burton, the David B. Falk professor for sport management at Syracuse University, "is taking more and more control."

The control that Burton alludes to comes in several forms. One way the individual fan expresses him or herself is through webcasts, podcasts, blogs, or social media (see Chapter 9). The second has to do with the fan's choice in how they view games. As Burton says:

> "The new medium is coming in, and instead of it being a residential box that is immoveable [television], the new generation has moveable boxes and screens so they can watch on their phone, their laptop, or their tablets. This is the logical evolution to the next way of consuming sport media. The younger generation is going to it and it ultimately could become the dominant way in which people view sports."

> "You need to understand how the 18-year-old is consuming sport. The 18-year-old doesn't just watch the game. He or she might also be playing a video game at the same time where *they* run the team or they're veering off into fantasy sports leagues like rotisserie baseball or fantasy football. There are a lot of people nowadays who are consuming [sports] media on three screens simultaneously. They're sitting with a phone and tweeting to friends, they may have a laptop in front of them and they're blogging or they're in a chat room and they may have a *third* screen—a TV that's further away where they may periodically glance up at to see if anything interesting is happening in the game."

The "multiple screen phenomenon" might have a fan viewing a game, checking out fantasy stats on a webpage and tweeting out comments on the game all at the same time. Comcast Sportsnet Philadelphia, like many national and regional sports networks, has implemented software platforms that complement television coverage of the game. While watching on TV, fans can view multiple, integrated webpages with graphics, text, photos, constantly updated game information, and a list of tweets and Facebook posts about the game.[31]

Burton says, "this is not an Armageddon call that sports is in trouble or the world is ending, it's just to say the consumer is a lot different than when I was growing up."

FUTURE OF RADIO

The increased ability of fans to follow sports while they're on the move is, ironically, a promising trend for the oldest medium in sportscasting: radio.

"In this day and age," says Dr. Murali Balaji, an assistant professor of media studies and production at Temple University, "you have a lot more people who are mobile. So they're listening to the games on the radio."

Advances such as digital technology, on-demand radio applications like Stitcher and the ability to embed those applications in car radios have or will help radio to stay current.[32]

"'I don't think radio is going away,' says Tom Boman, broadcast manager for Learfield Sports, a syndicator of college play-by-play sports broadcasts. "The way people consume radio is changing. Some people will continue to consume the way they have for years and years with traditional over-the-air radio, some people will consume it digitally online, via smartphone and some of our broadcasts are distributed via satellite. On a given game day you can have four or five different outlets for your broadcast which would hit every type of consumer possible and not be pigeon-holed into the traditional radio format."

Technological advances are helping sports fans to access one of radio's growth areas: sports talk.[33] In 2012, both NBC and CBS took the plunge, forming their own sports talk networks as a challenge to ESPN's 20-year hold in that area.[34]

"What you have seen with sports talk radio is it has become a very easily replicable model for these major corporations," says Dr. Balaji. "Sports talk has, in many ways, rejuvenated radio audiences because it gives fans an opportunity to chime in, in ways that television cannot."

A LITTLE GLOBAL PERSPECTIVE

Table tennis anyone? What about men's field hockey? Japanese rugby? Badminton?

Spanning the globe to bring you the constant variety of sport used to be the purview of ABC's *Wide World of Sports* program on Saturday afternoons (see Chapter 1). Now, supplying this content on-demand includes entities such as One World Sports, a channel available on Dish Network which describes itself as "an English-language sports network delivered on all digital platforms targeting millennials and featuring exclusive, live world-class sporting events around the globe.''The Al Jazeera-owned beIN Sports not only streams Internet content but it is available on DirecTV, Dish Network, and Comcast cable, oftentimes at an extra cost.[35] It is trying to make its presence felt by emphasizing soccer.[36]

Soccer is also something NBCUniversal and the NBC Sports Group is banking on, England's Barclays Premier League to be precise. The company announced in 2012 it would be the new Premier League rights holder in English and Spanish in the United States, carrying all 380 league matches live in the 2013–2014 season across its array of television and digital properties.[37]

▪ In Case You Were Wondering . . .

Q. Can someone take down or at least level the playing field with ESPN?

A. That answer is complex and will take a while to be realized, though it may start to become clearer in 2016. That's when the league's national TV deals with ESPN and Turner Sports' TNT expire. A key for NBC, Fox, and others will be to outbid ESPN for college and professional rights as they become available.[38] Fox joined NBC and CBS when it launched an all-sports network in August, 2013.[39]

Q. Give me an example of "smaller, easier, cheaper" from a technical standpoint.

A. Products like Newtek's Tricaster, which is billed as a "complete live production and media publishing solution."[40] A company called Mamigo touts its GameView as "the first live event production system that takes high-end features of a major broadcast production and reduces it down to a compact, feature-rich, laptop application."[41]

Q. If I become a television sportscaster, will I always have to wear a tie?

A. Maybe not, if you're appearing online. This is according to Beet.tv, which covers a broad variety of online topics including video journalism. This revelation came out of a panel discussion convened by Beet.tv, albeit on video *news*. Reuters' head of global programming, Dan Colarusso and *The Wall Street Journal*'s digital network video director, Rahul Chopra both agreed that online video news differs from its traditional, more upscale big brother broadcast news, seen at times to recruit talent based on looks rather than journalistic ability.[42]

SOME FINAL THOUGHTS ON THE FUTURE

Twenty-five years from now, it is hoped that many of you reading this textbook will be in the prime of your sportscasting careers. Like a time capsule, it might be interesting for you to unearth this final section from its resting place on your book shelf or computer file and see what we forecasted 25 years before.

Bill Rasmussen, Founder of ESPN, on the Overall landscape

"I think there will be a lot more direct TV—in other words, direct from the production of the game right to the individual. My guess is cable is going to be pretty dramatically impacted by the over-the-top technology [content delivery without the benefit of cable or satellite delivery] and the new Internet-ready TVs that have been on the market. I think the games are going to look the same. But the programmers are going to have to figure out ways to deliver their product in ways other than cable."

"There are experiments right now in south Florida, Pennsylvania and New Jersey—people experimenting with high school games, even kids' games, just going directly to the households. Just bypassing everybody. As long as you have a producer and a way to get the game televised, you can send it to "Johnny the third baseman's home." That's pretty exciting. It's a cumbersome process, but it's possible by streaming them over the Internet."

"The national and regional sports networks will still have to produce the games, but it's going to be a lot different. Bottom line, there will be a picture and there will still be fans who want to watch."

Paul Gluck, Associate Professor at Temple University's School of Communications and Theater and a Former Major Market News Director on the Future of Sports Coverage on Local News Programs

"I think the future of sports on local newscasts will be market-dependent. There are markets where the hunger, the appetite for sports information among audience members is very high and those markets will continue to have the traditional module of sports on the late news. I think in some markets where it is less important to viewers, they'll look for non-traditional ways to do it."

"In broadcasting in general right now, with fragmented audiences, the view is yesterday's competitor is today's strategic content partner. You can see as more and more corporate mergers happen, there's a high likelihood that a centralized sports organization might be doing sports for multiple stations in a market or in a region, something like the Comcast Sportsnet concept [NBC Regional Sports Networks]. That's a high-quality, regional sports network that—who knows—may someday provide sports content for some of the NBC-owned stations."

"All of this said, there are more opportunities right now to be in sports television than there ever have been and I suspect that trend won't change as we populate new media platforms and social media becomes, if you will, more legitimatized with verifiable information and reporting. Five years from now, there may be a network that does nothing but drop live sportscasts onto your portable devices and to me, that's something to value for aspiring media professionals as getting a job on the dominant television station in any market."

Rick Burton, Sports Management Professor at Syracuse University, gives his philosophical perspective on the future of sportscasting

"I think it's going to be something approaching almost constant babble. Sportscasters will be on all the time. I don't want to say it's *Rollerball* [the futuristic, science fiction film of the 1970s], but we could be moving to a time where it won't just be about the game broadcast. I've talked to a lot of print guys and even they're talking about the fact that they have to be commenting on their subjects all the time [on various media outlets]. So I have to believe that sportscasters who become celebrities are constantly going to have to, say, go to dinner at the restaurants where the athletes are or as soon as the game is over go down the locker room and then after the locker room go to the bar and then the next morning go somewhere and report yet again because the consumption, even now, is on a minute-by-minute basis. Sportscasters could eventually become bigger than ever, but demand is going to become a lot more than what they're asked to do now. I think it's going to be non-stop."

NBC Sportscaster Bob Costas on the Future of Event Coverage and the Sportscasting Performer

"It's almost impossible to predict what the future will be like. Media and technology are changing at such a rapid rate. But I will say this, even as many aspects of how sports are covered have changed dramatically, some of it for the better and some of it for the worst, one thing that has more or less remained constant is that the big sports events are still on network television and they're still covered in a way that would more or less make sense to play-by-play announcers and broadcasters of earlier generations. Now, the picture may be more vivid, it's in HD, they have more cameras, there are more replay angles, more graphics, but still no one is coming out of the Internet world or no one's coming out of sports talk radio who can do what Al Michaels does. Joe Buck's frame of reference may be a younger frame of reference than his dad's was [the late sportscaster Jack Buck], but there's considerable overlap between what his dad did and what Joe Buck does. The basic skills required to call a baseball game are still learned by doing games in Nashville or Chattanooga or some place.

It seems like the rights to these big sports events and the rights to the leagues are still going to be sold to over-the-air stations. No matter how much the peripheral commentary about sports changes, both print and over-the-air, I think the actual broadcast of games themselves are still going to require the same, basic play-by-play techniques that have always been the standard of the industry for as long as I have been following it. Can I say 25 years from now it won't have changed? I can't say that. But I don't see it changing a whole lot in the foreseeable future.

That said, a lot of what surrounds it will change. Is it possible that pre-game shows and post-game shows will go in a direction much different from where they are now? Yes. But the coverage of games themselves, I think that's the part that will change the least."

POINTS FOR DISCUSSION

1. What do you think will become a bigger issue in the creation of new sports networks in the future, rights fees or distribution?
2. Imagine you are the head of a national sports channel. Craft a ten-year strategy to overtake ESPN's hold on the sportscasting landscape.
3. Will there ever be a saturation point where rights fees won't or can't go higher? Explain.
4. Take sides and debate this point: the poll results indicate that fans would rather watch sporting events on TV than live, is this a good thing or a bad thing?
5. Imagine you're the sports director for a nightly news program and the news director is threatening to shorten your sportscast or cut it altogether. What points would you argue to change his or her mind?
6. Try to predict what sport, league, team, or school will establish its own television network.
7. Sports programming is available on television as well as a number of other platforms like your computer, smartphone, or tablet. Debate whether one day there will be a "single box" to take the place of everything.
8. List all the skills that sportscasters of the future are likely to need in light of media convergence.
9. Do you think fans will gravitate toward channels like One World Sports or beIN sport and embrace the sports they show?
10. Give you're overarching view of the future of sportscasting.

ENDNOTES
19

ENDNOTES

1. Jonathan Berr, "Why the Hugely Profitable ESPN is Laying Off Workers," *MSNMoney*, May 21, 2013. http://money.msn.com/now/post.aspx?post=838233a0-ddb5-44c8-820e-a375ea682683, accessed June 10, 2013.

2. Carolyn Giantina, "The Future of 3D TV and Why ESPN Dropped Its Pioneering Channel," *Hollywood Reporter*, June 13, 2013. www.hollywoodreporter.com/behind-screen/future-3d-tv-why-espn-568445, accessed June 18, 2013.

3. Bob Fernandez, "About Half of Cable-TV Bills Go to Sports," *Philadelphia Inquirer*, November 19, 2012. http://articles.philly.com/2012-11-19/news/35187681_1_sports-chan nels-cable-tv-bill-college-sports, accessed June 15, 2013.

4. Brian Stelter, "Rising TV Fees Mean All Viewers Pay to Keep Sports Fans Happy," *New York Times*, January 25, 2013. www.nytimes.com/2013/01/26/business/media/all-viewers-pay-to-keep-tv-sports-fans-happy.html?ref=brianstelter_r=0, accessed June 13, 2013.

5. Derek Thompson, "If you Don't Watch Sports, TV is a Huge Rip-off (So, How do we Fix It?)" *The Atlantic*, December 3, 2012. www.theatlantic.com/business/archive/2012/12/if-you-dont-watch-sports-tv-is-a-huge-rip-off-so-how-do-we-fix-it/265814, accessed June 12, 2013.

6. Joe Flint and Meg James, "Rising Sports Programming Costs Could Have Consumers Crying Foul," *Los Angeles Times*, December 1, 2012. http://articles.latimes.com/2012/dec/01/busi ness/la-fi-1202-ct-sports-cost-20121202, accessed June 13, 2013.

7. Fernandez, "About Half of Cable-TV Bills Go to Sports."

8. Tim Baysinger, "ESPN Scores Most-Watched Men's College Basketball Season," *Broadcasting & Cable*, March 15, 2013. www.broadcastingcable.com/article/492365-ESPN_Scores_Most_Watched_Men_s_College_Basketball_Season.php, accessed June 14, 2013.

9. Fernandez, "About Half of Cable-TV Bills Go to Sports."

10. "Here's What ESPN Earns in Cable Fees Every Year," *Business Insider*, March 6, 2013. www.businessinsider.com/heres-what-espn-earns-in-cable-fees-every-year-2013-3?0=advertising-contributor, accessed June 15, 2013.

11. R. Thomas Umstead, "Sports Summit: Sports Programming Scores with Advertisers," *Multichannel News*, June 19, 2013. http://www.multichannel.com/index.php?q=mcnbc-events/sports-summit-sports-programming-scores-advertisers/143997, accessed June 27, 2013.

12. Bob Wolflie, "ESPN Continues to Lead Cable by a Mile in Terms of Subscriber Fees," *Milwaukee Journal Sentinel*, March 1, 2012. http://www.jsonline.com/blogs/sports/141097593.html, accessed June 12, 2013.

13. Dave Warner, "The High Cost of Regional Sports Networks," *What you Pay for Sports*, April 17, 2013. www.whatyoupayforsports.com/2013/04/the-high-cost-of-regional-sports-networks, accessed June 15, 2013.

14. Fernandez, "About Half of Cable-TV Bills Go to Sports."

15. "Survey: Local TV Newscasts Devalue Sports," *Penn State News*, August 17, 2006. http://news.psu.edu/story/201979/2006/08/17/survey-local-tv-newscasts-devalue-sports, accessed June 13, 2013.

16. Jane Kwiatkowski, "Tough Times for Local TV Sportscasts," *The Buffalo News*, March 29, 2012. www.highbeam.com/doc/1P2-31030197.html, accessed June 14, 2013.

17. "NACE Salary Survey: January 2013 Executive Survey," *National Association of College and Employers*, January 2013. www.naceweb.org/uploadedFiles/NACEWeb/Research/Salary_Survey/Reports/SS_Jan2013_ExecSummary.pdf, accessed June 23, 2013.
18. John Catsis, *Sports Broacasting* (Chicago: Nelson-Hall, 1996), 87–88.
19. Andrea Morabito, "Golf Channel Comes of Age," *Broadcasting & Cable*, January 14, 2013. www.broadcastingcable.com/article/491307-Golf_Channel_Comes_of_Age.php, accessed June 15, 2013.
20. John Skipper, Mike Slive, and Justin Connoly, "ESPN & SEC Press Conference to Announce Creation of SEC Network," *SEC Digital Network*, May 2, 2013. www.secdigitalnetwork.com/Portals/3/SEC%20Website/SECNetworkTranscript.pdf, accessed June 23, 2013.
21. Michael Smith and John Ourand, "ACC Panel will Study Whether to Launch Net," *Sports Business Daily*, January 14, 2013. www.sportsbusinessdaily.com/Journal/Issues/2013/01/14/Colleges/ACC.aspx, accessed June 20, 2013.
22. Christian Corona, "Longhorn Network Endures Growing Pains, DeLoss Dodds Hopeful it will be More Widely Distributed," *The Daily Texan*, February 26, 2013. www.dailytexanonline.com/news/2013/02/26/longhorn-network-endures-growing-pains-deloss-dodds-hopeful-it-will-be-more-widely, accessed June 28, 2013.
23. John Ourand, "Houston Numbers Could Hurt Sports in Carriage Battles," *Sports Business Journal*, June 10, 2013. www.sportsbusinessdaily.com/Journal/Issues/2013/06/10/Media/CSN-Houston.aspx?hl=sports%20channel%20distribution&sc=0, accessed June 25, 2013.
24. Gracie Lawson-Borders, "Integrating New Media and Old Media: Seven Observations for Best Practices in Media Organizations," *The Journal on Media Management* 5 (2003), 91–98. www.mediajournal.org/ojs/index.php/jmm/article/viewFile/10/3, accessed June 24, 2013.
25. Martin Scott Sheerin, "Media Convergence: How are we Preparing Students of Journalism?" http://journalism.fiu.edu/lib/doc/faculty/SheerinResearch.pdf, accessed June 27, 2013.
26. David Pierce, "Why the Future of Live Sports is in ESPN's Hands," *The Verge*, November 14, 2012. www.theverge.com/2012/11/14/3643700/live-sports-tv-streaming-online-espn-war-for-tv, accessed June 13, 2013.
27. Tim Baysinger, "Sports Summit: Lazarus-TV Everywhere Protects Pay TV Ecosystem," *Multichannel News*, June 19, 2013. www.multichannel.com/distribution/sports-summit-lazarus-tv-everywhere-protects-pay-tv-ecosystem/143988, accessed June 29, 2013.
28. Mike Reynolds, "TV 3.0: ESPN's Skipper 'TV Everywhere' Authentication Process Must Become 'Uniform,'" *Broadcasting & Cable*, June 6, 2012. www.broadcastingcable.com/article/485614-TV_3_0_ESPN_s_Skipper_TV_Everywhere_Authentication_Process_Must_Become_Uniform_.php, accessed June 24, 2013.
29. Baysinger "Sports Summit: Lazarus-TV Everywhere Protects Pay TV Ecosystem."
30. Reynolds, "TV 3.0: ESPN's Skipper 'TV Everywhere' Authentication Process Must Become 'Uniform.'"
31. Peter Key, "Fans: Melding Sports on TV with Online Easy as OneTwoSee," *Philadelphia Business Journal*, June 1, 2012. www.bizjournals.com/philadelphia/print-edition/2012/06/01/fans-melding-sports-on-tv-with-online.html?page=all, accessed June 17, 2013.
32. John Paul Titlow, "Five Companies that will Define the Future of Radio," *ReadWrite*, December 12, 2012. http://readwrite.com/2012/12/12/5-companies-that-will-define-the-future-of-

radio#awesm=~oc94C0YdNxw89k, accessed June 23, 2013; Samantha Murphy, "The Future of Car Radio: Embeddable Apps" *Mashable*, June 25, 2013. http://mashable.com/2013/06/25/car-radio-embeddable-app/, accessed July 1, 2013.

33. "Jacobs Media's TechSurvey9: Speaking of Sports Radio," *AllAccess*, May 29, 2013. www.allaccess.com/net-news/archive/story/118869/jacobs-media-s-techsurvey9-speaking-of-sports-radi#ixzz2Up20N5KF, accessed June 23, 2013.

34. Kristina Elliott, "ESPN Might Take a Hit as CBS and NBC Move into Sports," *InVocus*, June 29, 2012. www.vocus.com/invocus/media-blog/espn-might-take-a-hit-as-cbs-and-nbc-move-into-sports-radio, accessed June 18, 2013.

35. "About One World Sports," www.oneworldsports.com/about.

36. David Trifunov, "Al Jazeera, beIN Sport Using Soccer to Win over US Audiences," *Global-Post*, August 31, 2012. www.globalpost.com/dispatches/globalpost-blogs/world-at-play/al-jazeera-bein-sport-using-soccer-win-over-us-audiences, accessed June 22, 2013.

37. Jack Bell "NBCUniversal All In for Premier League," *New York Times*, April 16, 2013. http://goal.blogs.nytimes.com/2013/04/16/nbcuniversal-all-in-for-premier-league, accessed July 6, 2013.

38. Michael McCarthy, "High Sports Prices Take Toll at ESPN," *AdAge*, May 26, 2013. http://adage.com/article/media/high-sports-prices-toll-espn/241699, accessed June 19, 2013.

39. Paul M. Banks, "Will Fox Sports 1 Enable Fox Sports to Eventually Compete with ESPN?" *ChicagoNow*, March 12, 2013. www.chicagonow.com/chicago-sports-media-watch/2013/03/will-fox-sports-1-compete-espn-621, accessed June 21, 2013.

40. "TriCaster 8000," www.newtek.com/products/tricaster-8000.html, accessed June 29, 2013.

41. "GameView for Sports and Entertainment," http://mamigoinc.com/Gameview.html, accessed June 22, 2013.

42. Dan Colarusso and Rahul Chopra, "Video News Panel: Online Shows More 'Dressed Down' Than TV," YouTube, June 14, 2013. www.youtube.com/watch?v=r8BjHA7Rt6M, accessed June 25, 2013.

INDEX